D1250884

My Old Confederate Home

MY OLD CONFEDERATE HOME

A Respectable Place
for Civil War Veterans

Rusty Williams

THE UNIVERSITY PRESS OF KENTUCKY

The University Press of Kentucky
Scholarly publisher for the Commonwealth,
serving Bellarmine University, Berea College, Centre
College of Kentucky, Eastern Kentucky University,
The Filson Historical Society, Georgetown College,
Kentucky Historical Society, Kentucky State University,
Morehead State University, Murray State University,
Northern Kentucky University, Transylvania University,
University of Kentucky, University of Louisville,
and Western Kentucky University.
All rights reserved.

Editorial and Sales Offices: The University Press of Kentucky
663 South Limestone Street, Lexington, Kentucky 40508-4008
www.kentuckypress.com

14 13 12 11 10   5 4 3 2 1

Library of Congress Cataloging-in-Publication Data

Williams, Rusty, 1948–
  My old Confederate home : a respectable place for Civil War veterans /
Rusty Williams.
      p. cm.
  Includes bibliographical references and index.
  ISBN 978-0-8131-2582-4 (hardcover : acid-free paper)
  1. Kentucky Confederate Home—History. 2. Soldiers' homes—
Kentucky—History. 3. Veterans—Services for—Kentucky—History.
4. Kentucky—History—Civil War, 1861–1865—Veterans—Biography.
5. United States—History—Civil War, 1861–1865—Veterans—Biography.
I. Title.
  E564.4.W55 2010
  976.9'03—dc22
                                    2010003208

This book is printed on acid-free recycled paper meeting
the requirements of the American National Standard
for Permanence in Paper for Printed Library Materials.

Manufactured in the United States of America.

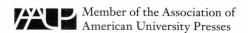 Member of the Association of
American University Presses

Contents

Acknowledgments

To write a book of history requires the assistance of many people in many different ways.

Conversations and correspondence with Jerri Conrad, Boyd Copal, Shirley Copal, Rebecca Myers, Susan Reedy, and other family historians helped me see the Home residents as more than names on ledgers. Recollections by Gin Chaudoin, Sis Marker, Bill Herdt, and other longtime Pewee Valley residents took me back to that village of almost a century ago.

The Kentucky Historical Society is a precious resource for every Kentuckian. Lynne Hollingsworth, Don Rightmyer, Charlene Smith, and Diane Bundy helped me navigate the library, the document collections, and the photo archive there. Reference librarians—particularly those at the Louisville Free Public Library, the Lexington Public Library, the Dallas Public Library, the Kentucky Department for Libraries and Archives, and the Filson Historical Society—are the smartest people in the world, and they helped me find what I often didn't know I was looking for. Robin Wallace (Filson), Jason Flaharty (University of Kentucky), Amy Purcell (University of Louisville), and Elizabeth Hogan (Notre Dame) helped me locate just the right photos in their collections.

Early readers Darryl Allara, Jim Chambers, Ken Freehill, Marty Prakope, Anna Ray, Ann Williams, and Phillip Wuntch provided valuable early criticism. Earl Williams, Stephanie Shelton, and the rest of Mr. Chung's Beltline crew stimulated the writing process with endless cups of coffee.

Acknowledgments

Always clear, supportive, and enthusiastic, Laura E. Sutton and the entire team at the University Press of Kentucky walked the story of the Kentucky Confederate Home through the publishing process. My every encounter with the editorial, sales, marketing, and publicity departments demonstrated their professionalism and passion for this story. Donna Bouvier's meticulous editing was done with an unerring eye toward clarity and scholarship. All have helped create a book much better than the manuscript they started with.

Pat Williams, Julian Williams, Ann and Brien John, and Alan and Bette Stone provided special encouragement. Meagan Alma and Ava Kai were always on my mind.

A native of Anchorage, Kentucky, my wife, Holly, insisted that this story be told—and told well. From first word to last edit, she has been my best critic, avid fan, and tireless cheerleader. Her love and support mark every page.

Introduction

In the 1940s, as the United States entered World War II, our nation recruited or drafted sixteen million citizen soldiers. We trained them, armed them, and sent many of them into combat. At war's end we discharged them, provided transportation back to their homes and farms, and gave them a booklet explaining their rights as veterans.

"By your service in this war you have done your share to safeguard liberty for yourself, your family and the nation," it said. "The nation salutes you."

The booklet listed privileges the veterans would enjoy for having spent years in service to their country. "They are yours," it told them. "You have earned them just as you have earned the respect and gratitude of your fellow citizens."[1]

Many of the veterans enrolled in schools, the cost of tuition, fees, books, and supplies paid by the U.S. government in appreciation for their years in uniform. Some purchased houses, using loans whose favorable terms were arranged—and guaranteed—by a grateful government.

Veterans could, if they wished, present themselves to any of 150 veterans' hospitals for medical, surgical, or rehabilitative care, all at no cost to themselves. If they became disabled—even if the disability was unrelated to their time in uniform—they might receive a monthly pension or other benefits in recognition of their military service.

"You have earned them," their nation told them.

As these veterans of seventy years ago pass away, they are offered a burial plot in a national cemetery and a uniformed military honor

1

guard to mark their final passage. Their family receives an American flag folded into a tight triangle. Accompanying the flag is an embossed certificate bearing the president's signature and expressing the nation's grateful recognition of the veteran's service in the U.S. Armed Forces.

"You have earned the respect and gratitude of your fellow citizens."

Too often in our history we have engaged in warfare to assure our sovereignty, to defend our territory, or to assist weaker nations against brutal aggression; sometimes we have fought for reasons that are tragically unclear. During these times of conflict we often ask our fellow citizens to take up arms on the nation's behalf, requiring them to defend the nation and its people to their final breath, their last drop of blood.

The young men and women who fight our nation's wars provide a special service, and we deem them entitled to a respectable place in the country's history and heart. We often promise special compensation or benefits to those who perform military service; we honor their memory and celebrate their sacrifices.

Like other civilized nations, America has a legacy for caring for the veterans of its wars. The Pilgrims of Plymouth Colony in 1636 pledged lifetime care for any soldier injured in defense of the colony, and the Continental Congress promised mustering-out pay and bonuses for soldiers who served through the end of the Revolutionary War. Veterans of the War of 1812 were given land grants in return for their service. In his second inaugural address, President Abraham Lincoln entered into a pact with Union draftees and enlistees when he asked Congress "to care for him who shall have borne the battle and for his widow, and for his orphan." We honor that pact.[2]

Today's military veterans continue to earn the respect and gratitude of their fellow citizens. The United States now spends $70 billion a year to care for 63 million eligible military veterans, spouses, survivors, and dependents. We may denounce the wars in which they fight, but we demand that men and women who take up arms on our nation's behalf be supported, honored, and treated with respect.

My Old Confederate Home tells of a time in American history when military veterans—enlistees and draftees who had absorbed bullets with their bodies, lost limbs, saw ghastly sights, and lost four years of family life—came home from war to find little institutional assistance.

For Americans who swore their oaths to the Confederate States of America in the 1860s, their nation did not exist at the end of the Civil War. There was no national treasury to pay these veterans for a train ticket home, compensate them for their service, assist them in their old age, or provide them with a respectful burial.

There was no nation to provide them a respectable place in its heart and history, no nation to salute them.

Most Confederate veterans returned home to live quiet, productive lives. But some—due to lingering war wounds, mental confusion, disability, infirmity, age, or just plain bad luck—were unable to support themselves. Jobless, invalid, and impoverished veterans of Confederate military service became an all-too-common sight on the streets of Southern cities; most small towns knew of at least one veteran unable to feed himself or his family.

Absent any assistance from a national government, and with only minimal aid from states financially strapped by years of war, ex-Confederates began caring for their own. Informally at first, then as part of organized groups, Confederate veterans throughout the South reached out to provide for their less fortunate comrades.

The Commonwealth of Kentucky never joined the Confederacy, opting instead to accept occupation by Federal troops. Nevertheless, more than 40,000 Kentuckians wore Confederate gray during America's Civil War, and a share of them were unable to cope with postwar life. So Kentucky's more successful Confederate veterans—men who, at the dawn of the twentieth century, were building a New South over the ashes of bitterness and occupation—joined with sympathetic women—the mothers, wives, and daughters of veterans—to build a place of refuge for the unfortunates. With the support of a sympathetic state government, they created, financed, furnished, and operated the Kentucky Confederate Home, a charitable institution for needy Confederate veterans.

"The young men Kentucky gave to the Confederate army rendered their state some service and are . . . entitled to a respectable place in its history," said one of the orators at the opening of the Kentucky Confederate Home in 1902. Kentucky's Confederate veterans intended the Home to be a grand gesture of fraternal benevolence, a respectable institution far superior to the publicly funded almshouses, poor farms, and asylums typical of the time. Nearly a thousand Confederate veterans who had need of sustenance or care would find comfortable refuge at the elegant Pewee Valley home from 1902 to 1934.

The story of the Kentucky Confederate Home demonstrates the camaraderie of the campfire, the unbreakable bond linking military men who have drunk from the same canteen. But the story of the Home is much more than a story of men acting charitably toward their less fortunate brothers at arms.

The Kentucky Confederate Home was built on and supported by three distinct pillars: energetic Confederate veterans' groups, a sympathetic public, and a generous state government.

Kentucky Confederate veterans and their families were quick to organize after the war. They recovered their dead, built monuments, and remembered their wartime experiences. By the end of the nineteenth century, more than 3,500 ex-Confederates and 4,000 women were active in local United Confederate Veterans camps and United Daughters of the Confederacy chapters. Despite its reluctance to join the Confederacy, Kentucky's memory of a Union occupation that was often oppressive resulted in the commonwealth's becoming more "Southern" in the postwar years than it had ever been during the war.[3] Kentucky politicians recognized the public's sympathy for their Confederate veterans, especially when ex-Confederates helped Democratic governor J. C. W. Beckham secure his hold on the statehouse following the assassination of Governor William Goebel.

My Old Confederate Home describes the construction and eventual erosion of these supports as the men and women who created the Kentucky Confederate Home and the men who lived there aged and died, and public interest waned. The Home would eventually become politically inexpedient, its expense outweighed by more general need as Kentucky wrestled with the effects of the Great Depression.

The opening of the Kentucky Confederate Home in 1902 coincided with a closing of the wounds of sectionalism that had festered in Kentucky's political flesh for more than forty years. The years during which the Home operated marked an increasing respect for and pride in Southern heritage among Southerners. At the same time, women were assuming a more active role in social aid programs and politics. Thousands strong, Kentucky clubwomen demanded a greater involvement in, and responsibility for, the well-being of the old men of the Confederate generation. In telling the story of the Home, I hope to provide insight into early-twentieth-century attitudes toward honor, duty, aging, the role of women, social welfare, and the mythology of the Lost Cause.

The story of the Kentucky Confederate Home—the final chapter of Kentucky's Civil War history—has never been told at length.

Many of the Home's operational documents were lost in a 1920 fire, and original documents generated afterward were destroyed after careless filing and microfilming in the 1950s. However, Kentucky United Daughters of the Confederacy files and personal histories recently processed by the Kentucky Historical Society shed new light on the founding, operation, and people of the Home.

I also draw on unpublished letters and family stories collected from descendants of individuals who lived in or were employed by the Home during its operation to complete the history of this unique institution.

My Old Confederate Home includes the stories of a daring cavalryman turned bank robber, a senile ship's captain, a prosperous former madam, a dapper banker, and a small-town clergyman whose concern for the veterans cost him his pastorate. These individuals, and a dozen others, professed and acted upon deep personal and cultural respect for men who, decades earlier, left their homes and families to fight for a cause that was lost before the first battle was joined.

Most of all, though, the story of the Home is the story of the hundreds of men who lived out their final days there. The stories of an old man who loses his burial fund when the banks fail, a prisoner who trades one institution for another, and a black Confederate, among others, illustrate the unique lives and special needs of the veterans sheltered in the Home. They were farmers, factory workers, trainers, traders, politicians, and professionals who asked for and received help at a time when acceptance of public assistance was seen by some as an act of moral insufficiency.

The veterans who lived in the Kentucky Confederate Home were military men for no more than four years of their long lives (though few who have served in the military would claim that their few years in service did not mark the rest of their days in some manner). *My Old Confederate Home* seeks to remind us that those who take up arms on their nation's behalf are unique individuals; yet they are human beings with aspirations, dreams, and frailties similar to our own. As veterans, they have earned the respect and gratitude of their fellow citizens, but their military service does not define, ennoble, or excuse the rest of their existence.

Still, the men and women who fight our wars deserve a respectable place in our history and in our hearts.

"The nation salutes you."

Chapter 1

The Cripple and the Banker

Attorneys, banking officers, city officials, presidents of manufacturing firms, and other members of Louisville's business elite crowded the downstairs rooms of Billy Beasley's tiny rented home for his funeral on a late winter morning in 1898.

A hundred mourners, shoulder touching shoulder, listened in respectful silence as the Reverend Charles R. Hemphill, pastor of the city's prestigious Second Presbyterian Church, spoke a brief memorial tribute to Beasley.

The day was unseasonably warm. Every window of the small house at 227 East Madison Street was open, but the humidity from earlier rain showers and the close quarters caused the men in attendance to perspire under their black woolen suits. Despite wilting collars and sweat at the smalls of their backs, the men remained at solemn attention around Billy Beasley's open casket during an a cappella solo performed by Mrs. John S. Morris.

Then the Confederate Quartet, standing outside the parlor window, sang an upbeat medley of old soldier camp songs, ending with:

The same canteen, my soldier friend,
The very same canteen.
There's never a bond, old friend, like this!
We have drunk from the same canteen.

At a signal from Rev. Hemphill, Beasley's wife and daughters were escorted through the crowd and out to the street. Eight men stepped forward to close the casket, and then silently carried it to a horse-drawn hearse waiting outside.

John Hess Leathers, president of the Louisville National Banking Company, picked up the large floral arrangement—hothouse carnations and roses arranged in a design of the Confederate stars and bars—which stood at the headplate. He carried it behind the casket to the waiting hearse.

On March 6, 1898, an honor guard of Confederate veterans, all prominent Louisvillians, carried fifty-six-year-old William W. "Billy" Beasley, the crippled and impoverished owner of a street-corner cigar stand, to his final resting place.[1]

During the years following Lee's surrender at Appomattox, surviving Confederate soldiers struggled to cope with the consequences of having fought on the losing side in a long, bitter, ugly war.

America's Civil War permanently marked the generation of men who fought its battles. One in five white Southern men of military age—fathers, brothers, and sons—didn't survive the war; more than a quarter-million were killed in battle, died of wounds they received, or succumbed to disease. Of those who came home, 20 percent were visibly wounded, or crippled, disfigured, or disabled in some manner that would impair them for the rest of their lives. Tens of thousands more were disabled in ways less visible, but no less debilitating.[2]

William W. "Billy" Beasley was one of the visibly wounded.

Twenty years old and employed as a typesetter in Selma, Alabama, Beasley enlisted on April 21, 1861, in Company A, Fourth Alabama Infantry. Within a fortnight he was marching into Georgia with ten thousand other Southern boys caught up in the awful excitement of war. By first frost he had tasted battle at Manassas Junction, almost within sight of Washington City.

For the next three years Beasley and the Fourth Alabama fought in most of the major engagements of the eastern valleys: Seven Pines, Cold Harbor, Malvern Hill, and Gettysburg. At Chickamauga he was named color-bearer for his regiment and given a sergeant's chevron. Confident in his stripes, Beasley was, at twenty-three, an experienced infantryman with a long, drooping mustache and hair already showing gray.[3]

At one of the battles of the Wilderness Campaign in May 1864, Beasley took the soft lead ball that would cripple him. It was a side-to-side belly wound, breaking his right hipbone, destroying the left hip joint, and mostly missing the major organs in his abdomen. Through some miracle of battlefield medicine he survived, but for the rest of his life he would be tormented by bowel and kidney infections. And Sergeant Billy Beasley of the CSA would never again walk upright.

Eventually, Beasley and the rest of the surviving soldiers of the beaten Confederacy staggered home—most hungry, barefoot, half-naked, sick at heart, and without a penny in their pockets—to confront the hell that had been visited on their homes.

To be a citizen of the Old South in April 1865 was to suffer a psychic loss not unlike that of a farmer who emerges from a root cellar the morning after a tornado to see the things he had grown and owned now flattened or gone. The heady confidence of 1861 was replaced by shock, then a grim realization of the butchers' bill paid and the need to replant and rebuild.

In 1860 six Southern states were among the top ten states in the nation in per capita income. Twenty years later there would be no Southern state in the top thirty. Four years of war destroyed a century of Southern economic development.

Most Confederate veterans—sickly, wounded, disabled or not—simply stood up, spat out the ashes of defeat, and did what they had to do to care for themselves and their families. One by one, day by day, they put aside memories of that awful time as best they could and went back to work. There was plenty of work to be done and too few people to do it.

Nearly a million men who had worn the gray of the Southern Confederacy returned home after the war, and the victorious U.S. government felt no need to award its former foes any manner of medical care, pension, or assistance. The Fourteenth Amendment to the U.S. Constitution prohibited payment of pensions or compensation to ex-Confederates, and Republican congressmen were positively gleeful at its ratification in 1868. (Congressman Thaddeus Stevens regretted only that the punishment was too lenient for traitorous Rebels. "A load of misery must sit heavy on their souls," he said.)

In state after state, Reconstruction governments refused to consider the payment of pensions to Confederate veterans (or promptly rescinded the few programs that were enacted). Even as the strictures of Reconstruction were eased, most Southern states were hobbled by debt and the costs of rebuilding. Few local governments were in any better position to provide significant relief to disabled Confederate veterans.[4]

Shortly after the outbreak of hostilities, the federal Congress enacted a pension plan for its own injured veterans (and for the widows and children of those who would not survive the war). Throughout the 1860s and 1870s, Congress passed a series of acts that provided pensions of up to $31 a month for disabled Union veterans. Any Union veteran disabled by injury, disease, or conditions resulting from his service was entitled to a monthly pension or a lump-sum payment for the time since his discharge. A national organization of Union veterans, the Grand Army of the Republic (GAR), was founded in 1866 and evolved into a formidable political machine, lobbying for increased benefits for soldiers of the winning side.[5]

Some Southern states offered artificial limbs or enacted modest pension programs; ex-Confederate soldiers in Kentucky, however, received nothing.

By the 1880s age and the debilitating effects of their time spent in uniform began to impair the ability of many Confederate veterans to earn a living. Disabled veterans grew more visible on the streets and in the alleys of Southern cities. Some were able to eke out a slim living; others were unemployed and homeless. Whether due to lingering pain in body or soul, many turned to liquor or laudanum for relief.[6]

Sergeant Billy Beasley was one of the all-too-visible cripples. He could walk, but only in tiny half-steps from the knees down, as if his thighs were cinched together with harness strap. Pain and poor balance kept him stooped at the waist like a bowing manservant. Beasley was a skilled typesetter, his fingers fast and his eyes strong. He found regular employment at print shops and newspapers, but periodic bouts of infection and a weakness for strong drink regularly cost him the jobs those skills had earned.

He drifted from job to job, city to city, northward through Tennessee and finally into Kentucky.

As Beasley and other disabled ex-Confederate soldiers drifted, the United States was providing military pensions and medical care to more than 200,000 Union army veterans. (The pension office paid an estimated $88 million in 1889 alone.) Veterans' benefits were becoming the largest single item in the federal budget, accounting for almost 18 percent of the total.[7]

For the tens of thousands of crippled, impoverished, or soul-sick ex-Confederates like Sergeant Billy Beasley there was little public assistance in Louisville, Kentucky. If these veterans were to receive a helping hand, it would have to be from one that had shared the same canteen.[8]

Many ex-Confederates, however, had no need of help. Through some inexplicable formula involving education, family connections, special skill, determination, or just plain luck, they managed to side-step the awful and lasting personal consequences of four years of civil war.

On Good Friday, March 30, 1888, banker John Hess Leathers left his office at the Louisville Banking Company and walked three blocks to the offices of the *Louisville Courier-Journal.* There he delivered a handwritten notice to the editor with the soft-spoken request that it be published as soon as possible in the newspaper.

The notice appeared on the front page of Sunday's edition: "You are respectfully invited to attend a meeting of ex-Confederate soldiers, to be held on Monday evening, April 2, at 8 o'clock, in the City Court room, City Hall, entrance on Jefferson Street, for the purpose of forming in this city a permanent Society of ex-Confederates."[9]

More than sixty well-dressed men milled around the room on Monday night when ex-Confederate George B. Eastin called the meeting to order. Eastin was well known to the others in the room.

He had been a Confederate cavalryman and had ridden with General John Hunt Morgan. Captured during Morgan's Ohio raid, Eastin was imprisoned at Camp Douglas in Chicago but escaped, and made his way into Canada to join Confederate conspirators there. (Though he could have been hanged had it been known in wartime, by 1888 it was common knowledge that Eastin was one of the out-of-uniform saboteurs who infiltrated Yankee-occupied St. Louis for the purpose of destroying the docks and bridges there.) Eastin was now a prominent Louisville attorney with an extensive corporate practice.[10]

Eastin opened the meeting by acknowledging other familiar faces in the room. He introduced two judges, an Episcopal bishop, two company presidents, a newspaper publisher, and others, all to loud applause.

We have all been comrades around the campfire, Eastin told them, and today we are comrades in business and commerce. He reminded his listeners of the comrades not in attendance that evening because they lacked streetcar fare or appropriate dress, or because of their infirmity or misfortune. He spoke of men who had already passed away, who were buried in paupers' graves without dignity or the honor due them.

"I have gathered an organizing committee," Eastin said, "to establish an association of men who were honorably engaged in the service of the Confederate States of America. As in the past, if no others should help us, we shall help ourselves."

The room erupted in cheers.

The eight men of the organizing committee sat at the head table with Eastin, all men with impeccable Confederate and civic credentials. But it was the bullet-headed man in the fashionable dark suit sitting to Eastin's right who had assembled the committee, served as the group's secretary, and drafted the constitution presented to the veterans that evening. Major Eastin was at the podium, but former Sergeant-Major John H. Leathers was the one who got things done.[11]

Like Billy Beasley, John Leathers was born in 1841, and both had been Confederate infantrymen who earned their sergeants' stripes in combat. The similarities ended there.

Leathers was born in northern Virginia, son of a cabinetmaker and the youngest of seven children. Working in his father's shop, writing bills of sale, delivering invoices, and keeping inventory, Leathers showed an early aptitude for numbers and organization. By age sixteen he was clerking at a dry goods store in Martinsburg, a crossroads town on the eastern slopes of the Appalachian Mountains just ten miles south of Maryland and the Potomac River.

In 1859 young Leathers came to Louisville, having been called there by an uncle for employment with a retail druggist in the city. A year later he became bookkeeper in the wholesale clothing firm of William Terry & Company.

At the first news of war Leathers put down his ledger books, returned home, and enlisted in the Second Virginia Infantry of Lee's Army of Northern Virginia. By the time Leathers returned to Louisville in the autumn of 1865, having healed from an injury suffered at Gettysburg, his old employer had founded a new firm and was holding a position open for the returning veteran. Leathers needed only to buy a new suit of clothes and settle in to manage the firm's accounts.

During the five years he kept books for the wholesale clothing firm of Jones & Tapp, Leathers built a reputation as a tight-vested young man: composed, controlled, and diligent at balancing assets and liabilities to the penny. It became apparent that Leathers's business skills extended beyond account books, and in 1870 the twenty-nine-year-old ex-Confederate was admitted as a partner in the renamed firm of Tapp, Leathers & Company.[12]

Because of his business, Leathers adopted the habit of wearing stylish suits and cravats of the best fabrics. And he wore them well. Leathers seemed to stand taller than his five-foot, ten-inch height, largely because of his broad shoulders, slim waist, and rigid posture. His hair was a sandy brown, cut slightly shorter than current fashion. Older men wore their beards full, but Leathers shaved to a neat mustache and an imperial, a pointed tuft of beard on the lower lip and chin. Even at a young age, John Leathers exhibited the demeanor of a serious man.

Throughout the 1870s and early 1880s Leathers managed the

operations of Tapp, Leathers & Company while his partner, P. H. Tapp, a native of Florence, Alabama, cultivated customers. By 1885 more than 500 employees under Leathers's supervision were manufacturing Kentucky jeans and lines of men's and boys' dress clothing for retailers throughout the country.

In 1885 Theodore Harris, a successful Louisville financier, moved his Louisville Banking Company to a new building at the corner of Fifth and Market Streets. Harris had narrowly avoided the financial panics of the 1870s and was now poised for aggressive expansion throughout Kentucky. He was looking for a man with "all the snap and dash of Young America" to direct the growth of his bank. On April 1, 1885, Harris and his board of directors convinced John Leathers to oversee day-to-day operations of the Louisville Banking Company.[13]

Three years later, by the night of the organizational meeting of ex-Confederates at Louisville's City Hall, Leathers's "snap and dash" had resulted in the tripling of deposits of the Louisville Banking Company. The forty-four-year-old former infantryman was head of Kentucky's largest financial institution.

At Eastin's nod, Leathers distributed printed copies of the constitution he and his committee had drafted for discussion by the veterans present. Louisville city court judge W. L. Jackson moved that the constitution be read aloud and approved section by section.

John Weller, a local attorney and former Confederate infantry captain, began his reading with Article I: "This association shall be known as 'The Confederate Association of Kentucky.'"

Within three hours the constitution of the new association had been debated and approved. Most of the debate centered around such extraneous items as the meeting schedule—four times annually "on the second Monday of April, July, October and January"—and the means by which men who had brought dishonor on the Confederacy could be excluded—"five black balls shall reject any application" for membership.

Article II remained just as Leathers and his committee had drafted it. The first object of the association, the constitution read, "shall be the cultivation of social relationships" and "to preserve the fraternal ties of comradeship." But the organization also pledged to "aid and assist those of the members who, from disease, misfortune or the infirmities of age, may become incapable of supporting themselves or families," to "pay a decent respect to the remains and to the memory of those who die," and to "see that no worthy Confederate shall ever become an object of public charity."

Much of the rest of the document was organizational boilerplate, but Article IX had been inserted at Leathers's suggestion: "This association shall have power to receive and hold any property, real, personal or mixed, that may be donated by any person for the use of the relief fund or for other purposes of the association."

The wording was sufficiently vague so that the article caused little comment on the evening of ratification; but this single paragraph would—more than a decade later—allow for the establishment of the Kentucky Confederate Home.

The proposed constitution was ratified unanimously.

The next bit of business for the evening was the election of officers. Reading from a sheet that had been prepared for him, Judge Jackson nominated Eastin for president, Leathers for vice-president, and newspaper editor Thomas D. Osborne for secretary. The slate was approved by acclamation.

At the end of the evening sixty-eight men answered the first roll call, affixed their signatures to the new constitution, then turned and saluted their new officers. They were the charter members of Louisville's new Confederate Association of Kentucky.

In the aftermath of the war, some veterans wished never to speak of it again. Others sought to regain the comradeship of others who, like them, had faced the cannon and have the chance to share stories of their wartime experiences.

The South's surviving upper class—the more affluent, the better educated, the least affected by lasting hardships—were forming the first regional veterans' clubs almost before the ink dried at Appomattox. The Army of Northern Virginia Association was organized in 1870, its membership consisting primarily of Robert E. Lee's former staff officers. There was the Society of the Army and Navy of the Confederate States, a Society of Ex-Confederate Soldiers and Sailors, and even an Association of Medical Officers of the Army and Navy of the Confederacy.[14]

The Association of the Army of Tennessee (AAT), founded in 1877, provided an opportunity for well-heeled veterans to meet in a different city each year for extravagant banquets, cigars, music, and evenings of drunken storytelling. (The bill of fare from one of these banquets lists a choice of ten wild game entrees, eight oyster dishes, and fourteen desserts.)[15]

Though these early organizations may have espoused noble ideals, most were elitist in their membership and were formed for little more than social purposes. Few expanded beyond their regional roots.

The founding of Louisville's Confederate Association of Kentucky in 1888, however, marked a change in the nature of Confederate veterans' organizations that was beginning to occur throughout the South as veterans aged and their needs increased. The new Louisville association would certainly serve a social purpose, but its membership was sworn to aid, honor, and support their less fortunate comrades.

The veterans who chartered the Confederate Association of Kentucky were lawyers, physicians, legislators, educators, judges, bankers, and business owners. They were members of Louisville's commercial and social elite and could certainly afford the association's $5.00 initiation fee—the equivalent of a week's wages for a factory worker—and dues of $1.00 at every meeting. The organization's money would not be spent on elaborate banquets and bands, however. Instead, the funds would be banked (at Leathers's bank, of course) in separate accounts, with initiation fees designated for relief and dues used to pay the group's minimal operating expenses. From time to time, amounts not used for organizational expenses would be moved into the Relief Fund. The Confederate Association of Kentucky was strict about spending its money on relief and not revelry. During its first nine years the group collected $7,500, spending all but $425 on relief and memorial work.[16]

The association's bylaws empowered the officers of the organization—including Eastin, Leathers, and Osborne—to examine applicants for need and worthiness, then make their recommendations for assistance to an executive committee.

When Billy Beasley, disabled and destitute at forty-eight years of age, arrived in Louisville with his two-year-old daughter in the humid summer of 1889, no public assistance program was available to him. But Beasley and his family would receive the help of some of Louisville's most prominent citizens.

P. H. Tapp, John Leathers's former partner in the clothing business and a native Alabaman, may have introduced Billy Beasley to the banker. Or perhaps Beasley wrote his own letter of introduction to Leathers, who was fast becoming one of the most prominent ex-Confederates in the state.

By whatever means the introduction occurred, Beasley and Leathers met at Leathers's office off the main lobby of the Louisville Banking Company in November 1889. Beasley needed help, and Leathers would give a serious hearing to any man who had worn the gray.

Leathers and Beasley had been born just two months apart. Both grew up practicing a trade, and both might have lived fulfilling lives as tradesmen had not the war intervened. But in 1889 it would be difficult to find two men more different.

Leathers stood tall. Freshly barbered, with his made-to-order suit and shined shoes with thin leather soles, he radiated the vitality of a successful capitalist in the process of building a New South. The cork soles of Beasley's shoes scuffed across the floor as he hobbled into Leathers's corner office. He was bent at the waist, barely able to look Leathers in the eye, a secondhand derby in his hand.

The first order of business between the two men was to establish Beasley's bona fides as a Confederate veteran: date of enlistment, units served, marches, encampments, and, finally, the battle that put a ball through Beasley's hip. Beasley produced his discharge and parole papers.

Discussion then turned to Beasley's need for assistance and his worthiness for relief.

The bent man told of his years since the war: constant pain, increasing disability, a growing familiarity with alcohol, and the loss of job after job. Like a guilty traveler emptying his suitcase before a customs inspector, the Alabaman laid out the sad highlights of his life story for Leathers.

Beasley had married for the first time in Nashville three years before. She was a churchgoing woman for whom Beasley had forsaken alcohol completely, but his bride had died in childbirth. Now, with hands too tremorous and brain too slow to find employment sorting type for a printer, the crippled veteran was left with a baby to raise and the hope of finding occasional odd jobs to support them both.

As a bank manager, Leathers was accustomed to hearing tales of woe, and he shared a conviction common to successful men in the nineteenth century. An individual's character—not his upbringing, not his current circumstance, and certainly not society—made him responsible for his own acts. The "worthy" man is one whose character is sufficiently strong to avoid the pitfalls of alcoholism, drug addiction, financial mismanagement, or moral dissolution. Or, if so ensnared, the worthy man has the strength of character to return himself to a virtuous path with the assistance of others.[17]

A veteran like Beasley had shown his strength of character on the battlefield by carrying a rifle and following the bugle. He had further demonstrated the inner strength necessary to give up alcohol and drugs, and take responsibility for his family. Beasley's indigence was, therefore, not a result of poor character. By this measure, Leathers and the Confederate Association of Kentucky deemed the crippled and unfortunate Sergeant Beasley worthy of assistance.

Within days of his meeting with Leathers, Beasley began receiving a temporary stipend of $2.00 a week to provide food for himself and his daughter. He received a letter telling him of a vacant apartment owned by Thomas Osborne in which he could live rent-free for six months. And he received a $100 loan from the Louisville Banking Company—guaranteed by Leathers, of course—to open a news and cigar stand at the corner of Market and Fifth Streets in Louisville.

Seven years later, in the winter of 1896, Mrs. Nannie H. Williams of Guthrie, Kentucky, came to Louisville for a stay at her son's home. One day during her visit, Mrs. Williams was sharing tea with callers, and the women were recalling war days in Kentucky.

Her son told the visitors of an acquaintance, a Confederate veteran who kept a little cigar stand on the corner of Market and Fifth Streets. "He was wounded in one of the battles of the Wilderness," the son said, "and can't walk a step; but he is always there, cheerful and pleased to serve his customers."

"We women soon had on our bonnets," Mrs. Williams later wrote, "for this one considers herself a Confederate veteran, and that story had touched a sympathetic chord."[18]

Nannie Williams, her friends, and her son boarded a streetcar for the trip downtown to meet Billy Beasley.

"The inevitable stand was by the wall of the great bank (doubtless by courtesy of some friend within)," she wrote, "and an old gray-haired Johnny Reb with keen eye beneath his shabby derby hat was perched on his high seat, ready to sell cigars, chewing-wax or anything in his line."

Billy Beasley had made the most of his last chance. With the help of the Confederate Association of Kentucky he had opened a little cigar, news, and snack stand, a wooden lean-to nestled next to the granite stairs outside the entrance to John Leathers's Louisville Banking Company. He had taken a sobriety pledge and joined a church. There he met and later married a widow, also with a daughter, and the family of four lived simply in a small rented home on East Madison Street.

Beasley became a celebrity of sorts in the fall of 1895, when 150,000 Union veterans descended on Louisville for their annual Grand Army of the Republic reunion. Beasley's downtown newsstand was a popular destination for the swarm of Yankee veterans, and out-of-town newsmen found the crippled but cheerful Rebel a good subject for the feature stories they dispatched to newspaper editors back home.

At her son's introduction, Mrs. Williams stepped forward to shake Beasley's hand.

"My best friends have always been the ladies," said Beasley with a warm smile and a quick wink.

Nannie Williams was charmed by the little man, and Billy Beasley, proud to have escaped the poverty and uselessness that had dogged him through his middle years, was gratified by the attention.

"When you go to that hospitable city of Louisville," Mrs. Williams advised, "find the old sergeant at his stand. You will be none the poorer to invest in some of his offerings."

On the humid afternoon of March 6, 1898, John H. Leathers met the hearse carrying Billy Beasley's casket at the entrance to Cave Hill Cemetery. A persistent abdominal infection related to the wound he suffered years before had finally overcome the crippled merchant with the shabby derby, even after six weeks of hospital care.

W. B. Haldeman, John Castleman, Bennett H. Young, Thomas D. Osborne, John Pirtle, William O. Coleman, Harry P. McDonald, and dozens more of Kentucky's business, social, and political elite—Confederate veterans all—formed ranks to escort the body of Sergeant Beasley to its final resting place in the cemetery's Confederate lot.

Leathers lingered by the graveside for a few moments after interment, one of Kentucky's most prominent bankers paying final tribute to the unfortunate cripple. As newly elected president of the Confederate Association of Kentucky, Leathers would soon approve bank drafts paying the bills for Billy Beasley's hospital care, funeral service, floral tributes, cemetery plot, and headstone, all in fulfillment of the group's promise to "pay a decent respect to the remains and to the memory of those who die."

Three decades after the end of the war, Kentucky's Confederate veterans were caring for, supporting, honoring, and burying their own.[19]

Chapter 2

The Private and the Clubwoman

The afternoon air smelled of blooming dogwood, fresh-cut flowers, and raw pine lumber on Saturday, June 10, 1893. Fourteen men and women sat in folding chairs on a wooden speakers' platform erected the day before on a hillside in the Confederate section of Lexington Cemetery.

A thick carpet of greenery and cut flowers encircled the platform. Some of the flowers were formal arrangements; most were snipped from gardens that morning, gathered into proud bouquets and laid against the others. Blue, white, and red ribbons fluttered from the arrangements. Outside the colorful perimeter a patient crowd of some two thousand people milled about, meeting friends, sharing greetings, waiting for the festivities to begin. Here and there, families spread picnic fare on quilts in the shade among the gravestones.

From his seat on the speakers' stand, John Boyd looked down on the frivolity with a vague expression of disapproval. He said nothing, but sat rigid on his wooden folding chair, back straight, palms resting flat on his knees, head up, eyes moving only to appraise the crowd. He was a stiff-necked man in his fifties, of average height but with a slight excess of weight. An impressive mustache drew attention from his thinning gray hair, receding hairline, and thickening jowls. As was his practice during public appearances, Boyd wore a dark woolen suit of generous cut, a boiled white shirt, a black silk four-in-hand, and a lapel button that identified him as a veteran of the Army of the Confederate States of America.

Seated near Boyd, Adeline Allen Graves twisted and turned left and right to chat with other dignitaries on the platform, a social ballet at which the slim brunette was particularly adept. She spoke to those near her with an easy familiarity; at one time or other she had asked most of the women surrounding her to chair a volunteer committee and most of the men for a charitable donation. Adeline Graves —everyone knew her as "Addie"—was one of Lexington's most active clubwomen, and if she was not speaking with people nearby about Confederate veteran business, she was certainly conducting the business of some other civic or service organization. On this day she wore an expensive china silk dress, stylish for the new season but not faddish, the muted colors appropriate for a public ceremony honoring Lexington's Confederate war dead.

At 4:00 P.M. sharp John Boyd consulted his pocket watch; then, closing it with a snap, he stepped to the podium to begin this ritual of the Lost Cause.[1]

The formation in 1888 of Louisville's Confederate Association of Kentucky reflected a desire by ex-Confederates to revisit what for many was the most significant experience of their lives.

In towns and villages throughout the South in the decades following the war, ex-Confederates began gathering for small meetings and reunions. At first, the meetings were impromptu and informal—old friends meeting at a country graveyard, a local grillroom, or the county courthouse to speak quietly of the sights they had seen and the faces they would never see again. "You go to reunions," said one old veteran of another war, "and you find yourself trying to remember what you've spent the last fifty years trying to forget."[2]

Kentucky's postwar economy fostered a new middle class— business owners, shopkeepers, physicians, lawyers, skilled workers —in the smaller cities and towns, and these men began to organize into formal local groups. The ex-Confederates met to celebrate the fellowship of their shared experience in wartime, but, like their counterparts in more urban areas, found it difficult to overlook the disabled and impoverished veterans in their own communities.

These local Confederate veterans' groups were more inclusive than the elite national associations of former officers that sprang up immediately after the war. They flourished as social and political organizations (though most publicly disavowed any political purpose), and many provided some manner of personal relief for their aging and less fortunate comrades: a box of groceries for a neighbor too sick to plow or enough cordwood for a one-armed man to get through winter.

By the end of the 1880s the rebuilt South was dotted with hundreds of independent small-town groups, and some began to coalesce into statewide organizations. Groups in Georgia rallied under the banner of the Confederate Veteran Survivors Association, South Carolina groups formed the Old Survivors Association, and Virginians launched a campaign to assemble their Grand Camp of Confederate Veterans.[3]

At a statewide reunion of veterans of Kentucky's Orphan Brigade held in Louisville in September 1889 (and hosted by Louisville's new Confederate Association of Kentucky), banker John Leathers proposed that Kentucky's ex-Confederates establish auxiliary branches of the Louisville group. Local branches of the statewide organization would pay dues into a common fund, elect a slate of officers, and adopt bylaws dedicating themselves to the care of members in distress and to honorable burial of the deceased. Visiting veterans saw the benefit of affiliating with Louisville's Confederate Association of Kentucky, and appointed a committee to make it happen.

"It is likely," said the enthusiastic committee chairman, "that nearly all of the ex-Confederates in the state will be members of the Association by [next year]."[4]

The committee chairman failed to account for the determination and salesmanship of one former Confederate private from Lexington.

John Boyd of Lexington was, by all accounts, one of those men for whom military service becomes a defining moment in life.[5]

A native Kentuckian, Boyd was born in 1841 in Richmond, thirty miles south of Lexington, but his family moved to Texas during the first years of the Great Southern Migration of the 1850s. A yellow fever epidemic killed some of his family and sent the rest scurrying back to Lexington three years later.

There, Boyd attended public schools and worked horses—caring for them, training them, and trading them—until he joined the army of the Confederate States when it occupied central Kentucky in 1862. He served as a private in the Buckner Guards, a cavalry unit of the state militia.

A private soldier in combat learns quickly that his immediate world is divided into two parts: one for himself and one for the officers. The officer is always warm, dry, clean, and safe; the private is invariably cold, wet, and a mile from food or relief.

During days on the march and nights in camp Boyd shared cold, wet, and hunger with other men of the lowest ranks. He formed lasting friendships with Kentuckians who knew what it meant to sleep under a pine-bough lean-to while officers slept on cots in taut canvas tents. He trusted his life to the men standing next to him in the battle line, not to the officers who viewed combat through spyglasses. Boyd's unit surrendered in North Carolina at the end of the war, and he joined the rest of the exhausted veterans on the long walk back to Kentucky.

After his return to Lexington, Boyd supported himself as a saddlemaker and an investor; but he comported himself as a soldier. He was said to be an absolute teetotaler with a clear and unequivocal view of right and wrong.

During the postwar years, when garrulous generals were describing the wisdom of their battlefield strategies in books and magazines, Boyd felt compelled to celebrate and honor the common soldier. He organized the effort (and paid much of the cost) to relocate the bodies of fourteen Lexington soldiers from poorly marked graves on distant battlefields to new burial plots under the crabapple trees in Lexington Cemetery. Boyd's collection of Civil War–era photos, engravings, and artifacts was said to be the finest private collection in Kentucky.[6]

For the best of motives, perhaps, Boyd distrusted the founders and leaders of Louisville's Confederate Association. They were officer types, he reasoned—high-sounding, inflated, and not to be trusted by the common soldier.

In 1890 Boyd formed his own Kentucky veterans' organization.[7]

He enlisted former comrades-at-arms from twenty rural counties to serve as chairmen, each responsible for helping to organize a local veterans association. After less than a year of ardent correspondence, personal visits, and recruitment, Boyd had assembled twelve newly organized groups into his own statewide organization, the Confederate Veteran Association of Kentucky, on November 29, 1890. (The Louisville association of ex-Confederates was not invited to affiliate.)

"Your [Executive] Committee . . . will be pardoned the pride they have in the success of the organization," Boyd wrote to members shortly after founding the new organization. "Our Association has steadily grown from its birth, scarce ten months ago, until now its Veteran and Honorary membership has reached more than three hundred in number."

From the beginning, Boyd was dismissive of any social purpose for his new statewide association. The strenuous efforts of the association, he wrote, quoting from the group's bylaws, are to be directed toward "the permanent establishment and endowment of a home for those who, 'from disease, misfortune, or the infirmities of age, may become incapable of supporting themselves or families.'"[8]

Boyd's more immediate goal, however, was to affiliate his group with a new national organization, the United Confederate Veterans.[9]

A quarter century after the founding of the Grand Army of the Republic, the organization of Union veterans, representatives of a dozen Confederate veterans' groups from Louisiana, Tennessee, and Mississippi met in New Orleans in 1889 to form a national association for ex-Confederates. The small group chose a name, United Confederate Veterans (UCV), and began gathering the smaller, independent Confederate groups (called "camps") and fledgling state organizations into a single national association.[10]

Under the UCV umbrella, small camps would share similar bylaws, dues structures, and membership requirements quite different from the more elitist, big-city associations with their $5.00 initiation fees and $1.00-a-meeting dues.

Not surprisingly, the UCV operated under a military structure. The chief national officer was the "commander-in-chief," and all other officers were given a military rank in the organization. The chain of command provided for three geographical departments, and each department was divided into state divisions (although individual camps were virtually autonomous).

The UCV provided its members a national standing, an affiliation with small-town former Confederates throughout the country. Members of a nine-man camp in Ringgold, Georgia, could join with counterparts in Honey Grove, Texas, or Rosedale, Mississippi, or any of the hundreds of other communities throughout the rebuilt South to raise money for a national memorial or share stories at one of the popular annual reunions.

By 1892, when the fifteen camps of John Boyd's Confederate Veteran Association of Kentucky affiliated with the United Confederate Veterans, the UCV commanded more than two hundred camps and was the fastest-growing fraternal organization in the nation. At the national meeting in New Orleans in 1892, Commanding General John B. Gordon commissioned John Boyd Major General, Commander of the Kentucky Division.[11] The zealous former private soldier of Lexington eagerly adopted his UCV rank and thereafter would be known as Major General John Boyd.[12] Yet "this is not a military organization," John Boyd told a reporter, "but is merely a brotherhood or fraternity with benevolent intentions."[13]

While it was true that the members of Boyd's Kentucky Confederate Veteran Association and other early UCV camps were not armed combatants, they surely liked to march in their uniforms.

More than 150 members of the Confederate Veteran Association gathered outside the gates of Lexington Cemetery on Saturday afternoon, June 10, 1893. Most of the men wore a gray suit: matching pants and jacket cut and ornamented to look like a military uniform. In its early days, the UCV had no standardized uniform for members; any ex-Confederate who could afford it would engage a tailor to create a uniform as ornate and fanciful as the veteran desired.

Men like John Boyd, however, were irritated by the inconsistency of dress, and often designated a local clothier as the sole source of member uniforms. (Globe Tailoring of Lexington did a booming business in Confederate veteran uniforms at $30 each.)

Outside the cemetery, Boyd formed his men into a line of march. It was becoming traditional among veterans' groups to arrive at their events on parade. The marching column echoed their service in the military and—especially if accompanied by a band—placed them at the center of attention.

For this march, the veterans formed up in pairs, the first two being the chaplains of Lexington and Winchester camps. The next two were Boyd and U. S. congressman W. C. P. Breckinridge, the featured orator for the day. Boyd barked a command, and an honor guard of the Brown Light Infantry led the column of men (which marched mostly in step) through the heavy iron cemetery gates, along the lanes between the gravestones, to the Confederate lot, with its sprays of fresh-cut flowers and a speakers' platform. ("The march was strikingly impressive," according to one observer.)[14]

Arriving at the Confederate section, the marchers broke ranks, and Boyd and Breckinridge took their seats on the platform. The remainder of the veterans joined the crowd of two thousand to await the dedication of their statue and the celebration of Confederate Decoration Day, two of the New South's most common Lost Cause rituals.

In the latter decades of the nineteenth century, Southerners began transforming their collective memory of utter defeat and total destruction in the Civil War into a myth-history known as the Lost Cause. Taking its name from *The Lost Cause: A New Southern History of the War of the Confederates*, an 1866 book by Virginia newspaperman Edward A. Pollard, the mythology of the Lost Cause allowed Southerners to downplay the calamitous outcome of the war while celebrating the manner in which it was fought.

"Whatever opinions may exist as to the right or wrong of the long and bitter controversy that culminated in the War Between the States, one thing can be confidently affirmed," a Lost Cause orator of the time declaimed: "That the annals of our common history bear no greater chapter than that wherein is written the record of Confederate valor and constancy."[15]

Valor and constancy.

As years passed, reverence for the Lost Cause would grow into something akin to a new civil religion that rendered Southerners the true believers, a people set apart in their willingness to fight and die for independence.

Lost Cause writings and activities reinforced the bravery of the common Confederate soldier, his prowess at arms, and his chivalry toward women and the cause of the weak. Lost Cause oratory praised the Confederate soldier for his devotion to comrades and his life-long fidelity to principles of individual and sectional independence.

Kentucky became an active supporter of the federal government during the war. But twenty-five years later, Kentuckians embraced the myth of the Lost Cause more firmly than it had ever embraced the Confederate cause during years of conflict.

In 1861, as other slaveholding states bolted the Union, Kentucky was led by a pro-secession governor and a pro-Union state legislature. Meeting in a special session called by the governor to organize a secession convention, Unionist legislators balked, voting instead for an official policy of neutrality in the coming conflict. Unwilling to accept neutrality, two hundred pro-secession legislators and other citizens from sixty-five counties met shortly after in Russellville to pass a sovereignty resolution, voting Kentucky out of the Union and into the Confederacy. (Jefferson Davis and the Confederate Congress accepted the action of this rump legislature and admitted Kentucky as the thirteenth state of the Confederate States of America.)[16]

The official neutrality policy lasted only until Kentucky's shooting war began, when the pro-Union state legislature created a military force to expel the Confederates. By early 1862 Federal troops controlled the state's major cities, river ports, and rail centers; by the end of that year the Federals owned the state.

Kentuckians of every political stripe chafed under the wartime measures of the military occupation. Censorship, loyalty oaths, seizure of goods and crops, conscription, and restrictions on movement led to a smoldering resentment toward the Federal occupiers.[17] With every Federal outrage (or rumored outrage), more Kentucky men left their homes and drifted southward to join the Confederate forces.

At the end of the war, when crisp Union soldiers marched northward to home and their victory parades, Kentucky's Confederates returned to the Bluegrass State battered, worn to rags, and, in many cases, bearing the scars of vicious combat.

Kentucky was spared the harsh restrictions of Reconstruction, but the drastic changes brought about by Emancipation, the objectionable operations of the Freedmen's Bureau, and an unwise military administration evoked sympathy even among the state's Unionists. In the first postwar elections, Kentuckians thoroughly repudiated the party of Lincoln to elect a solidly Democratic state legislature and state house. No Republican would again hold statewide office for almost three decades.

In the main, Kentuckians accepted the destruction of slavery and the renunciation of state sovereignty, but many adopted the historiography of the Lost Cause. They decried the war, but ennobled the higher principles for which it was fought and exalted the warriors who fought it. Johnny Reb, an earnest Kentucky farm boy with a squirrel rifle in 1861, had become, by the 1890s, a knightly warrior with "illustrious courage and splendid patriotism and unselfish consecration to the cause of liberty."[18]

The civil religion of the Lost Cause spawned its own rituals: the veterans' solemn march through the cemetery, soaring oratory at patriotic or memorial gatherings, the dedication of a public statue to the Confederate soldier, decoration of the graves of Confederate dead.

In Lexington Cemetery on June 10, 1893, at 4:00 P.M. sharp, according to John Boyd's pocket watch, the bittersweet Lost Cause celebration began.

Opening the ceremony, Boyd called to the podium Rev. E. L. Southgate to invoke a Christian blessing on the afternoon's events. Next, a local vocalist sang "A Conquered Banner," a Lost Cause anthem that brought tears to the eyes of some in the audience.

Then Congressman W. C. P. Breckinridge took the podium.

William Cabell Preston Breckinridge came from a prominent Bluegrass family, and his Confederate military service had propelled him to a successful career in law and politics. Breckinridge was currently serving his fifth consecutive term in Congress and had every expectation of winning reelection for a sixth. He was known (without a speck of irony) as "the silver-tongued orator of Kentucky," and his appearance at this dedication added to the importance of the event.

Breckinridge opened his speech by pointing at the statue to be dedicated, still hidden under a white drapery. He spoke of those who contributed money to purchase the statue, and of their desire to honor Confederate heroes under the gaze of this noble figure.

At his signal, two young women pulled ropes to unveil the marble monument, a larger-than-life Confederate soldier standing on a seven-foot base. The figure wore a neatly blocked hat and knee-length greatcoat, a rifle resting before him. ("The dress is of better style and fit than the real soldier ever wore or saw on his proudest day," an observer remarked.)[19]

Breckinridge spoke of the valor of the Confederate soldiers represented by this marble figure: "History did not record more daring or braver soldiers." He spoke of the constancy of their devotion to the cause, describing them as "heroes who had fought desperately and given their life blood for what they believed was right." He preached reconciliation: "Though the memories of the past are dear to Southerners, we are American citizens." And patriotism: "The love we now hold for the Union is second to none."

After an emotional conclusion, in which Breckinridge described what he would say to his comrades when he met them again in heaven, the silver-tongued legend returned to his seat amid cheers from the crowd.[20]

To cool the heat of Breckinridge's passionate oratory, a choir sang "We Will Cross over the River and Rest under the Shade of the Trees," a mournful Lost Cause standard written by Sidney Lanier, based on the final words of General Stonewall Jackson:

Thou land whose sun is gone, thy stars remain!
Still shine the words that miniature his deeds.

O thrice-beloved, where'er thy great heart bleeds,
Solace hast thou for pain!

After a respectful silence for the sentiment of the hymn, Boyd stepped to the podium to introduce Addie Graves. The clubwoman would preside over the next part of the ritual.[21]

As in centuries past, women took care of the war dead.

In one of the hundreds of mostly forgotten battles of the Civil War, a Union force met three Confederate brigades on a rainy January morning in 1862 near Mill Springs in Pulaski County, Kentucky. By the end of the day, more than two hundred men lay dead on the ground of a small meadow. The bodies were separated—blue on one side, gray on the other—and hastily buried as the armies moved on to other killing fields.

After the war, Federal employees returned to Pulaski County to disinter the Union dead. Some of the remains were shipped back to the soldiers' homes; the rest were reburied in individual plots of a neat cemetery. The Confederate dead remained in their mass grave, covered with earth, stone, and logs, largely forgotten.[22]

But a child who grew up in a cabin adjacent to the battlefield didn't forget.

Each spring, as others gathered at the nearby cemetery to honor Federal dead, Dorothea Burton collected roses from her mother's garden, fresh fern branches, and mountain flowers to lay in tribute on the brushy mound that marked the Confederate mass grave. Year after year she enlisted others to join her, and they brought still others, until Dorothea's annual decoration of the burial pit and its nameless dead became a regular community event.[23]

Throughout the postwar South, women memorialized their lost sons, husbands, and fathers. Recalling ancient tradition, the women marked soldiers' graves with flowers, then later erected monuments to Confederates living and dead. This memorial work continued a tradition of volunteerism demonstrated by Southern women during the Civil War. While men fought, their wives, daughters, and mothers formed hospital associations, sewing circles, relief societies, and food lines in towns and villages throughout Kentucky.

Women of South Carolina claim to have organized the first formal postwar memorial society. Members of the Charleston Ladies Memorial Association walked to the city cemetery under the hostile glares of occupying Federal troops in May 1865 to decorate the fresh graves of their Confederate dead. Memorialization was an activity that could be restrained by only the most callous of military authorities during Reconstruction, and springtime tributes at Confederate gravesites proliferated throughout the South. By 1868, when the United States designated a national Memorial Day, hundreds of Southern communities were already celebrating a Confederate Decoration Day on the last weekend of May or the first weekend of June.[24]

As local economies recovered, civic organizations, often driven by women, began to commission formal monuments to their Confederate dead. More than three thousand ladies' memorial associations—many in Kentucky—would sprout throughout the South to honor Confederate dead in the decades following the war.

Kentucky's earliest Civil War monument was erected in Cynthiana in 1869. The Cynthiana Confederate Memorial Association installed a twenty-five-foot-tall marble obelisk on the grounds of the city cemetery and surrounded it with the graves of forty-eight Confederate dead from seven states.[25]

It was in the Lexington Cemetery, however, not far from where Boyd's Confederate Veteran Association statue would be unveiled twenty years later, that the Ladies Memorial and Monument Association of Lexington in 1874 placed one of the most touching memorial statues of the period. The memorial sits on a pedestal carved to look like a pile of stones. Atop the base stands a rough-hewn Christian cross of logs; a broken flagstaff and drooping banner leans against the cross. The monument, with its themes of death and mourning, evokes the feeling of sadness and loss that drove Kentucky's earliest memorialization efforts.

By the 1890s, however, firsthand memory of the war years was fading. A new generation of women, daughters of ex-Confederates and the Confederate dead, turned from the personal grief symbolized by a broken flagstaff and drooping banner to a celebration of the valor and constancy of their living veterans and the mythology of the Lost Cause.

Addie Graves had the personality, inclination, and household income necessary to be an active clubwoman.

By the end of the century, Kentucky women, even in the smaller towns, were enjoying increased leisure and prosperity. A woman with a new indoor cast-iron cookstove and the ability to fill a mop bucket without having to draw water from a well had more time to contribute to the social needs of her community. Women's clubs dedicated to increasing literacy, improving health care, reforming prisons, preserving heritage, and promoting temperance were forming all over Kentucky. (In 1895 women of Lexington would form the Kentucky Federation of Clubwomen to help coordinate the good works of all these women's organizations.)

Addie Graves was a one-woman civic organization: a preacher's daughter brought up with a natural gregariousness and a proclivity for involvement in social causes. Her social skills were faultless, she wrote a good hand, and her stationery was exquisite. Addie Graves was active in a dozen clubs and organizations where, depending on the need, she could lead with grace or follow with enthusiasm.

Addie was married to James M. Graves, chief operating officer of Lexington's City National Bank. Their children were grown, but she and her husband cared for his ninety-six-year-old mother. James, a Confederate veteran, seldom spoke of his military service. His mother, Polly, however, spoke often of the two sons she had lost to the war.[26] John Boyd had honored the elderly Polly Graves and her contributions several times, so when Boyd asked her daughter-in-law Addie to assist the Lexington veterans' organization, the younger woman accepted.[27]

In 1893 Addie Graves was president of the Honorary Confederate Veteran Association and was responsible for Lexington's Decoration Day ceremonies.

"It is hoped all will exert themselves in bringing all the flowers which they can possibly spare," she wrote in a newspaper announcement published the day before the ceremonies. As she sat at the podium on Decoration Day in her china silk dress, she was surrounded by blossoms and greenery.

After the hymn and Boyd's introduction, Addie Graves nodded at the choir, which began to sing "Rest, Comrades, Rest." Thirteen young girls, each one the daughter of a Confederate veteran, came forward and took bouquets of flowers from around the podium and began decorating the nearby graves of Confederate soldiers. The crowd was still as the choir sang and the girls spread blossoms around the gravesites or wove greenery around the headstones.

The choir then began "Nearer My God to Thee," and the vast audience joined in. Members of the crowd picked up flowers and, still singing, walked off to join the girls in decorating more graves.

When the flowers were gone and the hymn was complete, John Boyd, Addie Graves, the veterans, the dignitaries, and the crowd walked silently through the gathering twilight and out the gates of Lexington Cemetery.

Confederate veterans' organizations were men's clubs, the price of admission being honorable military service to the Confederate States of America. Despite their wartime and memorialization activities, women would never gain full membership in that elect group.

Still, women did have a place in the veterans' organizations.

On behalf of Louisville's Confederate Association of Kentucky, John Leathers invited "any . . . woman whose sympathies were with the South during the struggle, or the wives and children of Confederate soldiers and sailors" into an auxiliary organization. John Boyd also appealed to the wives, sons, and daughters of veterans to become honorary members of his Confederate Veteran Association.[28]

Women were invited to participate in the various brigade and regimental reunions (usually as hostesses), but they were limited to "honorary" or "auxiliary" status in Kentucky's two main veterans' groups. "Fifty young ladies, principally the daughters of ex-Confederates, clad in white dresses with red sashes over their shoulder, will take upon themselves the duty of serving the veterans at the table," organizers of a Kentucky Orphan Brigade reunion announced in 1889.[29]

Not content with merely serving the veterans at their tables, independent Southern women eventually established their own private club. Correspondence between Caroline M. Goodlett, a native Kentuckian and president of a woman's auxiliary to the Tennessee Confederate Soldiers' Home, and Anna D. Raines, a member of the women's auxiliary of Georgia's Confederate Veteran Association, led to the formation in 1894 of a nationwide service organization unifying hundreds of women's auxiliaries and ladies' memorial associations. Goodlett and Raines envisioned a national federation to foster the social, historical, monumental, and benevolent purposes of existing independent clubs while instilling in the people of the South "a proper respect for and pride in the glorious war history."

"The ladies of the South ought to organize in one broad sisterhood," Goodlett wrote Raines, "and band themselves under one name, and throw around it such restrictions as would exclude all persons and their descendants who were not loyal to the South in her hour of need."

Goodlett and Raines invited representatives of women's clubs to Nashville to draft a constitution. Delegates approved a constitution, elected officers, approved the design for a club badge, and chose a name for their new organization, the United Daughters of the Confederacy (UDC). The constitution provided that new chapters would be numbered in the order in which they entered the federation.[30]

In October 1896 fifteen clubwomen of Lexington, including Addie Graves, were admitted as the charter chapter of Kentucky into the United Daughters of the Confederacy. Theirs was the twelfth chapter to enter the new national organization.[31]

The groups represented on the speakers' platform by John Boyd and Adeline Graves that day in 1893 would gain in size and social influence as Kentuckians moved toward the end of the century.

John Boyd's single-mindedness drove the statewide growth of the Confederate Veteran Association of Kentucky to thirty-seven camps by 1897. The group maintained a healthy treasury (which Boyd invested in Lexington city street bonds) and an enthusiastic membership. That same year, Louisville's Confederate Association of Kentucky—still not affiliated with Boyd's group—applied for membership in the national United Confederate Veterans organization, bringing total enrollment of active ex-Confederates in Kentucky to more than 3,500 by 1900.

The United Daughters of the Confederacy drew together disparate women's groups in Kentucky into a single organization that was thousands strong. The corresponding secretary of Lexington's new UDC chapter reported in 1896 that the "Lexington Chapter now numbers one hundred members." She added that "Richmond has a large chapter, and Winchester and Georgetown have organized."[32] By 1900 more than 4,000 Kentucky women (under the statewide presidency of Addie Graves) would hold active membership in the United Daughters of the Confederacy.

The United Daughters of the Confederacy and the United Confederate Veterans provided a national canvas on which the culture of the Lost Cause could be painted large. In addition, news of successful Confederate veterans assistance programs in other states could be shared with (and replicated by) Kentucky veterans' groups and the women of the UDC.

This combination of active ex-Confederates and sympathetic women, all working as part of strong statewide organizations, would in just a few years result in the establishment of the Kentucky Confederate Home.

Chapter 3

The Boat Captain and the Bank Robber

Captain Daniel G. Parr had been a hearty man in his earlier days, but at seventy-six years of age, his arms and legs were as thin as dowel rods. Barely balanced on a scrawny neck, old Dan Parr's head started as a broad, bald dome, then tapered to a pointed chin with wispy white chin whiskers. Between brow and beard were a pair of dark, piercing eyes with just a touch of confusion about them and, below, an expressionless slice of a mouth with thin and bloodless lips. His was a triangular face, gaunt, and beginning to show the skull beneath. Taking his daily exercise down Louisville's Fourth Street on an April morning in 1901 with the help of an ebony walking cane, the stick-thin man with the oversized head looked like nothing less than a giant mantis in a black wool suit.

With a black body servant at his elbow, Captain Parr wobbled down the street as if he owned it—which, in fact, he did. Daniel G. Parr, a steamboat captain and boat owner who discovered that the real money was to be made with warehouses and the property on which they sat, was by the start of the twentieth century one of Louisville's largest owners of commercial real estate. He was known as "The Pioneer of Fourth Avenue," and the Parr blocks on Fourth Street south of the new courthouse had recently been valued at more than a half million dollars.

On the morning of April 11, 1901, Captain Parr and his black helper halted to meet another man, younger and taller than he.

"You're the Confederate?" Parr asked.

"I am, sir," the younger man answered.

"Then meet me at my office soon, sir," the capitalist commanded. "I have in my mind to do something for the Confederates." The manservant made a note in a small leather daybook, and Captain Daniel Parr's appointment with Bennett Henderson Young was set.[1]

When John Leathers inserted language in the constitution of his Louisville Confederate veterans' group allowing that organization to receive and hold real estate, and when John Boyd wrote that a purpose of his statewide veterans' organization was to be the "permanent establishment and endowment of a home" for indigent ex-Confederates, both men were acutely aware of Virginia Hanson's failed home for Confederate veterans, widows, and orphans in Georgetown.

Virginia Hanson was the widow of beloved General Roger W. Hanson of Lexington. Hanson had served as a U.S. Army lieutenant in the Mexican War before returning to his law practice in Kentucky. Elected to the state assembly as a staunch supporter of states' rights, he lost a close election for a seat in the U.S. Congress in 1860. As Kentucky teetered on the brink of secession in 1861, Hanson raised a regiment and rode south to join the Confederate army.

Hanson was a commander who led from the front ranks, shouting personal encouragement to his men as he dodged Union shot and shell during combat. On January 2, 1863, his luck ran out: Brigadier General Roger W. Hanson fell, mortally wounded, during the battle of Stones River.[2] His wife, Virginia, was left a childless widow with a comfortable estate near Mt. Sterling.

Following the war, men of her husband's command would visit the widow Hanson to pay their respects to their fallen general's memory. It was through them that she began to hear stories of broken fortune and financial distress among the men who had followed her husband into battle.

She met a private in her husband's command "who was reduced by wounds and disease and is now in the Fayette County poorhouse." She knew a family of six children, she said, "their father dead and their mother in a lunatic asylum. These children are scattered among poor relations who are unable to support or educate them."[3]

In 1881 Virginia Hanson and Captain James E. Cantrill began soliciting donations to establish the Confederate Soldiers' Home and Widows and Orphans Asylum in Georgetown. They wanted to provide a temporary shelter where the men of her husband's command—or their widows or children—could build lives free from the stain of pauperism. The Georgetown home would be a combination work camp and trade school; men and women could work as they were able, and children would be taught the industrial arts or home-making skills.

Initial contributions allowed Hanson and Cantrill to acquire the buildings and property of a former girls' school for their asylum, and the first residents arrived in November. Bourbon County appropriated $150 to send Mr. and Mrs. A. Gunsaulte to live in the former schoolhouse, where the couple was expected to "do some light work in raising table supplies."[4]

Mrs. Hanson was counting on pledges from ex-Confederates to support and endow the asylum, and she enlisted the support of her husband's former officers. She was tireless in crisscrossing the state to solicit donations at reunions, political rallies, and other assemblies where she might find a sympathetic ear.[5]

But private contributions and good intentions alone weren't enough.

The Georgetown home enjoyed warm public support, but it lacked strong, local Confederate veteran organizations to sustain interest and fundraising. Municipal and county governments were willing to pay for hometown indigents, but the Kentucky legislature showed no desire to fund the home.[6]

Strangled with debt and out of money, Mrs. Hanson closed the home in 1883 after less than two years. The remaining residents were returned to the meager support of the county poorhouses or less-then-welcoming relatives.[7]

Just as Leathers and Boyd were familiar with the failed Georgetown home, so were they and their fledgling veterans' organizations familiar with attempts in other parts of the country to establish institutions for Confederate veterans who had fallen on hard times.[8]

Although there was no coordinated national Confederate Home movement, veterans in many of the states of the old Confederacy (and several of the border states) began to establish their own asylums for indigent and invalid comrades. Fifteen homes had been attempted or opened by the time the nineteenth century wound to a close, and the means by which these early institutions were organized and funded differed state by state as ex-Confederates learned how (and how not) to finance and operate such a major undertaking.

The Lee Camp Soldiers Home in Richmond, Virginia, resulted from a nationwide fundraising effort by Confederate and Union veterans in that city. Former combatants, now business associates, sought donations from comrades across the country "to establish a Home at said city for disabled ex-Confederate soldiers who are unable to take care of themselves, and whose helpless and pitiable condition calls for a liberal charity."[9] With money raised from Northern philanthropists, theatrical benefits, charity bazaars, and gifts from Confederate veterans everywhere, the home opened in February 1885.

Confederate veterans in Austin, Texas, raised enough money to buy and equip a seven-room house on fifteen acres near the state capitol in 1886. The Texas Confederate Home for Men struggled for five years until the Texas legislature (in contravention of its own state constitution) voted regular funding in 1891.[10]

Like Kentucky, Louisiana experienced its own false start at a home for indigent Confederate veterans. The Louisiana legislature in 1866 voted to fund a home, but reversed itself before a permanent place could be established. Twenty years later, after a series of political knife fights, the state again appropriated money to supplement local contributions, establishing a Confederate soldier's home in New Orleans in 1884.

Wealthy veterans of the Baltimore Confederate Association established a home in Pikesville, Maryland, in 1888, but were unable to sustain it through their own contributions. They scrambled to drum up statewide support through most of the 1890s.

Ex-Confederates in North Carolina organized, reorganized, and struggled for more than five years to raise money for a home in that state. It wasn't until 1891, when the state provided property and voted an annual appropriation, that the North Carolina Soldiers' Home in Raleigh first welcomed nine needy ex-Confederates.

As local Confederate veteran camps in Tennessee and Arkansas joined into statewide organizations under the United Confederate Veterans banner, they began to organize their own institutions. Tennessee Confederate veterans convinced the state to lease them Andrew Jackson's former estate in Nashville and provide a cash grant. Tennessee's first needy ex-Confederates moved into the Hermitage with the opening of the Tennessee Soldiers' Home in 1890. Arkansans set out to raise $50,000 and, with the first $9,000, bought an old homestead south of Little Rock. The Arkansas Confederate Home opened officially in December 1890.[11]

The thriving United Confederate Veterans (UCV) organization shared news of each fresh fundraising committee, false start, successful opening, and failure through *Confederate Veteran*, its monthly magazine, and the news spurred a regional competitiveness. As new chapters of the United Daughters of the Confederacy (UDC) were organized, wives, sisters, and daughters of veterans added their voices to the call for statewide homes of care and refuge.

By end of the 1890s it was apparent that the number and needs of invalid and indigent Confederate veterans were simply too great to be met by local assistance or niggardly pensions (in the states that could afford to provide them). It was one thing to bestow the temporary assistance that could help a crippled comrade reclaim his life, as John Leathers and Louisville's Confederate Association of Kentucky had done with Billy Beasley; it was quite another to provide rehabilitative care for entire families, as Virginia Hanson had attempted at Kentucky's short-lived Georgetown home.

Southerners also took note of the residential care provided to Union veterans by the U.S. government. Even before Civil War battle flags were furled, the U.S. Congress had appropriated monies to establish asylums "for the relief of totally disabled officers and men of the volunteer forces of the United States." In 1866 a board of managers acquired a bankrupt resort hotel near Augusta, Maine, and opened the first of thirteen institutions for Federal veterans of the Civil War. The homelike facilities provided residents with organized recreational activities, libraries, theaters, and regular religious services. (No ex-Confederates need apply, of course.)[12]

Viewing the successes and failures of Confederate homes at the end of the century, it was apparent that the construction of a successful institution required three distinct pillars: a unified and energetic statewide Confederate veterans' group, a sympathetic and enthusiastic public, and a generous state government.

By 1897 these factors were coalescing in Kentucky.

Active UCV camps and UDC chapters were part of the civic fabric in most large Kentucky towns. The two statewide organizations—John Leathers's Confederate Association of Kentucky in Louisville and John Boyd's Confederate Veteran Association of Kentucky, headquartered in Lexington—while not always acting in tandem, shared a commitment to care for needy veterans. And in the spring of 1897 John Leathers and his Louisville association applied for membership in the United Confederate Veterans, affiliating with Boyd's Lexington group. Boyd was nominally in charge of the statewide organization, but with 250 active members, the Louisville camp would set the agenda.[13]

At the same time, an ever-increasing United Daughters of the Confederacy membership began speaking up for a Kentucky Confederate home. At the first statewide meeting of Kentucky's UDC chapters in 1897 the president spoke of an urgent need for "a place of refuge and care" for Kentucky veterans.

As the veterans and Daughters waved the bloody shirt at every opportunity, more Kentuckians were expressing their sympathy for the plight of their state's indigent Confederate veterans.[14]

All that was lacking was a political commitment, and John Leathers had a plan for that.

Leathers, now commander (president) of one of the largest United Confederate Veterans camps in the country, appointed an executive committee to explore the subject of a statewide home for disabled ex-Confederates.[15] He enlisted Louisville attorney Bennett Henderson Young to draft the committee's report.

Bennett Young's roots were deep in the Bluegrass. Born in 1843 on the palisades overlooking the Kentucky River near Nicholasville, he was the child of a family that had crossed the Cumberland Gap when Kentucky was still part of Virginia. He attended nearby Bethel Academy and graduated in 1861, at age eighteen, from Centre College, intending to study for the ministry.[16]

As Kentucky balanced on the knife-edge of war—with Federals digging in along the Ohio River and Confederates marching northward from Tennessee—Bennett Young enlisted as a private under a charismatic cavalryman who would come to be known as the "Thunderbolt of the Confederacy": General John Hunt Morgan.

Morgan was an Alabaman who had settled in Lexington, where he formed a mounted state militia before hostilities broke out between North and South. At the outbreak of war, he gathered 500 young men who, like Bennett Young, were of good breeding, at home in the saddle, and burning with a patriotic fire. During the early years of the Confederacy, Morgan's men seemed to appear everywhere throughout the hills of central Kentucky and northern Tennessee, harassing poorly defended Union encampments and disrupting supply lines. Even as the Southern campaign in Kentucky collapsed, Morgan conducted raids—some authorized by the Confederate high command, some not—deep into the Bluegrass. To Confederate sympathizers in Kentucky, he was a Robin Hood, sweeping into a village at dawn with no warning to steal Federal supplies, horses, and gold.

Bennett Young rode with Morgan on his final raid into Kentucky in July 1863. Now a brigadier general, Morgan—without direct orders—chose to lead more than 2,500 men northward, crossing the Ohio River into Indiana. Once into Indiana, he turned eastward toward Ohio, perhaps intending to join Lee's Army of Virginia, which was then advancing on the town of Gettysburg in Pennsylvania.

Morgan's Raiders (as they were described by fear-stricken Northern newspapers) drove east toward Cincinnati, where civilians panicked at the thought of gray-clad cavalrymen sacking that city. The men continued eastward on horseback, south of Columbus, north of Chillicothe, and past Zanesville, pressing for the Pennsylvania border. But Federal troops, state militiamen, and a hostile civilian populace bit into Morgan's flanks like hyenas into a gazelle. On July 26, 1863, after eighteen days and almost 500 miles in the saddle, General Morgan surrendered to Union troops near East Liverpool, Ohio. (For the next seven decades, men would tell anyone who asked that their life's most valiant accomplishment had been to follow General John Hunt Morgan on that ill-fated Ohio raid.)

Morgan and his officers were imprisoned in Columbus, and the enlisted men—including Bennett Young—were transported to Camp Douglas, a Federal prison camp near Chicago. There, with 5,000 other prisoners on seventy acres surrounded by twelve-foot walls and armed guards, Morgan's men were expected to wait out the rest of the war.[17]

Bennett Young couldn't wait. After just four months in prison, he escaped from Camp Douglas and made his way 300 miles across enemy territory into Canada.

A thriving Confederate expatriate community awaited Young in Toronto. Confederate officials put him in command of a company of men and ordered him south to Richmond. Young and his men sailed to the West Indies, boarded a blockade runner, and slipped past Federal ships into Chesapeake Bay. At the Confederate capital, Bennett Young was commissioned a first lieutenant in the Confederate army and received secret orders for the infamous St. Albans raid.

The former ministerial student was about to become a bank robber.[18]

St. Albans, Vermont, was a drowsy little town twenty miles from the Canadian border and sixty miles south of Montreal. On Wednesday, October 19, 1864, teams of armed men hurried into the three banks of St. Albans, demanding gold from the vaults. Outside, another group of armed men herded passersby to the town green.

"We are here to take possession of this town in the name of Jefferson Davis and the Confederacy," the men are reported to have shouted to a dumbstruck citizenry as the raiders removed their outerwear to reveal uniforms of butternut and gray.

The raiders reassembled on the town green, pockets and satchels bulging with banknotes and gold. A running gun battle between the score of men led by Lieutenant Bennett H. Young, CSA, and a few armed citizens erupted as the Confederates mounted up and attempted their getaway. A building was torched and more shots were fired as Young and his raiders raced north toward the Canadian border with a reputed $208,000 in bank loot.

The St. Albans telegrapher keyed out a dispatch to all points that Rebels were sacking the town, and an impromptu posse saddled up to follow the men northward. Infuriated St. Albaners might have chased the raiders well into Canada and hanged them from the nearest maple tree had not a Montreal sheriff, alerted by the telegraph operator, ridden south and taken the Confederates into protective custody.

The U.S. government was infuriated at the audacity of the raid. This was not a legitimate act of war, Washington officials claimed, but a capital crime against private citizens. The U.S. State Department sent officials to Montreal seeking the extradition of the raiders for return and trial.

The Canadian government—officially neutral, but actually pro-Southern—held a trial of fact and determined that Young's actions were sanctioned acts of war and not common criminality. Canada refused to extradite Young and his raiders to the United States and certain execution, but instead released them from custody.[19]

Lieutenant Bennett Henderson Young—not yet twenty-two years old—was cheered throughout the now-dying Confederacy for his audacious raid into New England. (History would record it as the northernmost action of the Civil War.) But Young earned only notoriety in the United States of America and an enmity that would last long after Lee's surrender. After Lincoln's death, President Andrew Johnson issued amnesty proclamations that specifically excluded the St. Albans raiders. Worse, Federal officials in Kentucky posted a large reward for "evil minded persons who have crossed the border of the United States . . . and have committed capital offenses against the property and life of American citizens."[20]

After almost a year of cooling his heels in Canada, Young sailed for Britain, where he socialized with other Confederate exiles. Uncertain as to whether he would ever again be able to return to the

United States, Young enrolled at Queens University at Belfast to prepare himself for the practice of law. (Some later said that his expenses were paid with St. Albans gold.) The young cavalryman was an apt student, and he graduated with first honors in the study of English common law.

It was not until 1868 that the exiled Young was allowed to return home and establish a law practice in Louisville. The former bank robber quickly became one of the foremost railroad attorneys in the United States at a time when companies were making huge investments in rebuilding rail systems throughout the South.

His law practice thrived during the last three decades of the nineteenth century, and Bennett Young became more active in capitalistic endeavors. He took the lead as investor and partner in the construction of a cantilever bridge spanning the Ohio River at Louisville in 1886; he promoted and built the Louisville Southern Railroad, which broke the monopoly of the L&N line; and he launched the Presbyterian Mutual Insurance Fund. These enterprises required a great deal of public speaking, and Young honed his oratorical skills in front of crowds of interested investors and others who merely wished to catch a glimpse of the storied St. Albans raider.

Meanwhile, he involved himself in a number of public enterprises. In 1876 he was appointed by the governor to represent Kentucky at the Paris Exposition. Young also assisted in the founding of the Louisville Colored Orphans' Home, served as superintendent of the Kentucky Institute for the Education of the Blind, and was elected president of the Louisville Library Association.

Young served as a delegate to Kentucky's state constitutional convention in 1890, partly to protect his railroad interests and partly because he saw the need to streamline a turgid state government. (His reference manual for delegates, *The Three Constitutions of Kentucky*, drove the creation of a decidedly populist new constitution.) His participation in the constitutional convention also resulted in his becoming acquainted with two up-and-coming politicians, William Goebel and J. C. W. Beckham.[21]

Through 1890, however, Young took no public role as an ex-Confederate.

Perhaps the ex-raider feared renewed interest by the government in Washington or retaliation by St. Albaners, but Bennett Young's official biographies from the time make little mention of his service as a Confederate cavalry officer, and he chose not to participate in the formation of the Confederate Association of Kentucky. By 1894, however, he had employed a manager to seek speaking engagements for him and was contributing publicly to Confederate monuments and causes. The handsome cavalryman-turned-bank-robber-turned-attorney was soon in demand as featured orator at memorial dedications and Lost Cause celebrations throughout the state.[22]

Thus, when he was asked by John Leathers in 1897 to assist in the organization of a Kentucky Confederate veterans home, Bennett Young brought impeccable credentials as one of Kentucky's most politically adept and well-connected ex-Confederates.

By the late 1890s, Kentucky's Confederate veterans were aching for a veterans home of their own—especially after seeing the way Tennesseans gloated over theirs.

The Kentucky-Tennessee Reunion in Nashville in 1896 brought together Confederate veterans of the sister states, many of whom had fought side by side on battlefields in both states, and served as a promotional event for the Tennessee Centennial Exposition. Two thousand Kentucky veterans and their families enjoyed the hospitality of their Tennessee comrades, including a tour of the Tennessee Soldiers' Home on the grounds of Andrew Jackson's old estate. The two-story brick building with broad covered galleries and all modern amenities sat among towering oak and hickory trees, looking like a cross between a college classroom building and a resort hotel. A parade the next day featured more than fifty uniformed residents of the Soldiers' Home riding decorated wagons, sitting like pashas on pillows, waving to the adoring crowd.[23]

Tennessee built an Elysium for its needy veterans; Kentucky had done nothing.

Returning to Louisville, John Leathers immediately appointed a committee to explore the feasibility of establishing a Kentucky home for needy Confederate veterans. He asked Bennett Young to

advise the group on political matters, and the committee met spo-
radically throughout 1897.

Successful efforts of ex-Confederates in Missouri to open a home
in Higginsville in 1891 provided an organizational blueprint to
Young and the Kentucky Confederate veterans for the eventual establishment of Kentucky's Confederate home. The Missouri establishment was a ten-year effort, requiring the unified statewide
support of ex-Confederates and their female auxiliaries (later the
state UCV camps and UDC chapters) and the public at large. That
support, along with significant seed money to buy and furnish a
home, was enough to convince the state legislature to accept the
deed to the property in exchange for funding the operation of the
Confederate Home of Missouri for at least twenty years. This was
the plan Kentucky Confederates hoped to emulate.[24]

"Confederate Home Wanted in Kentucky," the *Confederate Veteran* trumpeted to its national audience. Bennett Young and his ex-
ploratory committee, reporting at the camp's first meeting of 1898,
recommended that all of Kentucky's United Confederate Veterans
camps join with Louisville in an effort to establish a home, that the
cost of the home and its furnishings be provided through private
subscription, and that the home be supported by state aid. Members
received the report enthusiastically, then moved that Leathers appoint still another committee "to take such steps as may be deemed
best" to get the plan underway.[25]

The Louisville Confederates cheered the plan, passed the motion, and then—for two long years—did nothing about it.

To be fair, much occurred during those years to distract Kentucky's
Confederate veterans and sympathizers from the business of establishing a statewide home for their needy comrades.

Major General John Boyd, commanding general of the state
Confederate veterans' organization, chose to ignore Louisville's
plan in favor of one of his own. Still distrustful of the Louisville
contingent, the former private used his old campfire connections to
build support for a massive memorial hall in Lexington. The state

United Daughters of the Confederacy chapters, now presided over by Addie Graves, signed on immediately. She urged her membership "to bend every energy to the erection of the Memorial Hall proposed by Gen. Boyd, in which he offers his valuable collection of relics on condition [that the hall be placed in Lexington]."[26]

Confederate home or memorial battle abbey? Kentucky's Confederate loyalties were split, and as a result, the veterans took little action on either front.

At the same time, Kentuckians were sniffing the first smoke of a wildfire that was about to sear the political landscape and threaten the traditional Democratic majority for the first time in thirty-five years. Kentucky's Democrats, split over the issue of bimetallism, were deserting the party in droves. Political fire bells were ringing, statehouse observers warned, and it wasn't a good time to ask nervous lawmakers to appropriate funds for former Confederates.

Louisvillians, meanwhile, were turning their attention to capturing the biggest Confederate plum of all: the United Confederate Veterans' annual meeting and grand reunion.

The annual UCV national meetings were becoming huge events for the cities that hosted them. Houston estimated that the event brought 50,000 visitors to its city in 1895; Nashville boasted 100,000 veterans and friends in attendance at the 1897 reunion. A four-day reunion of old vets could fill hotels to overflowing and stuff the cash registers of restaurants, beer halls, and entertainment venues in the host city. Louisville's business community wanted a piece of that.[27]

Supported by the editor of *Confederate Veteran*, the business community, and the local newspapers, John Leathers and the Louisville UCV camp prepared a bid to host the 1899 reunion. Louisville was a long shot; Kentucky had never been an official part of the Southern Confederacy, and Louisville was farther than some of the southernmost UCV camps wanted to travel. In the end, the Louisville lost its bid to Charleston, South Carolina.

But at the 1899 reunion, Bennett Young was tapped to deliver the funeral oration for Winnie Davis, venerated daughter of Jefferson Davis and the original "daughter of the Confederacy." Young's soaring Lost Cause rhetoric all but canonized the departed woman and transported his audience—men and women alike—from sobs of grief to tears of joy. It was a speech ex-Confederates and UDC members would talk about and quote from for decades.[28]

Now accepted on a national stage, Young was invited to plead his case for Louisville directly to the assembled delegates. Young promised the delegates that if they should come to Louisville, "Kentucky's homes and hearts, Kentucky's wealth . . . her tenderest lambs and fattest beeves, and the contents of her granaries, transmuted by Kentucky magic into *liquid corn and rye*" would be theirs. He would personally lead "the old Confederates beside the *distilled* waters."[29]

Young knew his audience. The veterans roared their approval, and Louisville won the 1900 UCV reunion.

The Louisville reunion—the first of the new century for the United Confederate Veterans—was as extravagant and successful as Bennett Young had promised. Everyone pitched in. Citizens opened their homes to out-of-town veterans, local businesses pitched in $70,000 to sponsor reunion events, and Bourbon County farmers shipped carloads of smoked hams to Louisville to feed veterans who couldn't afford their board.[30] "There is only one wish in every heart here," Young told the 150,000 visiting veterans, "and that is to make you as happy as possible while you remain with us."[31]

A favorite activity at any reunion of old Johnny Rebs was storytelling, spinning yarns—some true, some told as truth—about the war years. And one of the better storytellers was John W. Green, former sergeant-major, Ninth Kentucky Infantry, CSA. Johnny Green would tell anyone who asked about his return to Kentucky at the end of the war.

When he arrived in Nashville with little money in his pocket, Green would say, he heard he could get free rail transportation home to Louisville if he swore his oath of allegiance to the United States. Not yet ready to do that, he wandered down to the wharf, where he spotted a familiar steamboat and boat captain.

"Pay your passage and keep your mouth shut," the captain snarled. "You can travel on my boat without taking the oath."

Gratefully, Johnny Green climbed the gangplank and returned, unreconstructed, to his family in Kentucky aboard the riverboat *Tempest* with Captain Dan Parr in the wheelhouse.[32]

Daniel G. Parr told his children he was born in France in 1825 and brought to America as a babe by his father, a decorated veteran of Napoleon's army at Waterloo. True or not, Parr left the family farm in Kenton County, across the Ohio River from Cincinnati, to become a riverman while still in his teens. He learned the shipping trade, probably as a roustabout, on the boats and barges that transported goods along the Ohio and its tributaries. At age twenty-two Parr bought a boat of his own and promptly lost it to creditors. By then, however, he was well on his way to developing the heart of hard, black coal necessary to be a successful riverboat captain.

Parr found other investors and, by 1860, was operating a fleet of twenty river vessels. He spent the Civil War years transporting people and goods for whomever controlled the Ohio, Tennessee, Mississippi, and Kentucky Rivers at the moment, but he made little effort to disguise his Southern sympathies. When Federal troops seized one of his favorite boats for the assault on Fort Donelson, Parr refused to operate the vessel, earning six weeks in a Federal prison.[33]

In 1863 Captain Daniel Parr's thirteen-year-old daughter, Virginia, was aboard one of her father's boats at the Louisville wharf. Nearby was a transport steamer filled with Confederate prisoners who were bedraggled and unfed. Virginia stood at the gangway of the Federal wharf asking all who passed for contributions to benefit the prisoners. Parr's Rebel daughter must have raised some eyebrows among the blue-coated soldiers, but "quite a handsome sum was realized through the efforts of the child."[34]

After the war, Parr established a ferry company on the Ohio, earning himself a fortune. He then plowed that fortune into Louisville commercial real estate. His daughters goaded him into philanthropy, and most of his gifts at first benefited the Baptists. He supported Louisville's Baptist Orphans' Home and gave $10,000 for a bell tower at Walnut Street Baptist Church. His will provided for a trust fund for Broadway Baptist Church and endowed Parr's Rest, a home for unfortunate women.[35]

At seventy-six, Parr was no longer actively involved in his investments, but the old boat captain had more money than he could spend in the rest of his lifetime. His Rebel daughter had an idea about how Dan Parr could distribute his money.[36]

The day following their April 1901 meeting on Fourth Street, attorney Bennett Henderson Young called at Captain Parr's for their appointment. Young later described his meeting to newspapermen: "[Captain Parr] stated that his daughter, having come to live with him, would not need the house in which she had resided."

Parr wanted to flip the property back to his ownership, then turn it over to Louisville's Confederate Association of Kentucky.

"I suggested to him that he would be doing a most magnificent work if he would do this in such shape that it would be the basis for a Confederate Home," Young said.

The attorney wasted no time in drafting an agreement to Captain Parr's specifications, and on April 15, 1901, the two men met again at the county clerk's office where they executed the deed and handed it over for record.

"In consideration of the regard . . . for the Confederate cause and its surviving soldiers," Captain Daniel G. Parr put into the hands of nine trustees—John Leathers, Harry P. McDonald, and Bennett Young included—a house and lot at 421 East Chestnut Street in Louisville, a fourteen-room house valued at more than $5,000 on the tax rolls. According to the terms of the deed, the trustees were to use the house—or proceeds from the sale of the property, if they saw fit—"for the purpose of securing and maintaining a home for Confederate indigent and disabled soldiers in the State of Kentucky."[37]

This was the spark the veterans were waiting for.

Within eighteen months of the meeting between Captain Daniel Parr and Bennett Young, veterans would be dedicating the Kentucky Confederate Home.

Chapter 4

The Auditor and the Stockman

On September 24, 1902, General Fayette Hewitt sat at the oak desk in his office at State National Bank of Frankfort, reviewing the morning's correspondence. Sunlight pouring through the large windows fronting Main Street illuminated the neat stacks of paper and bundles of envelopes on his desk.

Hewitt disposed of the usual banking business first—loan applications, title reports, a daily balance sheet. He was nothing if not good at processing paper and money. He scanned the balance sheet, noting yesterday's cash receipts; he initialed the loan applications and checked the title reports for the proper seals and endorsements. He managed the paperwork of his bank with the mechanistic efficiency of a dedicated high-level bureaucrat.

Paper and money. Money and paper. General Fayette Hewitt had spent most of his adult life accounting for both.

A native Kentuckian, he was appointed to the Post Office Department in Washington in 1860. At the outbreak of hostilities between North and South, he volunteered his services in Richmond and was tapped by President Jefferson Davis to help organize a postal service for the fledgling Confederate nation. Commissioned as an adjutant-general, Hewitt served on the staffs of Generals Albert Pike and John Breckinridge, helping manage the requisitions, paperwork, and currency that equipped, fed, clothed, and paid the soldiers in their commands. Returning home at the end of the war, he practiced law until he was appointed quartermaster general of the Kentucky state militia in 1867.[1]

Hewitt won statewide election for state auditor in 1880, then spent eight years accounting for the tax dollars Kentucky residents sent to Frankfort to do the state's business. A $250,000 embezzlement by the state's attorney general dropped a tinge of soot on the auditor's house, and General Hewitt resigned in 1889 to found State National Bank. Hewitt's partners named him president, and the bank flourished on the strength of deposits from state accounts.[2]

On this September morning of 1902, after completing his banking business, Hewitt turned to the remaining piles of correspondence that occupied an increasing amount of his time.

The envelopes bore postmarks of towns throughout Kentucky, though a few were from out of state. Hewitt would have recognized many of the return addresses; they were from leaders of Confederate veterans camps or local politicians Hewitt met during his own statewide election campaigns. Most of the envelopes contained checks or cash, and all would require a personal reply.

More money, more paper.

So Fayette Hewitt, former adjutant-general of the Confederate army and former state auditor of Kentucky, opened a ledger book labeled "Kentucky Confederate Home." He sorted through the envelopes stacked in front of him and began to record the paper and money.

Until Captain Daniel Parr deeded his house and lot to the ex-Confederates in April 1901, Kentucky veterans had made little real progress toward the establishment of a Confederate veterans' home. A lack of strong statewide leadership of the ex-Confederate groups accounted for some of the delay, while political turmoil in Frankfort made it difficult to achieve a consensus in the General Assembly.

Then, sometime near the end of the nineteenth century, General John Boyd disappeared—literally disappeared.

Like a ball of string wound too tight, Boyd began to unravel when it appeared that his Lexington battle abbey would never be built. His behavior became increasingly erratic, he was prone to fits of irrational rage, and his personal appearance deteriorated. Concerned officers of Lexington's Confederate Veteran Association staged a surprise "retirement" party for him in 1896, giving him a gold watch and passage to Cincinnati, where it was hoped he would seek treatment by specialists for whatever ailed him.[3] Sometime in 1899 John Boyd packed his bags, told his wife he had urgent business in Texas, walked out the door, and was never heard from again.[4]

Confused and dispirited, Boyd's ex-Confederate brethren chose J. M. Poyntz, a former Confederate surgeon from Richmond and close friend of Bennett Young, to head the statewide veterans' organization.[5]

As remarkable as Boyd's disappearance was, however, it merited just a few column inches of newspaper space compared to the forests of newsprint used at the time to report the political developments in Frankfort.

William Goebel, a progressive state senator from northernmost Kentucky, surprised traditionalists when he won the Democratic nomination for governor in 1899 with his populist platform and naked demagoguery. In the general election, 50,000 disgruntled Democrats, including many prominent ex-Confederates, crossed over to the Republican side and, by the narrowest of margins in a very dirty fight, elected Goebel's opponent. The state's Democratic General Assembly, however, refused to certify the election and appeared ready to reverse the results when Goebel was shot in the back by a sniper hiding in the office of the secretary of state. Goebel was mortally wounded, but lingered long enough for the General Assembly to overturn the popular vote and name the dying man governor.[6]

Goebel's death on February 3, 1900, elevated his running mate, J. C. W. Beckham, a thirty-year-old former public school principal from Bardstown, to Kentucky's highest office.[7] Although inexperienced, Beckham was politically astute, and as the political fires in Frankfort cooled, the boy governor signaled his willingness to deal with the old-line Democrats.

A more stable political environment, Daniel Parr's real estate gift, and the increasing influence of Louisville's ex-Confederates on the statewide veterans' association put some heat under stalled plans for a Kentucky Confederate home. John Leathers and other prominent ex-Confederates (again) recruited Bennett Young to get the project back on the rails.

It is not surprising that an organization of former military men—particularly when its field commander is an accomplished cavalry-man-turned-bank-robber-turned-political-advisor—would devise a textbook military strategy to accomplish its objective.

Bennett Young and other Louisville veterans spent the spring and summer following the announcement of Dan Parr's gift traveling the state and meeting influential ex-Confederates. They scouted the territory, determined the likely field of engagement, and placed their batteries on the most propitious terrain before any potential opponents knew that a battle was to be joined. Young quietly enlisted the support of Governor Beckham and buttonholed key state legislators.

With firm expressions of support in hand, Young and his cohorts prepared for the annual gathering of the state Confederate veterans' organization in Louisville in October 1901. The estranged Louisville and Lexington camps had joined together under the national United Confederate Veterans banner, and for the first time, delegates from sixty-seven local organizations representing 3,500 members would gather for a business meeting.

Henry Watterson, legendary editor of the *Courier-Journal* and a Confederate sympathizer, fired the first salvo in the morning paper with a front-page story headlined "Johnny Rebs Will To-Day Again Capture Louisville." Lest anyone doubt the primary order of business, the subhead promised, "Definite Action Will Be Taken on a Home." Interviewed the night before the meeting opened, Young cagily allowed that the state legislature might be persuaded to appropriate a per capita allowance to fund operation of a home if the Confederates were to ask.[8]

A thousand Kentucky Confederate veterans converged on Louisville's Exchange Hall Tuesday morning, October 22, 1901, streaming through the double doors to find seats on the main floor while a popular local band played marches and old Confederate songs. Pictures of Lee, Davis, Jackson, Morgan, and others hung on the walls to either side of the dais; red, white, and blue bunting draped the balcony rails and covered the front of the stage.[9]

Major General J. M. Poyntz, now heading the state Confederate organization, sat at center stage. John Leathers and other staff officers who governed the now-united Kentucky Division of the United Confederate Veterans flanked him on the platform. With cigar smoke already thick in the air, Poyntz hushed the raucous crowd and called the business meeting to order at a quarter past noon.

After a short invocation, Poyntz tantalized his audience with an opening address that called attention to the plight of destitute Confederate veterans. "Age, like the silent night, progresses," he intoned. He spoke of the increasing physical infirmity, mental distress, and poverty among Kentucky veterans. "Compelled by this decline, the aged soldier must have help to make his last days comfortable."

Offering no specific solutions, he adjourned the meeting for lunch.

At the afternoon session Poyntz called on a series of speakers intended to whip up support for the establishment of a home. (Young had recommended the speakers to Poyntz and had helped craft their speeches.)

Judge R. H. Cunningham of Henderson touched all the Lost Cause bases before asking attendees to give their less-fortunate and aging comrades "a home where ease and comfort shall be theirs." A member of the newly formed Sons of Confederate Veterans, Reed Emery of Danville, spoke as a representative of the young men of Kentucky. He urged the men of his father's generation to care for their disabled and decrepit contemporaries so that "we have done all that love could do to make their last days ones of happiness and peace."[10]

Cheers echoed around the hall as Poyntz—appearing to bow to the will of the assemblage—opened the floor for suggestions about how to found and fund a home. Well-meaning but unprepared attendees responded enthusiastically with half measures and half-baked suggestions until Poyntz (according to plan) called on Bennett Young.

Young strode to the podium, crisp in his new gray UCV uniform, and proceeded to dump ice water on the mawkish sentiment expressed thus far.

The audience may have expected to hear Bennett Young the orator, but instead got a dose of cold reality from Bennett Young the attorney. Sentiment is a beautiful thing in its place, he warned them, but it wouldn't dispose of the poverty and want experienced by Kentucky veterans.

"Remember, comrades," he said, "men who can support a Confederate home grow fewer each year, while men who need a Confederate home will increase each year."

He spoke as if arguing to a jury of the problems Kentucky and other states experienced in maintaining a home from the pockets of the veterans alone. "The Confederate Veteran Association of Georgia with its 30,000 members did not sustain its Confederate home," he reminded them.

Young cited the successes in Missouri and Maryland, where local veterans built and furnished fine homes, then asked their state legislatures for an appropriation to maintain the residents. "Why shouldn't we ask Kentucky for this appropriation?" he asked the crowd. "Does not Kentucky owe much to the soldiery she furnished the South?"

Of course she does, the audience roared in response.

Young introduced a formal resolution—distributing copies printed the night before—calling for Kentucky veterans to raise $25,000 to build and equip a home for indigent veterans while simultaneously asking the state for funds to maintain it. He proposed that a steering committee of twenty-five members from all parts of the state see the project through to completion.

"Let us put up fine houses, well equipped for our needy comrades. Then let us say to the legislature, 'here is our home, well fitted out.' Kentucky will do the rest," he assured them. "We have delayed this work thirty-five years. It is needed now more than it ever was or will be again!"

Veterans erupted in cheers, and several rushed the stage for the privilege of seconding Young's resolution. According to plan, however, John W. Green (representing the Orphan Brigade) seconded the motion. Poyntz opened the floor for discussion, and camp after camp endorsed Young's resolution.

One delegate, however, expressed reservations.

Alpheus Washington Bascom (though everyone, including his wife, called him "A. W.") was a fixture in Bath County with a statewide reputation. Like his grandfather and father before him, he had served terms in the state legislature, but he was most widely known as a successful stockman. Bascom bred and sold the finest specimens of Bates shorthorn cattle in Kentucky. He was a generous man, and he shared his wealth with the Owingsville Christian Church, the Ladies Memorial Association, and any down-on-his-luck neighbor who needed help. A short, solid fireplug of a man, A. W. Bascom was a plain speaker who was as straightforward and honest as the manure on his boots.[11]

When A. W. Bascom rose to speak about plans for a Confederate home, he spoke of his concern for indigent veterans whose wives were still living. What will happen to the wives of veterans who might be left without care if their husbands were to enter a home? At the very least, Bascom urged, we might build modest cottages in different parts of the state so the old vets would not have to live apart from their needy wives.

Apparently unprepared for the objection, Young glibly assured Bascom that the committee would consider the matter, then called for a vote. Rebel yells from the crowd cut off any further discussion, and Young's motion was passed. The Kentucky Confederate veterans were committed.

The next day Major General Poyntz named members of the Committee of Twenty-Five, a steering committee responsible for raising $25,000 and securing favorable legislation. Ex-governor J. B. McCreary, State Supreme Court Chief Justice J. H. Hazelrigg, and State Senator William O. Coleman brought political sway; Walter N. Haldeman, founder of Louisville's *Courier-Journal*, and Lot D. Young of Lexington assured a favorable press. Geographic balance came from T. M. Barker (Christian County), Judge R. H. Cunningham (Henderson County), Charles L. Daughtry (Warren County), and James B. Rogers (Bourbon County). John W. Green represented Kentucky's Orphan Brigade. In a nod to his dissent, A. W. Bascom, the plainspoken stockman from Owingsville, received a seat on the committee.[12]

Altogether, Poyntz appointed twenty-four of the most recognizable names in Kentucky politics, commerce, and society—ex-Confederates all—to join him on the committee. Bennett Young was named chairman, and he chose John Leathers as treasurer.

At its first meeting the Committee of Twenty-Five discussed how its members were going to raise $25,000.

Amid the frenzy at the statewide meeting, $25,000 seemed like an easy goal.

The Louisville camp had Parr's house, and it was estimated that the Chestnut Street property would bring $7,000 to $10,000 at sale. Half a dozen veterans at the state meeting pledged $50 or $100 on the spot. One camp pledged thirty acres of land on which to build the home. Everyone seemed to know someone—some prosperous benefactor back home—who would be proud to lay out $500, $1,000, maybe $5,000 for the old boys in gray.[13] Surely it would be snap to raise $25,000.

But Bennett Young and the Committee of Twenty-Five knew better. Seasoned fundraisers for political campaigns, monument drives, and charitable institutions, the committee members knew they would likely have to scratch for every dollar. John Leathers opened an account book where he would record firm promises ("subscriptions") by individuals to collect or pay a specific amount toward building and equipping the veterans' institution.

Returning home to Bourbon County, committee member James Rogers provided his local newspaper editor a printed letter signed by all committee members. This "Appeal to Kentuckians" described the intention of ex-Confederates to build a home and asked "such people in Kentucky or elsewhere as sympathize in this movement to aid it by early and liberal contributions."[14]

The appeal was printed in the *Bourbon News* and a score of other newspapers across Kentucky in the first weeks of November 1901, and it aroused a favorable response everywhere. Ex-Confederates and their supporters were simultaneously writing state legislators and passing resolutions in favor of a veterans' home. *The Lost Cause*, a monthly magazine for Kentucky's UDC chapters, urged every Daughter of the Confederacy, "with heart, hand and purse, [to] help this splendid movement." Mrs. James M. Arnold, current Kentucky UDC president, mailed her own personal appeal to every chapter, asking for their active support.[15]

In the spirit of reconciliation and comradeship, Union veterans and their supporters pitched in, too. A letter from the national commander-in-chief of the Grand Army of the Republic to the Kentucky GAR camps encouraged their members to support the Confederate home effort. The Committee of Twenty-Five's printed appeal made mention of "the splendid provisions made by the National Government for the Federal veterans," a not-so-subtle reminder of the pensions and veterans' homes available to Kentuckians who had worn the blue.[16]

Though by December 1901 Leathers's subscription book still had plenty of blank pages, committee members could say that the money tree was blooming and the financial harvest was in sight. A constant drumbeat of favorable publicity, coupled with public confidence in the ability of veterans to raise their $25,000, was making the lobbying effort in Frankfort a lot easier for Bennett Young.

Young was no stranger to counting votes in the General Assembly. He had helped draft the current state constitution and written a procedures manual for state legislators. In addition, his years representing railroad interests in Frankfort had taught Young how and when to press for passage of a bill.

And now was the time to press.

Senators and representatives arrived at the state capitol on January 7, 1902, to be sworn in for the regular session of the Kentucky General Assembly. In the first week following the opening gavel of the new session, State Senator William O. Coleman, a Democrat and one of the Committee of Twenty-Five, introduced SB 41, a bill providing for the establishment and maintenance of a Confederate soldiers' home. Harry P. McDonald, a Democrat from Louisville and Bennett Young's longtime business associate, introduced an identically worded bill in the House of Representatives.[17]

The assembly was in firm Democratic control, but the acrimony that filled the capitol air two years before had largely dissipated, and the spirit of reconciliation wafted over the statehouse. Legislators looked forward to governing with reason, not rifles. And from a political standpoint, a home for decrepit Confederate veterans was a reasonable—and popular—cause to support.

"The heroes who followed the stars and bars to defeat," one Republican senator said when asked about the bill, "are as worthy of support in their old age and poverty as the heroes who followed the stars and stripes to victory."

"A Kentucky Confederate home is an absolute certainty," wrote one newspaper, and other editors predicted that the legislation would pass without a single vote against it.[18]

There were a few naysayers, however, even as the bills were under discussion in Frankfort. The *Lexington Leader* reported that the veterans' group in that city felt there was no deep support for the Confederate home plan and predicted that the legislation would be defeated. Instead, the Lexington veterans proposed establishing a state-funded pension program or general assistance fund, administered by a board of ex-Confederates, which would put state money directly into the hands of comrades who needed it. Two Lexington members of the Committee of Twenty-Five resigned, saying they were no longer in sympathy with the plan to establish a home.[19]

But the Lexington veterans were deaf to the statewide support that Young orchestrated.

Legislation establishing a home for Kentucky's needy Confederate veterans passed with only one dissenting vote and was signed by Governor Beckham on March 27, 1902. (Senator R. H. Fleming, a Federal veteran from Covington, explained why he voted in favor of the ex-Confederates. "I faced these men for four years," he said, "and I have an abiding respect for them.")[20] The new law created an institution to be known as the Kentucky Confederate Home, and it contained four key provisions.

First, the bill required that the Confederate veterans (or their friends or sympathizers) deed to the commonwealth an appropriate residence on at least thirty acres of land, fully furnished and ready for the care and custody of at least twenty-five persons. The ex-Confederates must convey clear title to the secretary of state, and the governor's office must inspect and approve the facility, before the state would make any payment for the operation of the Home.

Second, the state would provide $125 a year for every resident enrolled in the Home (or a lump sum of $10,000, whichever was greater) for operation of the Home. The state's $10,000 annual payment allowed the ex-Confederates to count on a minimum annual revenue; the $125 annual per capita payment protected the ex-Confederates in the unlikely event that more than 80 veterans sought refuge in the Home.

Third, all residents of the Home must be able to prove their active military service for the Confederate States of America and their honorable discharge or parole at the termination of the war.

And fourth, the governor would appoint an active and involved board of trustees consisting of ex-Confederates or their sons to manage the Home. The fifteen trustees would have complete financial and operational control of the Home, and they would not be paid for their services. The act required that the trustees elect their own board president, treasurer, and secretary. The board would meet at the Home at least three times annually and would provide a detailed financial accounting the first of every year.

Governor Beckham named his fifteen appointments to the Home's board of trustees within a week of signing the bill.

Bennett Young's appointment to the Kentucky Confederate Home board of trustees was no surprise. Neither were the appointments of Harry P. McDonald and William O. Coleman, the legislators who had introduced the Home bills in the General Assembly. Governor Beckham also appointed General Fayette Hewitt, former state auditor, in whose Frankfort bank much of the state's cash was held. The rest of the board members—all of them active ex-Confederates—were politically and geographically balanced, with trustees selected from the strongest Democratic counties of western and central

Kentucky. (Lexington's Confederate veterans were not represented on the board.)

The fifteen new trustees gathered for the first time at noon on May 6, 1902, in a conference room of the Courier-Journal Building in Louisville. They were serious men, all of them big fish in their respective ponds. Each had a nodding acquaintance with the others from business dealings, political conventions, or veterans' reunions; but only Bennett Young and Fayette Hewitt had statewide reputations. As a first order of business, a state clerk on hand for the occasion administered an oath of just, impartial, and honest service to the Commonwealth of Kentucky.[21]

No sooner had the clerk set down his Bible than William O. Coleman rose to nominate Bennett Young president of the board. With little discussion (and no dissent), Young was elected by acclamation.

The election of officers continued, with Fayette Hewitt named treasurer, Leland Hathaway of Winchester vice-president, and Harry P. McDonald secretary. These four board officers, along with former Confederate chaplain Dr. Lindsay H. Blanton of Danville, would serve as the board's executive committee.

Coleman stood again to offer a resolution, this time typewritten (with revisions already made in pencil in Bennett Young's handwriting). Coleman's resolution—also approved with little discussion and by acclamation—instructed the board's secretary to advertise for proposals from individuals or communities for property suitable for use as the Kentucky Confederate Home.

Following adoption of a final resolution thanking Governor Beckham and members of the state legislature for their "generous, kindly and brotherly act" in passing the Confederate Home bill, the board adjourned to await real estate proposals.

Sometime following that first board meeting, John Leathers turned over his subscription book of pledged contributions to Fayette Hewitt and showed him the bad news.

Early reports of successful fundraising and the passage of legislation providing payment to operate the Home may have convinced many Kentuckians that there was no need for further contributions. In fact, the ex-Confederates were still far short of their $25,000 goal. Furthermore, every penny of that $25,000 would be needed to acquire at least thirty acres of land, improve it, build the necessary structure, then furnish it for occupancy by no fewer than twenty-five residents. By the spring of 1902, however, subscriptions were stalled at about $8,000, not including the Parr house.[22]

Leland Hathaway took it upon himself to write the Kentucky UCV camps, urging them to dig deeper. Clearly, money was going to be a problem.

"The establishing of the Home would be a big thing for any place selected," one newspaper publisher wrote. "That this has been thoroughly understood is best evidenced by the variety of places applying. The chief towns all over the state want it."[23]

It didn't take long for communities (and entrepreneurs) around the state to realize that a state-funded institution in their midst could be an attractive proposition. The Home would provide local employment and business for local merchants. And communities could expect the Home to bring visitors who would eat in local restaurants and stay in local hotels.

Owensboro wanted the Home. Glasgow did, too. And Bowling Green. And Frankfort. And Versailles, Nicholasville, Winchester, Bardstown, and Franklin. All announced plans to prepare proposals for the Home's board of trustees.[24] Even the publisher of the *Lexington Leader*, ignoring the sentiment of his own local veterans, wrote that "Lexington should get to work to secure [this] valuable institution." He reminded merchants that the Home would "serve as a constant source of revenue to the inhabitants of the lucky town."[25]

The trustees knew they would be giving some town a windfall, so, with money short, they decided to squeeze bidders to sweeten their offers with incentives.

"To Communities and Individuals Desiring to Make Proposals for the Location of the Kentucky Confederate Home." An ad for site proposals was placed in newspapers around the state during May and June. "Each proposal must state the amount of land offered

[and] the amount of money to be given in case the location is accepted." The proposal also asked for information about existing buildings on the property, proximity to railroads, and water supplies.[26]

Some communities weren't shy about squeezing back.

In response to a fundraising letter, the commander of the UCV camp in Bardstown wrote Fayette Hewitt "that the members are too poor to subscribe to the Home, but that outsiders might contribute" if the Home were to be located in that county. (The board primly voted that the amount contributed by any camp would not influence the choice of location.)[27]

The mail brought the board more solid proposals, too—and plenty of them.

At their meeting on July 2, 1902, the board's executive committee opened bids on twenty-three properties in fifteen towns. (Promoters in Owensboro submitted proposals for seven properties; Louisville and Shelbyville, two each.) With proposals still rolling in, Bennett Young appointed a Committee on Visitation to inspect each of the properties and report to the board.[28]

By the end of July, with more than forty proposals in hand, the Committee on Visitation reported they wished to "respectfully call attention" to sites in Owensboro, Louisville, Frankfort, Bardstown, Harrodsburg, Hawesville, and Pewee Valley. The committee recommended that the full board physically examine each of the sites.[29]

Thursday, September 4, was a marathon travel and deliberation day for the board of trustees. Nine members boarded the train in Louisville at 6:00 A.M. They met the remaining trustees in Owensboro and were touring the properties there by 8:00 A.M. Back on the train an hour later, they made a brief stopover at Hawesville, then sped off for Frankfort. With barely enough time to walk the four blocks from the rail station to the proposed property and back, the fifteen men then caught the Harrodsburg train, then the shortline to Bardstown. Leaving Bardstown, they connected at Anchorage for the quick ride out to Pewee Valley and returned to a private dining room at the Galt House in Louisville that evening for a final vote.[30]

There was little need for discussion; they had talked on board the train. At that point, the board of trustees had about $10,000 in solid subscriptions, plus the Parr house (which, it was now understood, had a market value closer to $4,500, considerably less than its $7,000 assessed value). From those funds they were required to purchase at least thirty acres of land, build a facility suitable to house at least twenty-five veterans, and furnish the home to be ready for immediate occupancy. Though they might be able to raise more money during the coming year (or enter into some sort of loan arrangement), there was a consensus that the Home should be opened sooner rather than later.

The board agreed to take multiple ballots, with the site drawing the fewest votes to be eliminated before the next ballot.

Hawesville was eliminated first. A thirty-acre plot with house and outbuildings was offered for just $5,000 (and the town would pay $3,000 of that). But the land was swampy and the water supply uncertain.

The Owensboro offer was for a hundred level acres of tillable land, a large house, and outbuildings, all on high ground with a rail line running along the property line. But at $18,000 for the property alone, the cost was greater than the board's purse would allow. Owensboro was the second proposal to be cut.

Bardstown boosters offered two tracts of land, one of forty acres and the other of eighty. Each tract was offered at $6,000, but a citizens committee raised $4,300 to put toward the purchase price. The properties were attractive and the price was right, but building and furnishing a suitable home on the acreage might take a year or more. Bardstown lost on the next ballot.

Frankfort's bid was for eighty acres and the old Hendrix place, once a landmark home but now a creaking ghost's mansion overlooking the Kentucky River. The $15,000 price tag, coupled with the cost of renovating the old house, took Frankfort out of the running.

The final ballot came down to a choice between Pewee Valley and Harrodsburg.

The Cassell property in Harrodsburg included another landmark home, but this one was in good repair and large enough to house at least thirty residents. The property, home, and outbuildings had a price tag of $10,500, but the merchants of Harrodsburg pledged $3,000 for furnishings and improvements. Rail connections to Harrodsburg were spotty, but the town was close to the geographic center of Kentucky and almost equidistant to Lexington, Frankfort, and Louisville.

Pewee Valley, a little village of small businesses, modest houses, comfortable summer homes, and a population of about 450, was located just sixteen miles east of Louisville. Property owner Angus Neil Gordon was offering thirty-three acres and the Villa Ridge Inn, a bankrupt luxury resort hotel built years before. The old hotel had seventy-two guest rooms (all completely furnished), dining hall, kitchen, running water, steam heat, and gas lighting. Gordon wanted $8,000 in cash and Captain Parr's Louisville property.

The price was right; the trustees could divest themselves of the Parr property, pay Gordon, and still hold about $2,000 cash in hand. Pewee Valley was only thirty minutes by train from the busy Louisville railway hub, so it was accessible to visitors. Villa Ridge Inn could house up to 100 residents in a building meant for institutional use, and it was ready for immediate occupancy with just a bit of sprucing up.

The final ballot tallied six for Harrodsburg and nine for Pewee Valley. A committee was appointed to examine the title and complete the purchase.

But the long board meeting wasn't over yet. The trustees still had to select a superintendent, a salaried employee who would manage the Home and see to the care and control of its residents.

Ten men had presented themselves to the board for the position, among them board member and state senator William O. Coleman. Coleman had polished his share of apples on behalf of Bennett Young and the Kentucky Confederate Home. He had introduced legislation for the Home, served without pay on the board of trustees, nominated Young as board president, and made boilerplate motions as needed. He needed a steady income, and he wanted this job.

Most board members, however, favored Salem H. Ford, a Confederate veteran from Owensboro with a strong work ethic and none of Coleman's oiliness.

Young asked Coleman to leave the room for the vote. With one abstention, the remaining trustees voted in favor of Ford over Coleman, seven to six. Salem Ford would go to work immediately to transform Pewee Valley's Villa Ridge Inn into the new Kentucky Confederate Home. The board of trustees wanted to open the Home for occupancy in October, just one year following adoption of plans for the Home at the state convention.

After approving a statement that could be handed to a waiting *Courier-Journal* reporter, the weary board members finally adjourned their meeting and retired to their rooms in the Galt House.[31]

Breakfast was still being served in the Galt House dining room the next morning when a storm of protest erupted in Pewee Valley. Affluent Louisvillians maintained elegant summer homes in Pewee Valley, and they weren't at all pleased with news that a public benevolent home would end up in their backyard.[32]

"We are proud of the old Confederates," one resident said, "but the people of Pewee Valley believe that an institution of [this] kind must hurt the place."

Judge P. B. Muir led the opposition, and his first step was a personal appeal to Governor Beckham. When he couldn't reach the governor, Muir threatened an injunction to halt the sale. The choice of Pewee Valley "will not be allowed to stand without every vigorous protest that can be made against it," Muir vowed.

Harry Wiessinger, a Louisville investor and summer resident of Pewee Valley, sent a public telegram to the board withdrawing his $300 pledge to the Home.

A newspaper editor wrote, "The whole affair will become entangled in a miserable and damaging mess."[33]

Most veterans, however, thought the protest was a petty one in view of progress made by the board of trustees. "Notwithstanding there is some objection," one veteran wrote Fayette Hewitt in a note accompanying his $25 donation, "we must congratulate the committee in getting a place so well adapted for the home and ready for occupancy."[34]

In the end, the tempest blew itself out. The board of trustees patiently explained the benefits of the Pewee Valley site to newspaper reporters; the governor supported the choice; and plans continued to have the Home operational by mid-October.[35] A Richmond newspaper editor wrote the coda to the entire episode under the headline "Hard to Please," saying that "while . . . a dozen other towns are tearing their hair out in their efforts to secure the Confederate Home, the citizens of Pewee Valley raise a terrible howl because they have gotten it."[36]

Though Fayette Hewitt was receiving subscription payments every day, the Kentucky Confederate Home board of trustees was feeling the same cash pinch felt by every new homebuyer: purchase insurance, replace a balky water pump, commission another survey to satisfy the county clerk.

Cash ran so low at one point that Bennett Young was forced to sign a personal promissory note to take delivery of bed linens. Contributions of furniture, books, dishware, and wall hangings arrived daily, but cash was in short supply.

On October 2 the board announced another fundraising scheme: the sale of naming rights to rooms in the Home. For $50, anyone could name a room in the Home and decorate it as he or she wished. The offer had special appeal to the UDC chapters, and women from all over the state began showing up in Pewee Valley, bank drafts in hand, wanting to tour the Home and choose "their" rooms.

Despite this last-minute infusion of cash, the board was still scrambling to meet every contingency. Attorneys discovered an encumbrance on one tract of the Villa Ridge Inn property, and the ex-Confederates needed to ante up an extra $1,000 before they could gain clear title and turn the property over to the state.

The board of trustees didn't have an extra $1,000.

With hat in hand, Bennett Young and Harry P. McDonald called on Mrs. Basil Duke, president of the Louisville UDC chapter. The chapter was a wealthy one and had raised $1,000 to purchase furni-

ture for the Home. Young and McDonald explained that they needed the money right away, fully expecting the compliant ladies to
turn it over for the good of the Home.

Henrietta Morgan Duke was the sister of legendary general John
Hunt Morgan and the wife of his equally legendary protégé Basil
Duke. A disarmingly beautiful woman and a grand dame of Louis-
ville society, she had the cunning and tenacity of a panther.[37]

Over tea, Henrietta Duke dictated her terms to the men: the
chapter would provide the money in return for seats on a Home advisory board. The name of the Albert Sidney Johnston Chapter must
appear on the deed conveyed to Governor Beckham. The chapter
will receive naming rights to five rooms in the Home. And, by the
way, the board will grant the chapter permission to hold a private
reception at the Home shortly after the opening.

Young and McDonald were outranked, outflanked, and out of
options. Young accepted the terms and the check for $1,000.

Within days, however, unexpected donations from the Lexington and Louisville UCV camps (along, perhaps, with a little buyer's
remorse) allowed Young to return the bank draft to Mrs. Duke. The
deal was off, he said. Mrs. Duke promptly sent the check back to
Bennett Young, reiterating the terms of their agreement. Young
eventually asked John Leathers to return the check by depositing it
in the chapter's account.

Women of the Louisville UDC chapter seethed at Young's ef-
frontery for reneging on their agreement, and they spread the story
from chapter to chapter across the state. Bennett Young and his
board of trustees would regret the consequences of the perceived
indignity for years afterward.[38]

Meanwhile, ex-Confederates, Daughters, and their friends and
families were preparing for a trip to Pewee Valley for the opening of
the Kentucky Confederate Home.

A month before the opening of the Home, Fayette Hewitt, sitting at
the oak desk in his office at State National Bank of Frankfort, sorted
through the envelopes stacked in front of him. Most of the envelopes contained letters and money, expressions of compassion to-

ward fellow Kentuckians, men who decades earlier had left their homes and families to fight for a cause that was lost before the first battle was joined.

Money and paper.

Hewitt recorded the contributions and read the letters.

"Dear General," read the letter from A. W. Bascom, the stockman from Bath County who, a year before at the state reunion, expressed his reservations about the plan for the Home. "Enclosed find check for $300, a part of the money raised by me for the Confederate Home." Despite his reservations, Bascom served on the Committee of Twenty-Five, and he had personally raised more than $400.

"I am somewhat disappointed that there has been no provision made under which a needy comrade together with his dear old wife can be provided for," Bascom wrote. "Still, I hope that the managing board may in the near future be able and willing to devise some plan by which this oversight may be remedied."[39]

There had been so many struggles during the previous year. Despite the petty fights, heated arguments, and money worries, Kentuckians were about to open a comfortable home for disabled and impoverished ex-Confederates.

"Trusting and believing that the good work so propitiously begun may be pursued until we can have a Home of which all of us will be proud, I remain your comrade and friend, A. W. Bascom."

When it opened on October 23, 1902, the Kentucky Confederate Home would not be the home that every ex-Confederate had envisioned. But, working together, Kentuckians were poised to provide a respectable place for their comrades who needed it.

Chapter 5

The Governor and the Prisoner

Aboard a special train approaching the Pewee Valley depot, thirty-three-year-old Governor John C. W. Beckham was as nervous as only a politician facing uncertain reelection could be. His formal campaign wouldn't begin until spring, but on this trip rode a hope that he would be more than an accidental governor.

Normally self-assured for a man his age, today he was nervous. He needed the respect and support of the Confederate veterans waiting for him in Pewee Valley.

Waiting with the rest of the welcoming party on the platform of the Pewee Valley Depot, seventy-eight-year-old Lorenzo D. Holloway had time to reflect on the new governor. Thirty-three years old and managing a whole state. Awfully young to be a governor. When Lorenzo Holloway was thirty-three years old, he hadn't managed much more than the books of a small stable. At thirty-three, Holloway hadn't yet been in prison with 10,000 men. And he hadn't yet seen good men die in droves.

As dawn broke over central Kentucky on Thursday, October 23, 1902, the sky transmuted from black to indigo to cerulean blue, here and there buffed by wisps of low-hanging wood smoke. September had been unseasonably warm, and autumn was late arriving. It was a blackberry autumn, and the trees had held their fire through October.

Sixteen miles east of Louisville and about that far south of the Ohio River, Pewee Valley was a quiet village of well-bred estate homes, unpretentious stone church buildings, white fences, coffee-colored dirt lanes, and a population of fewer than 500. Originally known as Smith's Station, residents adopted the current name in the 1850s for reasons lost to legend. The pewee is a bird, a woodland flycatcher that may once have made its home in the brushwood and broomsage of the area. Pewee Valley sits 300 feet higher than Louisville, a topographic feature that accounted for the elegant summer homes built there years before by wealthy Louisvillians who thought altitude and cooler summer evenings would make them less susceptible to the night vapors blamed for most summer illness.

Two side-by-side rail tracks—one for the steam trains connecting Louisville and Frankfort, another for interurban electric rail service—bisected the hamlet; a county road paralleled the tracks. Near the center of the village was a small commercial district, including a dry goods store, a meat market, a post office, a bank, a blacksmith shop, and the rail depot.

Six hundred yards up the county road from the rail depot, the former Villa Ridge Inn stood atop a gentle hill surrounded by newly raked grounds, awaiting its dedication as the new Kentucky Confederate Home.

As a rising sun painted Pewee Valley with its daytime colors, farm families from neighboring areas were clip-clopping up the county road in work wagons and buggies. The farmers were the first arrivals for a daylong celebration of bands, bunting, dignitaries, spectacle, and Lost Cause oratory.[1]

The board of trustees was desperate to open the Kentucky Confederate Home to residents as soon as possible. Bragging rights were at stake, of course, sectional pride for having financed, legislated, equipped, and opened a Home just twelve months after the meeting at which the board members set their hands to the task. (Ex-Confederates in Virginia, Texas, Georgia, Missouri, Maryland, and elsewhere spent years to do the job.) But financial considerations provided the most pressing reason for urgency. Until the state took formal possession of the Home and residents moved into it, no money would flow from the state's funding tap. Every month the Home remained unoccupied cost the trustees almost $300 in utilities and maintenance, an amount their minuscule reserve wouldn't cover for long.

Superintendent Salem H. Ford and his helpers and contractors had been working for weeks to prepare the former resort hotel for occupancy. The rooms of the old hotel needed scrubbing, sweeping, patching, repairing, painting. The building was sound and generally in good condition, but it hadn't been occupied for five years. Ford had to flush out water pipes, recharge gas cisterns, test each lamp, and replace pump gaskets, all the while dealing with loads of gifts, furnishings, and provisions that arrived daily.

There was much left undone, but by Thursday morning, October 23, 1902, the old Villa Ridge Inn was ready to reopen as the Kentucky Confederate Home.

Early-arriving farm families hitched their wagons to fences and trees surrounding the Home and roamed the grounds, determined to make a day of the celebration. Some spread blankets and baskets of food near a speakers' platform that had been built at the top of the looping driveway that led up the hill to the Home's entry. Long wooden picnic tables dotted the grounds.

At midmorning Salem Ford hoisted a U.S. flag and a Confederate flag to fly side by side from flagstaffs atop the four-story building. Red, white, and blue bunting was draped along the speakers' stand and the Home's gallery echoed the colors of the two national flags flying overhead.[2]

By 11:00 A.M. the broad lawn surrounding the Home was teeming with more than 4,000 people. "In keeping with the true spirit of Southern hospitality," a visitor wrote, "ample provision had been made to feed all who had come."

Churchwomen of Pewee Valley set out food and lemonade on the outdoor tables, while clubwomen from throughout the state distributed hampers of picnic fare. A detachment of cadets from the Kentucky Military Institute gathered in rank to rehearse their duty as honor guard for the dignitaries who would arrive later. The lively sound of popular tunes and patriotic marches rose from a brass band that wove through the crowd.

Every hour, it seemed, another thousand men and women from all parts of the state arrived by cart, carriage, trolley, train, and the occasional motorcar. The rail companies offered a discounted round-trip fare to Pewee Valley for the day. The later arrivals were townspeople mainly, the shopkeepers, physicians, bankers, and small businessmen of Kentucky's increasingly influential middle class. They found seats at the outdoor tables or spread picnic blankets on the raked grounds. Families gathered with other families of the same town, until congregations of visitors from Kuttawa melded into the visitors from Carrollton and Hopkinsville and Prestonsburg and Somerset.

"When the crowds began to gather in numbers on the broad lawn and under the trees it was first feared there would not be enough to give all a plenty," a reporter observed. But the women of Pewee Valley continued to produce hampers, steaming dishes draped with tea towels, and platters of sliced meats for the new arrivals.

The veterans—men of the Civil War generation, now in their sixties, seventies, or older—were scattered among the throng, and many were in the company of their wives, children, and grandchildren. Some wore old gray jackets or hats, remnants of uniforms that had been saved in trunks for decades. Others wore newer gray suits of a martial cut, the now-standardized uniform of the United Confederate Veterans organization. Here and there an old man would let out an excited yip as he recognized, then embraced, another old man. "[The veteran's] elastic step and joyous laugh belied his age as he met in happy reunion with his old comrades in arms," noted one visitor.

Kentucky's major newspapers gave the dedication front-page play in the early editions, and by midday Pewee Valley was jammed with more than 10,000 visitors, the largest gathering of Kentucky ex-Confederates, sympathizers, family, and friends since the end of the Civil War.

A quarter mile away, Lorenzo D. Holloway waited on the platform of the Pewee Valley rail depot for the governor's train with Home superintendent Salem Ford. Holloway had been the first to register as a resident of the Home, and he would be among the first that day to size up Kentucky's Boy Governor.

Lorenzo Holloway was almost forty years old when he left his farm in Scott County and the horse ranch where he worked to join John Hunt Morgan's cavalry in the autumn of 1861. He was a well-read man, good with figures, and trusted by the younger men of Smith's Regiment, Fifth Kentucky Cavalry. In the summer of 1863, he was a captain and regimental quartermaster when Morgan's cavalry swept northward on the ill-fated Ohio raid. Holloway was captured and imprisoned with sixty-odd other officers—including Thomas Eastin, Basil Duke, and General Morgan himself—in the Ohio state penitentiary.

"I am becoming quite fond of my cell," he wrote his mother in October 1863. "I can eat as much as I want and no limit to sleeping. Can keep warm, dry, clean, read my Bible, sing in a whisper and pray for myself, my family, friends and enemies."[3]

Conditions at the Ohio prison may have been *too* relaxed, a situation some prisoners exploited in November 1863. Aided by smuggled weapons (and a bribed guard or two), Morgan and a handful of officers escaped from the penitentiary. Humiliated Federal officers sent Holloway and the rest of the remaining prisoners to Fort Delaware.

Located on a small island at the mouth of Delaware Bay, Fort Delaware was a recommissioned Union fort intended to hold the thousands of Confederate prisoners captured at Gettysburg and Vicksburg. By the time Holloway and the other Ohio prisoners arrived, Fort Delaware was a hellhole.[4]

The last years of the war produced a quantity of Confederate prisoners of war the Federal bureaucracy was simply unprepared to handle. Southern prisons (such as Andersonville) couldn't obtain the resources needed to feed, clothe, and house large numbers of Federal prisoners; Union prison officials couldn't get the resources in place quickly enough to care for the prisoners they were capturing. Fort Delaware was ill-equipped to handle the number of prisoners arriving there.

"I am very poor, bones nearly through," Holloway wrote his sister several months after arriving at Fort Delaware, "but by my regular habits and the grace of God, my health is unimpaired."

Thirty thousand prisoners were housed there; Holloway was fortunate to have a strong constitution. The death rate rose as high as 30 percent as overcrowded prisoners coped with smallpox, cholera, bad water, poor nutrition, and insect infestation, as well as sadistic guards.

Facing the winter of 1864–65 in prison, Holloway begged his sister to send him a few food items and a stout Kentucky comforter. "It may be the last act of kindness you may have to extend to an only and unfortunate brother," he told her. "If I should have to winter on this island, I don't want to have to freeze and die of rheumatism or pneumonia."

Thousands of younger men died of cold, hunger, or despair that winter in Fort Delaware; but forty-year-old Lorenzo Holloway survived. In May 1865 he was released from prison and returned to Kentucky.

Governor Beckham's special train arrived from Frankfort at the Pewee Valley depot near high noon. From the window of his private rail car, Beckham could see the welcoming committee jostle themselves into a rough receiving line on the platform.

Beckham had endured welcoming ceremonies at countless rail depots all over the state during the three years of his governorship. But in the year since President William McKinley was shot to death during a stop in Buffalo, these routine events carried more than a tinge of worry, particularly for a governor who had gained office only after his predecessor was gunned down.

But that was just one more layer of anxiety added to an already worrisome day. The young governor was facing his first real reelection campaign, and he needed the unqualified support of Kentucky's ex-Confederates.

The gunshots that killed William Goebel still echoed in Kentucky politics three years later. Kentucky's moderate Democrats—including Bennett Young, John Leathers, W. N. Haldeman, and others of the state UCV leadership—had bolted the Democratic Party to vote against Goebel in 1899, and they were lukewarm about Beckham. In a special election to fill Goebel's unexpired term, Beckham squeezed out a razor-thin margin of 3,700 votes (out of a half million votes cast), then set out to mend fences with the state's traditional Democrats. He slavishly supported Bennett Young's plan for the Kentucky Confederate Home and helped grease legislative skids in the General Assembly, all the while expressing his fealty to the Lost Cause—this despite rumors that Bennett Young was contemplating his own run for the governorship against Beckham.[5]

Kentucky's state UCV organization and local camps were avowedly apolitical, but the men of the Confederate generation were Democrats down to their bootlaces. Governor Beckham needed all their support, all their clout, and every one of their votes to keep his office in the upcoming election.[6]

Beckham and his mother appeared at the door of his rail car and stepped onto the platform of the Pewee Valley depot. Even from a quarter mile away, they could hear the noise of the growing crowd gathered on the grounds of the Kentucky Confederate Home. After a brief greeting by the chairman of the welcoming committee and an equally brief response, Beckham and his mother turned to the receiving line.

Lorenzo Holloway stood next to Superintendent Salem H. Ford on the depot platform, somewhere between a Pewee Valley town committeeman and several gussied-up ladies of the UDC, all waiting a turn for their handshake with the governor.

Holloway had spent the years since Fort Delaware working at a variety of state bookkeeping and auditing jobs. A widower, he left Frankfort to return to farming in Scott County when Fayette Hewitt resigned as state auditor, and his friendship with Hewitt earned him early acceptance to the Kentucky Confederate Home. Holloway arrived in Pewee Valley before the formal opening to help Superintendent Ford prepare the building for occupancy. He and Ford had been detailed to the depot to meet the governor.

Holloway's first impression of Governor Beckham was likely the same as all who saw him for the first time: he was so *young*. The governor was well barbered, beardless, with oiled hair parted down the middle in the current style for young men. Beckham was hatless; he dressed carefully and well without looking dandified.

But Beckham was no fragile youngster who had to be handled with sugar tongs. Despite his youth, Governor Beckham betrayed no lack of confidence as he worked his way down the receiving line, every move graceful and practiced without seeming so. He gave the impression of being someone who knew how the world turned and was willing to keep it spinning in the right direction. Maybe he was up to the job.

Within a few moments, Beckham had made his way down the receiving line. He, his mother, Senator J. C. S. Blackburn, and the other out-of-town dignitaries stepped into decorated carriages for a quarter mile parade to the grounds of the Kentucky Confederate Home, escorted by an honor guard of Kentucky Military Institute cadets.

Seventy-eight-year-old Lorenzo Holloway and Superintendent Ford walked back to the Home behind the parade of open carriages.

Thirty minutes later the special train from Louisville arrived, six cars carrying 100 boisterous state UCV reunion delegates and their own brass band. The band struck up "Dixie," and the ex-Confederates formed into ranks. Flag-bearers flanked the procession—Stars and Stripes in the place of honor at the head of the right-hand column, Stars and Bars on the left—as they marched in column (mostly in step) up the crushed-rock carriageway to the grand building they would later dedicate for the use of Kentucky's invalid and indigent Confederate veterans. Wild cheers from the crowd greeted the flags, the sound of "Dixie," and the waving veterans.[7]

Some of the arriving dignitaries joined Governor Beckham and Senator Blackburn to inspect the building. Visitors marveled at the sheer luxury of the Home, surrounded on three sides by a wide, comfortable verandah. At a time when only city dwellers knew such amenities, the Home had gaslight in every room, steam heat throughout, and roof cisterns that allowed for indoor bathrooms on the first and second floors. There were seventy-two guest bedrooms already furnished, two oak-paneled parlors, and a dining room that could seat 125 comfortably. The former lobby had been converted to a library, and more than a thousand volumes lined the shelves. Just the week before, movers had delivered a pipe organ and an upright piano, along with box after box of sheet music.

Governor Beckham pronounced the home "beautiful," a splendid place where noble old veterans could weather the storms of winter while receiving the necessities of life.

Bath County stockman A. W. Bascom and his wife, Mary, were among those who bypassed the tour. "Do you remember the band coming in from Louisville about one o'clock and the veterans marching behind?" Mary Bascom asked a friend later. "A. W. and I fell in just behind the standard bearers and wove on through the crowd and out to the tables for dinner. We then came back and stood twenty feet left from the speakers stand."[8]

Having been fed and entertained, the crowd was ready for the speechifying to begin.

At two o'clock, to the strains of "My Old Kentucky Home," the governor, the chairmen of the various dedication committees, and the invited orators filed onto a temporary platform erected on the driveway in front of the Home. Bennett Young, John Leathers, Leland Hathaway, and other officers of the state veterans' organization wore their gray UCV uniforms. (Major General J. M. Poyntz, commander of the Kentucky division, the man who had presided over the statewide meeting that sparked creation of the Home and who appointed the Committee of Twenty-Five, was absent. His only son had been shot and killed in a duel several days earlier, and Poyntz couldn't bear to leave his family.)

Six feet tall, ramrod straight, his hair and mustache shining white in the bright sunshine, Bennett Young stepped to the podium to begin a ceremony that would celebrate the ex-Confederates and honor their gift, while hitting all the notes of the Lost Cause ritual.

Young first introduced the state UCV chaplain, the Reverend

E. M. Green, who invoked God's blessing on the veterans, the Home, the Commonwealth of Kentucky, and the United States of America.

Next, Young called H. M. Woodruff, mayor of Pewee Valley, to the podium. Obsequious as a hotel desk clerk, Woodruff began with a clumsy apology for the town's earlier opposition to the Kentucky Confederate Home. "We feel somewhat like the old folks did when the daughter ran off and married the man of her choice: after the knot was tied, the best thing was to receive the young couple back into the bosom of the family." After a few more halfhearted words of welcome, the perspiring mayor returned to his seat on the platform.

But these were just the warm-up acts. As the band struck up "Dixie" once again, Colonel Leland Hathaway, vice president of the Home's board, strode to the podium.

"It is my duty and pleasure to introduce to you . . . a man who needs no introduction to Confederate soldiers," Hathaway began, "and a man who in days gone by needed none to our friends, the enemy."

Cheers broke out before Hathaway could finish. "I have the honor of presenting to you General Joseph H. Lewis of the Confederate army."

Whoops and yawps and Rebel yells exploded from the crowd, a thunderous ovation lasting a minute or more as Lewis rose from his seat on the platform and made his way to the podium.

Lewis needed no introduction. Every Confederate infantryman in Kentucky knew him.

Forty years earlier, Joseph H. Lewis had shuttered his law practice to recruit an armed regiment when Kentucky's rump convention seceded from the Union. Lewis's regiment joined with others to become the First Kentucky Brigade, under the command of Brigadier General John C. Breckinridge, former vice-president of the United States. This Kentucky brigade, organized and trained outside its home state, fought across the South, but would never return to fight in Kentucky. By the end of the war—following the deaths of Roger

Hanson and Ben Hardin Helm—Kentucky's Orphan Brigade was under the command of General Joseph Lewis.[9]

Most of the ex-infantrymen in Pewee Valley that day were veterans of the Orphan Brigade, Kentuckians who were never able to return as a unit during wartime to their home state. For those years they were "orphans," their only home the Confederate army.

General Lewis was brief in his remarks, and in less than five minutes touched all the Lost Cause bases. He praised the valor of his Confederate veterans ("the fight we made was a manly and upright one"), the constancy of their beliefs ("steadfast and true to our convictions"), ultimate reconciliation ("our ill will against the Union of States ceased"), and unremitting patriotism ("despite political ostracism attempted by mad men and bad men").

These men of the Lost Cause had proven themselves worthy, the general pronounced.

"The foundation [of the Home] teaches a lesson which should not be lost on our young men," the old warhorse concluded to more cheering. "It shows that men who do their duty honestly and fearlessly are not forgotten in their old age."

Bennett Young wanted to be sure the financial needs of the Home weren't forgotten, either. When applause for General Lewis subsided, Young stepped to the podium to receive a donation of $110 in gold from two Union veterans. In a few words, Young expressed his appreciation for the gift and the spirit of brotherly love in which it was rendered.

Veteran J. L. Haines, backed by the Confederate Quartet, brought the crowd to its feet once again with "Tenting on the Old Camp Ground" and a medley of old camp songs before Young returned to the podium to introduce Captain William T. Ellis.

Like Young, Ellis was one of those Civil War boy wonders whose fuse was lit by the war and whose career rose like a rocket. He enlisted in the First Kentucky Confederate Cavalry at age sixteen, returned home to Daviess County relatively unscathed after four years, then graduated from Harvard Law School by the time he was twenty-five. Ellis opened a law practice in Owensboro in 1870, and the same year won election as county attorney. In 1886 he mounted a campaign for U.S. Congress and served two terms in Washington. He was an active organizer of Confederate veteran camps in western Kentucky and a powerhouse in Democratic politics.[10]

An experienced stump speaker, Ellis knew how to grab an audience, even one made drowsy by a warm day and a heavy lunch. Grinning down from the podium at the hundreds of gray-clad veterans in his audience, Ellis broke the elegiac spell cast by earlier speakers.

"It is evident that all the young Kentuckians who, some forty years ago, served in the Confederate Army are not yet dead," he began, gaining an appreciative chuckle. "And if we're to judge from present indications, they have no intentions of voluntarily capitulating as long as their rations hold out."

From his years in politics, Ellis could deliver a respectable stemwinder. He quoted the Bible, cited scholars, and recited poetry, all in oratorical service to the Lost Cause touchstones of valor, constancy, reconciliation, and patriotism.

The crowd interrupted Ellis time after time with thunderous applause during his hour-long oration, but he earned the greatest roars of approval when he spoke of the debt his audience owed the men of the Confederate generation:

"The young men Kentucky gave to the Confederate army rendered their state some service," he bellowed from the podium, "and are, as they and their friends believe, entitled to a respectable place in its history."

As the congressman concluded his speech and the audience cheered, Bennett Young led a schoolgirl with a large box of flowers to the podium. She presented the flowers to Ellis, and Young introduced Miss Laura Talbot Galt to the audience, who recognized her name immediately. Little Laura had been turned out of her Louisville public school for refusing to sing "Marching through Georgia" in a school assembly. Indignant newspaper editorials throughout the South brought about Laura's reinstatement and the removal of the despicable Yankee song from schools throughout the Southland.[11]

For a full two minutes Laura stood at the front of the platform with Ellis's arm on her shoulder, the Lost Cause heroine and the Lost Cause orator enveloped by adoring cheers from the crowd.

To be a first-rate orator at the beginning of the twentieth century required lungs like leather saddlebags, a diaphragm as solid as a manhole cover, and vocal cords more resilient than piano wire. In those days before electronic amplification, a man—there were few top-tier women orators—had to address a group of people large enough to fill a minor league ballpark and make his every word heard and understood. Moreover, he had to modulate his voice sufficiently to convey emotion and maintain interest. And, to make things even more difficult, he often had to do this in an outdoor setting, his voice competing with crying babies, the natural rustle of a crowd, a whistling breeze, or even passing trains.[12]

Captain Ellis was an excellent stump speaker; but, by all accounts, Bennett H. Young was an inspired orator.

His eulogy for Winnie Davis in 1899 and his high-spirited invitation to Louisville for the 1900 UCV reunion earned Bennett Young a seat (literally) on the national Confederate veterans' stage. He had learned all the movements of the Lost Cause symphony, and it was a tune he could play by heart. Behind a lectern Young was scholar, storyteller, teacher, and poet. When he chose to turn on the charm, it flowed in irresistible waves; when he intended pathos, women sobbed and men reached for handkerchiefs. By 1902 there was hardly a monument ceremony, battlefield dedication, or Confederate reunion where Bennett Young wasn't invited to be the featured speaker.

Shortly before three o'clock he returned to the podium before the 10,000 men, women, children, and babies awaiting formal dedication of the Kentucky Confederate Home.

"Comrades, ladies and gentlemen," he began. "[Today] witnesses the speedy consummation of the most important enterprise ever inaugurated by the Confederate soldiers of this Commonwealth."

Young went into a brief (and prideful) recap of the founding of the Home. "It is less than a year since the state reunion of the UCV . . . declared its purpose and formulated plans to establish on a liberal scale and secure foundation a Kentucky Confederate Home."

Kentucky's Confederates have, in this and other ventures, Young reminded his audience, "reflected on the state nothing but credit and renown."

Turning to look at the building behind him, he mused on the nature of the men who would come to live there.

"There will be men here in this Home who, with their comrades, marched with unblanched cheeks into the fires which belched from Federal guns up and down the slopes of Chickamauga's hills."

A cheer arose from the veterans who remembered Chickamauga all too well.

"There will be men here to pass the closing years of their lives who charged down along the valley of Stones River on that dreadful afternoon of January 2, 1863."

More cheers from the men who survived that bloodbath.

"The men who will come here will be those who walked without fear amid the awful carnage of Shiloh."

Rebel yells now, and more cheers from a crowd that had been primed to respond to these legendary names.

"There will be men here to live out the closing days of their lives who rode with . . . the valiant Forrest."

The audience erupted over mention of Tennessee's brilliant cavalryman.

" . . . the peerless Breckinridge . . ."

The roar from the crowd was almost constant, but Young continued with the names of battles and leaders dear to Kentuckians' hearts.

" . . . the Federal lines at Harrisburg, Mississippi . . ."

The roar increased in volume.

" . . . that memorable campaign from Dalton . . ."

Louder still.

" . . . to Atlanta . . ."

By this point the call-and-response between speaker and audience was at a sonic volume sufficient to blow the windows out of any Baptist church. At the absolute crescendo of excitement, however, at the precise moment when this roaring mob of 10,000 seemed ready to strip bark from the trees in their frenzy, Young went silent.

The crowd was confused, and its sound spluttered away to nothing.

For a long moment Young simply stared at his audience, letting their attention focus on him alone. He spread his arms wide and finally, in a low, steely voice that was almost sepulchral, continued.

"Today we swing wide these hospitable doors and bid these heroes come in." Young slowly closed his arms to his chest, as if embracing the whole of the crowd.

"Here with sheltering love no want shall go unsupplied. . . . Here they can abide in peace, plenty, quiet and comfort until they shall answer the divine roll call and cross over to the unknown shore to keep company with the immortals."

As the audience cheered these words Young reached into the lectern to produce a set of golden keys. He displayed them to the crowd, then turned to Governor Beckham's seat on the platform.

"And to you, governor of our beloved Commonwealth . . . I tender these keys with unfaltering faith that Kentucky will never forget her brave and chivalrous sons, who at Shiloh . . ."

Again, the audience exploded at mention of that fateful name.

" . . . Hartsville . . ."

The call-and-response began once more, louder even than the first time.

" . . . Kennesaw Mountain . . ."

" . . . Jonesboro . . ."

" . . . Resaca . . ."

" . . . Murfreesboro . . ."

Men who had yelled themselves hoarse threw hats in the air and waved handkerchiefs; women swooned and kissed their hands to him; children stood paralyzed by the incredible explosion of noise surrounding them. Few heard (or needed to hear) the final few words of Young's dedicatory address.

When the audience finally regained its composure, they saw that Governor Beckham was standing at the podium, golden keys in one hand and a sheaf of papers in the other.

"There is a certain lady in this crowd who has me very much intimidated," the Boy Governor began. "During the war her work of sending supplies to the Confederate soldiers in the South was carried on to such an extent that it attracted the attention of Federal authorities, and she concluded that the climate of Canada would be more congenial to her than the prospect of a Northern prison. That lady was my mother."

The audience chuckled; most knew of Julia Tevis Wickliffe Beckham's wartime activities. She was the adventuresome daughter of Kentucky's beloved governor Charles A. Wickliffe and the sister of Louisiana's Governor R. C. Wickliffe. Now an attractive dowager, she enjoyed the rare distinction of being the daughter, sister, and mother of governors of states.[13]

Julia Beckham, former Confederate spy, acknowledged the polite applause without leaving her seat.

"She said that if I dared say anything that was not complimentary to the Southern soldiers or the cause they espoused, she would get right up and disown me," Beckham said with a shy grin. "So to avoid running the risk of anything of the kind, I have committed to paper what I have to say."

Beckham formally accepted the Home on behalf of the State of Kentucky. His speech was unremarkable, but it was well received by the ex-Confederates, lauding as it did their wartime patriotism and assuring them that the people of Kentucky would care for them in their old age. The governor's voice was confident and clear, and he did not attempt the oratorical flourishes or bombast that might have been more appropriate for an older man. Beckham read his speech rather than deliver it from memory. The youthful governor basked in the warmth, if not adulation, of the crowd, and he gave his mother no reason to disown him.

As the festivities wound to a close, Bennett Young motioned for a fragile old man to join him at the podium. Slowly, almost painfully, the man rose from his seat on the speaker's stand, his eyes sunken and lusterless. Assisted by his matronly daughter, a black manservant, and an ebony walking stick, he wobbled toward Young, looking not unlike a giant mantis in a black wool suit.

Captain Daniel G. Parr, whose gift of a house and lot sparked the final push for a Confederate veterans home eighteen months before, leaned close to Young in utter confusion as he was introduced to the crowd. On behalf of their family, Parr's daughter, Virginia Sale, presented a silk streamer—a red, white, and blue guidon inscribed "The Confederate Home"—and it was hoist on the flagstaff.

A final benediction sent the crowd on its way.

The ceremonies in Pewee Valley on October 23, 1902, marked a clear dividing line for Kentucky's ex-Confederates. In less than two years they had completed the tasks necessary to build a veterans' home. From that day forward they would have to provide for its management.

Governor Beckham and his mother departed Pewee Valley that afternoon on the governor's special train. He carried with him the golden keys, symbolic of his proprietorship of the Kentucky Confederate Home. Beckham would sleep that night in his Frankfort apartment, comfortable that he had done nothing to embarrass himself in front of the veterans. A year later he would win reelection, his victory ensured by the near unanimous support of Kentucky's ex-Confederates.

Lorenzo Holloway would sleep that night at what was now officially the Kentucky Confederate Home. As a young man he had spent three ugly years in a Federal institution, and he had chosen to spend the final years of his life in another type of institution. Under the management of the board of trustees and the eyes of other interested parties, the Kentucky Confederate Home promised to be a more benevolent institution than the one that imprisoned Holloway during the war years.

The Kentucky Confederate Home would be a respectable place, but an institution nonetheless.

Chapter 6

The Druggist and the Sheriff

Three inmates approached the door of the superintendent's office on the ground floor of the Kentucky Confederate Home and knocked politely. The man who answered was dressed in work pants and an old shirt, his spectacles coated with the same dust that seemed to cover every horizontal surface in the Home, a result of ongoing carpentry, scraping, sanding, and minor renovation projects.

The inmates handed the superintendent a formal resolution, the wording of which had been debated the evening before, then written on a crisp sheet of Home letterhead stationery. A second sheet, this one with the signatures of eighty-four veterans and Home employees, was affixed to the first.

The superintendent removed his spectacles, wiped them clean with his shirttail, and began to read the formal language.

"Whereas it has come to our knowledge that you have tendered your resignation . . ."[1]

The facility now known as the Kentucky Confederate Home was originally one of Kentucky's grandest (and least successful) summer resort hotels. Villa Ridge Inn was built in 1889, conceived as a luxurious getaway for Kentucky's elite.

Kentucky was dotted with pleasant little resort hotels, often built around natural springs. The Chalybeate Springs Resort Hotel in Union County attracted guests from Indiana, Illinois, and as far away as Texas. Swango Springs Spa and Hotel in Wolfe County operated as a posh resort through much of the nineteenth century.

And, just north of Pewee Valley in Trimble County, the Parker family promoted their Bedford Springs Hotel and its warm sulfur waters as a healing treatment for everything from arthritis to mange.[2]

Pewee Valley already had a reputation as a healthful place in which to reside when local entrepreneur Horace Smith spent close to $50,000 to build his 100-room summer resort in the Louisville exurb. With seventy-two guest rooms, Smith's Villa Ridge Inn was one of the largest hotels in Kentucky, and certainly the largest located outside a city. But Villa Ridge Inn wasn't so much about size as about luxury.

Located on the crest of a gentle slope just 600 yards from the Pewee Valley train depot, the resort hotel stood four stories high, sixty feet deep, and as long as seven rail cars. A wide veranda, furnished with comfortable rocking chairs and wooden gliders, surrounded the building on three sides, and it was said guests could enjoy a mile-long covered stroll. Second-story balconies and generous windows on every floor provided splendid views of area homes and churches as well as natural cross-ventilation. Atop the frame building was an octagonal cupola and, atop the cupola, eighty feet above neat flower beds, was a flagpole from which flew the U.S. and Kentucky flags.

The servants' quarters—a two-story dormitory for live-in help—was located behind the main structure, with a fully equipped linen laundry and steam boilers in the basement. The boilers fed a heating system that provided warmth to every room on cool spring evenings or chilly autumn mornings. Four brick-lined wells and a pump house provided water for the indoor bathrooms located on the first three floors. (One of the wells produced a sulfurous water flow that was too sporadic—and too foul-smelling—to be promoted as a healing mineral bath.)

On arrival at the Pewee Valley depot, hotel visitors could see the resort's tall cupola and flagpole above the trees. Uniformed porters loaded trunks and luggage onto carts as guests boarded open carriages for the short ride to the inn. As a guest's carriage entered the grounds and began its gradual ascent up the white gravel driveway, the visitor could easily mistake the Villa Ridge Inn—particularly at twilight, when warm gaslight shone from every room—for a luxurious White Star ocean liner, a vessel of aristocratic elegance planted somehow in the rolling hills of central Kentucky.

That first impression of upper-crust splendor continued when the visitor's carriage halted under the porte-cochere and a liveried doorman opened the oak-framed front doors.

Just inside the main entrance on the ground floor were a richly paneled lobby and a book-lined library. The parlor furniture was carved, massive, dark, and comfortable. Two additional parlors and a smoking room opened off a wide hallway that ran the length of the building to the dining room. Victorian paintings or pressed ferns hung on every wall, and sprays of fresh flowers appeared on every horizontal surface. Surrounded on three sides by large windows, the dining room could seat 80 for formal servings, but could accommodate more than 100 for casual meals, and the adjoining kitchen was equipped with institutional stoves, ovens, coolers, and prep tables.

Three curving wooden stairways provided access to the upper floors, one in the center of the building and one on either end. Upstairs sleeping rooms and bathrooms opened off central hallways of wide waxed floorboards; large linen presses and servants' pantries were hidden at convenient distances throughout the halls. The upstairs guest-room floors were covered with matting, while the hallways and all the downstairs rooms were carpeted.

During prime summer seasons Pewee Valley's Villa Ridge Inn was a place where fashionable men in three-button double-breasted sack suits, pretty young mothers in trailing skirts and parasols, and well-scrubbed little girls in ruffled white dresses with pink sashes and hair ribbons strolled the broad lawns and among the shady trees of the spacious grounds.[3]

Within six years of its opening, however, the luxury resort hotel fell into bankruptcy.

During its short life, Villa Ridge Inn was bedeviled by a combination of too many expenses and too little income. The hotel was overbuilt: money spent on the hotel's necessary staff and its modern heating, lighting, and plumbing infrastructure was far more than could be recovered with only six dozen guest rooms during a summer tourist season. And Pewee Valley was just too close to Louisville to be a compelling getaway location for that city's upper crust. (By comparison, the extravagant French Lick Springs Hotel and Spa in southern Indiana thrived during the same period. It was more than an hour away by rail, and the owners enjoyed income from their golf course, casino, local tours, and healing baths, in addition to hotel revenues.)[4]

"On the premises, we will sell at public auction to the highest bidder the property known as the Villa Ridge Inn." Falls City Insurance Co. of Louisville, as liquidating agent, put the property under the auctioneer's hammer (without reserve or limit) on Saturday, October 26, 1895.[5]

Real estate speculator Angus N. Gordon eventually acquired the property, but his White Star luxury liner was now more of a white elephant. He managed to lease the buildings to a private boarding school for several years, but by 1898 he was valuing the land and improvements at something less than $13,000. By the turn of the century Gordon had practically given the vacant hotel over to the use of Pewee Valley citizens for dances, musicales, and other legitimate entertainments. (Village residents provided the cash and maintenance services necessary to keep the facility heated, lit, and secure.)[6] So when Kentucky's ex-Confederates announced in 1902 that they were looking for a veterans' home site, Angus N. Gordon had just the right property at exactly the right price.

That the Kentucky Confederate Home was presentable on the day it was dedicated and suitable for occupancy by arriving veterans was due to weeks of personal oversight and dawn-to-dusk physical labor by a bookish sixty-eight-year-old druggist from Owensboro.

Salem Holland Ford was an odd choice to be named first superintendent of the Kentucky Confederate Home. He had spent most of his professional career in the drug trade at a time when the local druggist was as much a personal health care provider as was the country doctor. Some druggists of the period built fortunes by devising and marketing laxative syrups, catarrh salves, typhoid tablets, health drinks, and other patent medicines, but Ford had little interest in the entrepreneurial aspects of his profession. Instead, he was content with compounding and dispensing useful medicaments to those seeking relief from various ailments. Ford maintained an impressive pharmacological library, and he was a regular speaker at annual meetings of the Kentucky Pharmaceutical Association. He had no great political ambitions, but was willing to serve on the local school board when appointed by the mayor of Owensboro.[7]

Nothing about Ford's appearance was particularly awe-inspiring. He was a slight man, trim, with thinning white hair. Behind a broad, drooping mustache, his lips were pursed like a disapproving Sunday School teacher, and his watery blue eyes tended to squint when he wasn't wearing his wire-rimmed spectacles.

But Ford's military credentials were impressive.

At the outbreak of the Civil War, Ford crossed the Mississippi River into Missouri to enlist as a private in the state guard there. Within a year he was attached to the Confederate army and elected captain of Company F, General Joseph Shelby's cavalry brigade under Major General Sterling Price. For two years Ford and his men conducted lightning raids throughout Missouri, north Arkansas, and parts of the Indian Territory. (During his time in Missouri and Kansas he had occasion to command Frank James, brother of Jesse, and he formed a lifelong friendship with soon-to-be-legendary lawman Wyatt Earp.)

In combat and on raids, Ford was no reckless sword-waver, but a careful planner who maintained a quiet equanimity in even the most disordered situations. His troops trusted him; his commanders respected him. Near the end of the war, as Price's Trans-Mississippi Army faced increasing pressure in the north, Ford led his company on a 1,400-mile skedaddle around Union troops in Arkansas, through Indian Territory and Texas. Eventually, he surrendered and was paroled at Shreveport, Louisiana, on June 15, 1865.

Back in Owensboro in 1879, Ford organized the Monarch Rifles, a private military company in Daviess County formed under Kentucky state law. He was elected captain, and for the next decade he helped build the organization into one of Kentucky's best-trained local militias. He played an active role in establishing Owensboro's Confederate veterans camp, and by 1900 was on General Poyntz's staff of the Kentucky UCV organization.

The board of trustees voted to hire Ford as the first superintendent of the Kentucky Confederate Home at its marathon board meeting on September 4, 1902. He would receive a salary of $75 a month, plus free room and board at the Home for him and his wife. He had no experience running an institution of any sort—one of the other job candidates, Thomas Richards, was a career hotelier— but Ford was known as an energetic, well-organized man who said what he was going to do and did what he said. (By comparison, the other serious candidate, former state senator William O. Coleman, always seemed a little too unctuous and eager to please.)

It was not until the first week in October, however, when the purchase of the old hotel was completed, that Ford could commence preparing the building and grounds of the old Villa Ridge Inn for the dedication ceremony barely three weeks later.

First, he had to repair and clean the property. Most of the hotel guest rooms had been closed for several years. The entire facility required scraping, patching, repainting, and wallpapering. Ford oversaw the inspection, repair, and replacement of the gas and water lines. He called in local workers to make sure the pumps, tanks, and cisterns were operating properly and holding their seals. To prepare for the dedication and opening ceremonies, Ford saw that the trees were trimmed, the lawn was raked, and a new bed of crushed white gravel was spread over a dirt carriageway that led from the road to the front of the Home.[8]

Ford was assisted by several veterans who had arrived early at the Home: Lorenzo Holloway and others. He used these early arrivals to help oversee construction and manage outside workers, but Ford alone had to navigate the political spider web of purchasing and staffing.

As superintendent, Ford was "charged with the general management and supervision, [and] the employment of such help as may be necessary therein." Major purchases and key employees, however, were the responsibility of the board of trustees. Before Ford could buy so much as a replacement doorknob, he was required to advertise for bids, then submit the bids to the executive committee for action. In this manner he had to acquire the necessary furnishings, linens, dinnerware, and stores necessary to house, feed, and care for 100 residents and staff.

Dozens of businesses with ex-Confederate connections vied to supply the Home with what it needed (and sometimes didn't know it needed). Ford would listen patiently to every pitchman and drummer, interrupting occasionally to clarify a point or ask a question. Then, politely, he would direct the prospective purveyor to the Home's board of trustees.

On no more consultation with Ford than a buggy-maker might have with a horse, the board of trustees hired a matron (to supervise meals and cleaning) and a steward (to serve the residents and clean the facility). Ford would be responsible for managing these employees, but he lacked the power to discipline or replace them.

Still, Ford maintained an even temper and a calm demeanor.

In addition to the renovation and management challenges, there was the torrent of gifts that poured into the Home every day.

In testament to the statewide support of the Home and the old veterans who would live there, Kentucky residents sent gifts they felt would bring a bit of comfort or pleasure to the residents. Few days failed to bring an express wagon to the door of the Home, with a constant stream of drivers seeking to offload a carved easy chair, boxes of books, a tin of cupcakes, or some other precious item.

Growers in Madison County sent a hogshead of tobacco for use by the old soldiers; M. W. Oliver sent a large Bible; E. J. Elliott sent a box of games; and Mrs. Poyntz shipped a crate full of magazines and her husband's old summer clothing.[9]

"I had a . . . fern three feet across that I wanted to take down to the Confederate Home," an Owingsville woman wrote her cousin. (In the end, she decided to send it by rail.) Women of the Paris County UDC shipped a huge crate "containing cakes, candies, literature, stationery, tobacco and a liberal donation of money" with the promise of similar shipments in future months. Governor Beck-

ham and his mother sent an upright piano from their home in Bardstown to the Confederate Home's parlor, where it likely sat side by
side with a pump organ donated by a Louisville music store.[10]

Every gift required a note of thanks.

"I am in receipt of five strong, handsome hammocks," began one
such expression of appreciation. "The hammocks have been swung
in cool shady spots in our grove of wide-spreading oaks and beech-
es, and the 'old boys' will take great pride in them."[11]

Ford designated one of the downstairs parlors as a library, and
two Louisville women solicited 3,000 books from printers, book-
sellers, local businesses, and friends to fill the shelves with reading
matter.[12]

The Home library likely had a dictionary, and if the donor had
been particularly generous, the dictionary would have been *Webster's International Dictionary of the English Language*, published just
three years earlier. If one of the early-arriving residents happened
into the library one day to riffle through the pages of that new dictionary, and if his finger happened to stop on page 381 ("ink–
innerve"), he might have read the definition of the word "inmate" as
it was commonly used in 1902: "One who lives in the same house or
apartment with another, a fellow lodger; by extension, one who oc-
cupies or lodges in any place or dwelling." Thus, by the usage of the
day, ex-Confederates who lived voluntarily in the Kentucky Confederate Home were referred to as "inmates," a word used a century
later to denote *involuntary* residents of institutions such as prisons or
asylums.

There was nothing involuntary about the first men who would
be inmates of the Kentucky Confederate Home. They were eager to
get to Pewee Valley.

In late September, a month before the Home's scheduled opening,
board secretary Harry P. McDonald printed 200 copies of a one-
page inmate application form and mailed several to each of the
state's UCV camps. A few more copies were distributed to interested
UDC chapters and to veterans who requested them directly from
the board. McDonald's printed form was the first step of a four-step

admissions process that involved application, review, notification, and processing.[13]

A veteran desiring to apply for a place in the Kentucky Confederate Home first had to give information about his residence and military service. (According to the law that established the Home, all residents had to prove their active military service for the Confederate States of America and their honorable discharge or parole at the termination of the war.) The questions asked of the applicant were not unlike the questions John Leathers had asked Billy Beasley years before when determining Beasley's worthiness for assistance: Where did you enlist? In what commands did you serve? Were you imprisoned? Wounded? Where were you discharged or paroled? Do you still have your papers? An applicant was required to swear that "he is unable by reason of bad health or mental or physical inability to support himself." Further, "he says he is not addicted to the excessive use of intoxicating liquors" and agrees that he will abide by the rules and regulations of the Home.[14]

Applicants also had to provide a recommendation from two witnesses, men who were in a "position to know that the statements made in his application are true." The witnesses were also required to attest to the applicant's moral worthiness, that "he is not addicted to excessive use of liquors" and that "he is a proper person for admission to said Kentucky Confederate Home."

Finally, a physician must swear that he examined the applicant and that he "is not addicted to the use of intoxicating liquors to excess and that he is not insane."

Completed applications came flowing back to Harry McDonald almost as fast as he could mail out the blanks. On October 24, 1902, the executive committee formally approved its first batch of fifteen completed admission applications: "It affords me great pleasure to inform you that your application for admission to the Kentucky Confederate Home was favorably passed upon by the executive committee. The Home is now open for your reception at any time you may desire to enter."[15]

The committee sent form acceptance letters to sixty-three-year-old Peter B. Adams, a resident of Lexington and a veteran of John

Morgan's Ohio raid, and to S. G. Shumate, a slow-talking native of Virginia now living in Middlesborough on the charity of his friends. Seventy-seven-year-old Benjamin Thomas received his acceptance letter at his son-in-law's home in Louisville, where he was living with his daughter and her three children. Confederate veteran Stanford P. Ashford was an Arkansan when he enlisted in the Confederate infantry there, but he had tramped around quite a bit since the war and was living in Jessamine County when he received his acceptance letter. S. O. Foster lost his arm in Tennessee in 1863, but had been earning a decent living in Paducah until a stroke paralyzed his remaining arm. He made arrangements to leave for Pewee Valley right away.

At least two, and perhaps as many as five, old veterans took up residence in the Home prior to its formal opening, arriving early to help Superintendent Ford prepare the property. The rest arrived as soon as they could settle their affairs and gather up sufficient train fare for Pewee Valley.

George A. Miller of Trimble County, one-time cavalryman John Lynn Smith, and paralyzed veteran Otway Norvell arrived on November 1. By November 4 eleven inmates were living in the Home.[16] The next day, the executive committee voted to send letters of acceptance to twenty-three more applicants.

When the veterans launched their plan to create the Kentucky Confederate Home, no one was certain exactly how many ex-Confederates had need of such a place or would consent to live there. Even some proponents of a home felt it would be a difficult matter to practice charity upon ex-Confederate soldiers.[17]

On one hand, every UCV camp had a story of at least one comrade who was living in mean conditions on the charity of others. And Kentucky veterans had read of the number of indigent ex-Confederates who entered the Virginia, Texas, Arkansas, and Maryland homes. General Poyntz could say that Kentucky's camps had "many destitute Confederates," and the editor of *The Lost Cause* could write that there were "a number of aged Confederates in the public charitable institutions"; but no one could actually say what that number was.[18]

On the other hand, their own Lost Cause rhetoric convinced them that a noble Johnny Reb would be loath to accept all but temporary charity. ("Haven't you got any more sense than to think I am a beggar?" an indignant veteran reportedly responded when his UCV camp comrades offered assistance.) The U.S. pension program for Union veterans had become a graft-ridden national embarrassment, further dampening, it was believed, any desire for public charity. ("It is rare to find a pensioner who, with no blush upon his face, will look you in the eye and declare himself a pensioner," sputtered one ex-Confederate.)[19]

There was little the board of trustees could do but open the doors of the Kentucky Confederate Home and see who wanted in.

In early November Harry P. McDonald realized he had used up his supply of application forms. He placed a rush order to have more printed.

When a new inmate arrived at the Home, Salem Ford would take time off from whatever he was doing to greet the newcomer.

If the inmate was hungry, if he had missed a meal during his trip, or if the superintendent believed the new arrival had missed more than a few meals in prior weeks, Ford would walk the man to the kitchen for a plate of whatever food the cook could rustle up on short notice. Some men were in immediate need of a bath and new clothes, so Ford would dig around in the boxes of donated shirts, pants, and underdrawers to assemble a decent wardrobe. (Bennett Young observed that some men "were in such condition that they could not be admitted in the Home without the destruction of all their clothing.")[20]

Eventually, Ford would lead every new arrival back to his office to read them the Home rules and have them sign the inmate register.

The board of trustees recognized the need for some ground rules for the comfortable operation of the Home, basic rules of conduct meant to allow every inmate the quiet enjoyment of his new residence while showing respect for the rights of others. Treasurer Fayette Hewitt was assigned to draft the rules, and he did what any other bureaucrat might do when faced with a blank page: he revised someone else's rules to fit the needs of the Kentucky Confederate Home. Sometime, somehow, someone had acquired a copy of the "Rules and Regulations of Residents and Employees at Fitch's Home for Soldiers," and Hewitt set about editing those rules for the Kentucky Home. As a result, Salem Ford would read to every new inmate at the Kentucky Confederate Home a set of barely modified rules originally written for Union veterans living in a state-run veterans home in Connecticut.[21]

Section 2 of the printed rules required each inmate "to observe habits of order and cleanliness and good care with respect to his person, clothing and bed and bedding, and with respect to the building and premises, and a courteous demeanor to the other inmates."

Section 4 protected the inmates from any political or religious proselytizing by officers or employees of the Home and allowed inmates to hold nonsectarian religious services in the Home and attend (or not) any other religious services outside the Home.

Sections 5 through 8 set rules for access to the Home. Inmates were prohibited from leaving the grounds without permission, and a roll call would be conducted each morning and evening to assure compliance ("All inmates shall answer to their names, unless absent from the Home, sick or excused"). The doors of the Home would be closed and all lights extinguished at nine o'clock each night; all inmates were expected to be in their rooms and in bed by that time.

It was Section 3—the rules regarding alcohol—that would prove hardest for some inmates to follow. Intoxication was prohibited, of course, but so was the possession of alcohol anywhere in the Home. Further, inmates were forbidden to visit "places, stores or houses where intoxicating liquors are sold." Inmates who enjoyed a little taste of the spirits now and then would have to break the Home rules to get it.[22]

And for those inmates who broke the rules, Sections 10 through 13 spelled out the procedure for complaint, trial, and punishment—a lengthy process not unlike a military court-martial.

In his office, with the incoming inmate seated across from him, Superintendent Ford would carefully polish his spectacles and begin a slow, deliberate reading of the Home rules. At the end of each section he would look up from the printed page, squinting over the top of his spectacles, and ask the newcomer if he understood what had just been read.

Salem Ford used this time to size up the new man. Ford knew that most of the inmates came to the Home after years of living in rough circumstances, and like any good officer, he was taking responsibility for their well-being. By all accounts Ford was a patient listener, managing to convey sympathy without pity, concern without condescension, and the fact that he cared and would help.

Finally, when Ford was certain that the inmate knew what was expected of him, he would ask the man to sign the formal register, a bound ledger book that would be maintained throughout the operation of the Home.

Lorenzo D. Holloway's name is first in the register, written in a firm hand with rounded, well-formed letters typical of Spencerian script. Lee Beckham's handwriting is more cramped and jittery, and slightly left-leaning.

By Thanksgiving Day, November 27, 1902, forty-six more men had added their names in the register.[23]

"The Confederate Home at Pewee Valley did ample justice to King Gobbler on Thanksgiving Day," a newspaper reported. That first holiday banquet was a day of particular abundance: plenty to eat, plenty of heat, plenty of elbow room at the table.[24]

Bennett Young and Andrew Sea visited the Home that afternoon, bringing a box of celebratory cigars for the old vets. After four years of planning, arguing, fundraising, meeting, arm-twisting, and optimism, Young could be justly proud of helping create this respectable place.

The bill enacting the Kentucky Confederate Home mandated a facility spacious enough to house a minimum of twenty-five needy ex-Confederates. In their announcement of its purchase, the board of trustees said that the Villa Ridge Inn property was ideally suited for fifty residents, although Bennett Young maintained that it might have to shelter up to a hundred in a pinch.

It wasn't until the end of the first month of operation, however, that the board of trustees realized just how badly they had miscalculated. Application forms were still flying off Harry McDonald's desk, and there seemed to be no way to turn off the flow. Bennett Young and his board of trustees, after a year of raising money and promoting the Home, couldn't begin turning down the indigent and invalid Confederate veterans for whom the Home had been conceived. By December 1, the executive committee had approved more than eighty applications for admission.

As the number of inmates in residence grew—sixty-six ex-Confederates were living in the Home at the end of December—Salem Ford found himself overwhelmed by administrative and management tasks. During any given week, the cumbersome grocery purchasing process left him short of some staples and ruinously overstocked on others. He was trying to manage the day-to-day activities of ten employees while seeing to the medical needs of dozens of elderly men. His administrative paperwork was a mess, and to cap it all, the steam heating system was threatening to give out, forcing him to rely on expensive coal to heat the Home. At the same time, disciplinary problems were beginning to crop up among the inmates, problems the soft-spoken Ford was ill equipped to deal with.

The executive committee may have been sympathetic to Ford's difficulties, but they had a bigger problem to deal with: the Home was deeply in debt and sinking deeper every day.

Part of the problem was the committee's own doing. "Quite a large sum of money has been spent in procuring furniture and making outlays which will not be required again," Bennett Young admitted. Among other things, the board had voted to spend $2,500 to provide uniforms for poorly clad inmates. The cash reserve was gone.[25]

Another issue was the way the state appropriation was calculated —paid quarterly and based on the average number of residents during the previous quarter. With a skyrocketing inmate population, the ex-Confederates would be paying to house more inmates than the number for which the state would reimburse.

But the biggest issue appeared to be runaway costs, and due to

Ford's spotty record-keeping, it was difficult to determine exactly how far away those costs were running.

Just after New Year's, Young did what executives for the rest of the twentieth century would do when they were in trouble: hire a consultant.

George Milliken was a Louisville businessman who had been elected to several terms on the Kentucky Board of Prisons. He knew how state institutions worked; he came with an unsentimental, independent point of view; and he could write a good report. By the time he completed his investigation and reported to the executive committee on January 27, seventy-eight inmates were in residence at Pewee Valley.[26]

"The figures show an expenditure $7.23 in excess of the monthly appropriation per inmate," Milliken told the committee. The state had agreed to pay $10.41 per month—$125 annually—to feed and care for each Confederate veteran housed in the Home; the Home's management was spending $17.64 per month per inmate.

"The monthly bills deserving especial notice are for fuel, $275, for servants, $231, and for subsistence, $444."

Milliken felt the winter coal bill could be cut in half if Superintendent Ford would switch to the cheaper (but dirtier) furnace coal and contract by the carload at wholesale prices. He also recommended restricting the hours of heating certain areas of the Home.

The $231 monthly for "servants" paid the salaries of the cooks, waiters, and laundry helpers; Milliken suggested "employing a different class of servants." He noted, "At present the Home employs two men to do the cooking at a cost of $48 per month." According to Milliken, "Three Negro women could be employed to do the same work, with equal satisfaction, for $30 per month, thereby saving $18 per month." He also recommended that the male waiters be replaced with women ("Man's labor invariably costs from one-third to one-half more than a woman's labor").

Milliken found that Superintendent Ford's "present system of bookkeeping, duplicating, receipting and purchasing are quite irregular and wholly unsatisfactory." He advised a wholesale overhaul in the way staples were purchased, accounted for, and stored.

After listening to Milliken's report, the executive committee voted to implement every recommendation. They also directed Fayette Hewitt to seek $5,000 in short-term loans and asked Bennett Young to hire several commission-only professional fundraisers. The committee decided, reluctantly, to ask the Kentucky UCV camps and UDC chapters to step up their cash contributions.

Another result of that January 27 meeting may have been the resignation of Superintendent Salem H. Ford. Absent any written evidence, it is possible that the unflappable former druggist from Owensboro found the job of superintendent too large for him, or that, at almost seventy years old, he was simply tired of the constant struggles. But it is more likely that Bennett H. Young, lacking confidence that a man as good-natured as Ford could make the tough decisions necessary to turn around the Home's fortunes, asked the superintendent to fall on his sword.

The executive committee met again on February 10 to accept Ford's resignation and elect one of their own as commandant of the Kentucky Confederate Home: board member and state senator William Oscar Coleman.[27]

William O. Coleman was a man who never quite achieved in life what he felt he deserved.

At the start of 1903, his term as state senator was ending, and it was clear he wouldn't win reelection. He had hoped for an appointment to the Kentucky State Prison Commission, but he had irritated too many of the governor's friends for that to be a reasonable possibility. Free room and board and $75 a month to manage the Kentucky Confederate Home looked pretty good to the former sheriff of Trimble County. He needed the paycheck.

Born in 1839 to a farming family, Coleman left home and a young wife to join General John Hunt Morgan in 1861. There was little to distinguish his military service as an enlisted man, but on returning to Trimble County, he managed to parlay a minor war wound into election as county sheriff in 1868.[28]

Sheriff Coleman was Trimble County's chief law enforcement officer at a time when white families feared the retribution of their former slaves and resentful freedmen. Many local lawmen earned reelection by protecting their white constituents, usually at the point of a gun and occasionally with a threat of the rope. Coleman earned a reputation as a toady, a man who sought to advance his career by the flattery of more successful men and the intimidation of less powerful ones.

Coleman's physical appearance alone could be intimidating. He was six feet tall, with broad shoulders and powerful arms. His eyes were deep-set, dark, and glowering, and his hair remained unnaturally black for most of his life. He wore a full beard that fell to the middle of his chest and served to hide his thin neck.

Though he kept a farm, Coleman had no interest in farming, preferring government work instead. Between terms in the state legislature, he sought appointment as collector of internal revenue and Indian agent, but the jobs never materialized, despite his elaborate promises to patrons.

Coleman had introduced the Confederate Home bill in the Kentucky state senate and, as a result, earned appointment to the board of trustees. Perhaps he hoped to make a little money off the real estate or the purchasing of supplies for the Home, but those opportunities hadn't yet presented themselves. Meanwhile, Bennett Young had offered to Coleman a healthy percentage of all Confederate Home donations he could scare up, but Coleman had not yet set to the task when it became apparent that Salem Ford would be leaving the superintendent's position.

Bennett Young and the executive committee needed a tough-minded man who would do whatever it took to get the Home under control.

And William O. Coleman needed the paycheck.

"Therefore, we, the inmates of the Home, hereby express our implicit confidence in you as a man of irreproachable bearing and in your competent administration of the Home; and we must respectfully and earnestly request that you withdraw your resignation . . . believing that your continuance will be for the best interest of all concerned."

Seventy-five inmates and nine employees signed a petition urging their respected superintendent to change his mind and withdraw his resignation. A copy of the petition was mailed to the board of trustees, and a delegation of inmates called on Salem H. Ford in his office. But it was too late.

There was no ceremony to mark Ford's departure. The kindly, bookish man was gone by the time Coleman arrived on March 1, and Coleman's first priorities were to bring some discipline to bear on the inmates and some new money in the door.

Chapter 7

The General's Sister and the Stockman's Wife

A breakfast reception preceded the formal opening of the seventh annual convention of Kentucky's United Daughters of the Confederacy chapters in Owensboro on October 14, 1903. At tables decorated with roses, chrysanthemums, tiny Rebel flags, and hand-painted place cards, the 50 delegates representing 3,500 members of the state's UDC chapters exchanged social pleasantries over plates of sweet breads and toasted mushrooms. This was an event for mannerly conversation, but from time to time one woman might catch another's eye and share a brief glance and a nod to signal their support of The Motion.

The formal meeting opened at 2:00 P.M. in City Hall with an invocation and speeches of welcome. Mrs. James M. Arnold, the state president from Lexington, responded to the welcome and was presented a bouquet of Winnie Davis roses, a new variety of climbing tea rose with a salmon-pink center and outer edges of cream. Songs, a poetry recitation, and the reading of a brief historical essay occasionally interrupted the afternoon agenda of reports by officers and chapter delegates, but there was no formal mention of The Motion.

An evening reception held at Owensboro's new public library, with pink punch and white cakes served on cobalt blue glassware, allowed for easier conversation among the delegates. Henrietta Morgan Duke, president of Louisville's UDC chapter and former two-term president of the state organization, spoke graciously with old friends and greeted the women with whom she had corresponded during the previous year. Mary Bascom, wife of Owingsville stockman A. W. Bascom and the delegate representing the Bath County chapter, circulated among the delegates from the small towns, exchanging news of fundraising activities, chapter membership, and local celebrations. The reception allowed ample time for shared compliments, gentle gossip, and informal discussion of The Motion.[1]

The women gathered in convention certainly knew that an affirmative vote for The Motion the following morning would be seen as nothing short of a declaration of revolution. Their husbands, brothers, and fathers would view The Motion as an act of outright defiance.

That's what made The Motion so irresistible to them.

Upon replacing Salem Ford just three months after the Kentucky Confederate Home's opening, William O. Coleman and the board of trustees scrambled to bring about some measure of fiscal and operational control.

Coleman immediately implemented changes recommended by the board's consultant. He installed temporary partitions at first-floor stairwells, cutting off daytime heat to the upstairs bedrooms and limiting it to the first floor. Inmates found it necessary to leave their rooms in the morning and gather in the downstairs library and parlors in order to stay warm. Coleman fired the kitchen help and servers, replacing them with part-time black women from the area, in the process reducing the number of employees by half. Fearful that employees might steal food or supplies, he began a weekly inventory of the pantries, weighing every pound of sugar and beans, counting each pillowcase and box of soap, paring stores down to the bare minimum. Meals that had been varied and appetizing became grayer and more institutional.

Coleman's efforts received the full support of the board. They changed his title from "superintendent" to "commandant"—a title given the person in charge of a fort or other military institution—and the change allowed Coleman to take direct responsibility for hiring and disciplining Home employees. Commandant Coleman also intended to impose greater military discipline on his inmates.[2]

Beginning in February 1903, inmates were issued uniforms consisting of underdrawers, pants, shirts, jacket, a military-style waist-length dress cape, and a felt hat. Although the uniforms were originally intended for use during special ceremonies when visitors were expected, or to supplement everyday clothing, Commandant Coleman decreed that inmates should wear them at all times, whether they were strolling the grounds of the Home or napping in the library. Part of Coleman's reasoning involved increased efficiency: the Home's laundry staff could process standardized garments faster than they could wash, iron, and sort varied personal items of clothing. But the uniformity also served to reinforce a personal discipline that Coleman felt was slipping. Gone were the oddments of clothing; every inmate was expected to dress in full uniform at the morning inspection and remain so dressed throughout the day.

The new clothing was of top quality; it was supplied by Levy Bros. Department Store in Louisville. But it was the first time since leaving military service forty years before that these men had been required to wear uniforms. Bennett Young put a more positive spin on the uniform requirement: "It was thought," he later wrote, "that the Confederate uniform which they had worn with much honor and credit should be used by them now, in the declining years of their life, when they had come to enjoy the benefits of this State institution."[3]

Coleman also instituted a zero-tolerance policy for infractions of Home rules, particularly those involving the use of alcohol.

"Charges are hereby preferred against Stanford P. Ashford for drunkenness at Confederate Home on March 6 & 7," Coleman reported to the board before an April executive committee meeting. He included the specifications and a list of witnesses. In addition, E. J. Sanders was reported to be drunk at dinner on March 16, and Matthew Little was caught with a whiskey bottle on March 17. Both men were brought up on charges.[4]

The board's executive committee was required to hold hearings on the offenses. The men admitted their obvious guilt, but charges were "dismissed upon their positive promise that they would not repeat the offense."

Commandant Coleman wanted to make a special example of James Elbert, however. Elbert had been a whiskey drummer—a salesman representing local distilleries and bottlers to the retail trade. As the years went by, however, he spent less time selling his product and more time consuming it. By the time he entered the Home, he was long unemployed and practically homeless, nursing a mighty thirst for Kentucky's finest. On the evening of March 5 a drunken Elbert verbally abused Coleman, then staggered out of the Home before he could be restrained. Elbert made his way to Louisville for a four-day tear, and a county sheriff was dispatched to return him to Pewee Valley. At his hearing, he was unrepentant and, at Coleman's insistence, was expelled from the Home. The minutes of Elbert's court-martial by the executive committee state that "the Commandant was directed to furnish a railroad ticket to his former home and to give him lunch and $1 in money."[5]

Within weeks of Coleman's arrival, the Home was transformed from a comfortable lodging place with bountiful meals and an accommodating household staff to a chilly military installation that was becoming increasingly crowded with bored and disgruntled old men.

Meanwhile, the board members were struggling to dig their way out of a deep financial hole. Coleman's operational changes had reduced the costs of running the Home, but the board faced additional, extraordinary expenses as well as repayment of the short-term loans they had taken out in January 1903.

Bennett Young's plea to the UCV camps for additional financial help was bearing fruit. Members of the camp in Paducah voted to pledge 25 cents per member per month in 1903 to help the Home out of its financial jam, and the Confederate veterans of Lexington reinstated a $500 pledge that had been withdrawn a year earlier. W. J. Stone, an active veteran from Kuttawa, stood up at a meeting of the Little River Baptist Association to speak on behalf of the Kentucky Confederate Home. He raised $35, telling Fayette Hewitt he thought it was a pretty good sum, "considering that the crowd had been so thoroughly drummed for money for missions."[6]

With the board's approval, Young retained five independent financial agents, promising them a 25 percent commission on the money they raised. Florence Barlow, editor of *The Lost Cause*, was one of the agents, and she collected donations while speaking at UDC luncheon meetings around the state. J. W. Bird and Alexander Lawson traveled around Kentucky seeking donations, while C. C. Cantrell looked for big donors in Cincinnati, Cleveland, Chicago, and New York. (In April 1903 the *New York Times* reported that Cantrell was at the Broadway Central Hotel, "having come to New York to secure contributions for a fund of which the [Kentucky Confederate Home] is in immediate need.") William O. Coleman also drew a commission for any financial contributions he could raise, but Bennett Young said Coleman's duties as commandant had "prevented him from further pursuing these collections."[7]

The financial agents collected $4,600 during the spring of 1903. Those funds, added to other monies squeezed from here and there, allowed Young to report on May 6 that the executive committee had been "extraordinarily successful in raising money to pay off the deficit." Further, Young said, we are now "satisfied that the State appropriation will pay the running expenses of the institution."[8]

Confident as Young may have sounded in public, however, he had to have been aware that this financial stability was only temporary.

The Kentucky Confederate Home was operating at near capacity. By the end of June 1903, just eight months after the formal opening, the board of trustees had approved more than 140 applications for admission. Of those, 125 needy ex-Confederates had arrived at the Home and signed the register. The first winter in the Home had been hard on the old men: fourteen died and nine were under temporary care at various hospitals.

A hundred men were living in the Home that summer, and they were putting a strain on the facility. Water wells were barely keeping pace with the daily needs of the laundry and kitchen; a pump used to fill roof cisterns with water for storage and fire protection was failing, causing the wooden cisterns to dry out in the summer heat and develop leaks. Many of the inmates who came to the Home had no familiarity with indoor toilets, and plumbing clogs were a constant problem. (Commandant Coleman was forced to enlarge the septic beds and dig two outdoor privies to handle sewage.) In addition, the old resort hotel was constructed for genteel vacationers, not a hundred idle old men; spots of tobacco juice stained hardwood floors, heavy boots frayed the delicate carpets, and pocketknives whittled away sections of the wooden porch rail. Repairs and maintenance weren't immediately necessary, but they were imminent, and they would be costly.

Despite overcrowding at the Home and its precarious financial situation, there is no evidence that Bennett Young or the board of trustees ever considered limiting applications for admission. To do so would have broken faith with every UCV camp in the state, every Kentucky Confederate veteran who had pledged a dollar for the care of needy comrades. Suspending admissions would also betray the Home's political supporters, legislators who voted the Home's appropriation and who might be counted on to provide some future financial relief.

Winter was coming, and dozens more old veterans would need the warm beds and hot meals they were unable to secure for themselves and that had been promised to them. So the men responsible for managing the affairs of the Kentucky Confederate Home chose to squeeze every penny possible out of the operating costs while continuing to pack their indigent comrades into the strained facility.

And it was just this kind of stubborn male nonsense that led the United Daughters of the Confederacy to The Motion.

One of the earliest speeches in support of establishing a Kentucky veterans' home urged the men of the state's United Confederate Veterans camps to accomplish the hard work of financing, building, and running the home. "If we do our part in this," the (male) speaker said, "the noble women, the Daughters of the Confederacy, will see that [the indigent veterans] do not lack for ministering angels."[9]

But the women of Kentucky's United Daughters of the Confederacy didn't wait until the hard work was done before commencing their daughterly duty.

When the Committee of Twenty-Five first announced its goal of $25,000, the clubwomen organized bake sales, flower fairs, fetes, and market-day lunchrooms to raise funds. They encouraged other clubwomen to donate, then put the touch on husbands and friends. The women of Carlisle collected $100; the Newport UDC chapter pledged $500; the Louisville chapter raised $1,500 toward the purchase of the Pewee Valley property and another $1,000 intended for furnishings. Funds raised by Kentucky UDC chapters, sent directly to Fayette Hewitt or reported through local UCV camps, likely accounted for as much as half of the $10,000 originally used to purchase and improve the Villa Ridge Inn.

When Bennett Young and the board of trustees needed fast cash to close the purchase of the Pewee Valley property, UDC chapters paid more than $2,200 for room naming rights, then expended thousands more to paint, carpet, refixture, and furnish those rooms.[10]

And when the board of trustees finally opened the doors to the Kentucky Confederate Home, the ministering angels of the UDC flew in to provide luxuries and comforts for the old veterans. The women arrived at the Home with gifts of clothing, magazines, hard candies, fresh fruit, handkerchiefs, games, rocking chairs, and books. Women from the Paducah chapter staged monthly musicales for the veterans; the chapter in Winchester made deliveries of baked goods and special gifts. Within days of the formal opening, UDC member Virginia Sale—Daniel Parr's daughter—announced the formation of the Confederate Home Woman's Committee, an organization formed to "give all the sunshine possible to these men in their declining years." The state's UDC chapters vied to provide amenities to the Confederate veterans residing in the Home.[11] But in the first flush of excitement after the Home opened, the ministering angels seemed not to notice that many of the old men arriving in Pewee Valley—their "living heroes"—were too blind to read the books, too addled to enjoy the music, too sick to sit in rocking chairs.

"This Home is not intended to be a mere receptacle for men who are paupers," said one of the speakers at the opening of the Kentucky Confederate Home, "but as a comfortable, luxurious home for the honored ex-soldiers who are invalid."[12]

Oratory surrounding the opening of the Kentucky Confederate Home (and the speeches that helped raise money to pay for it) described the elegance of the facility and the creature comforts to be showered on those who would live there.

"Here, with sheltering love, no want shall go unsupplied," Bennett Young had promised. "Tender affection will anticipate every need."[13]

From the public words of Young and his board members, Kentuckians could reasonably expect that the Home would be a sort of Cockaigne, a sugar-cake palace of luxurious and idle living where distinguished old Southern gentlemen lounged away their final days. But the realities of overcrowding, financial shortages, and the precarious physical condition of many of the inmates quickly eclipsed the rhetoric.

Living conditions at the Home were indeed far superior to those a destitute old Confederate veteran would encounter at county-operated poorhouses or state asylums. (Residents of the Bath County poorhouse, for example, were forced to take their meals with criminals from the county jail, and a Clark County inmate, unable to tolerate conditions in the poorhouse there, attempted suicide by jumping headfirst into a rain barrel.) The state legislature would fail to pass a bill raising to $60 the annual mandatory minimum that Kentucky counties could spend on the care of each of their poorhouse inmates. Meanwhile, the state was paying $125 annually for each ex-Confederate inmate.[14]

But when the women of Kentucky's United Daughters of the Confederacy saw their Confederate Home in operation in the spring of 1903, they weren't happy.

Their immediate dissatisfaction arose from problems with the Home itself: insufficient water, poor sewerage disposal, irregular heating, poor food preparation, and tacky decor (not to mention the coarse deportment of the old inmates). Most women visitors could ignore (or were too modest to mention) the smell resulting from clogged sewer pipes (or the inmates' poor hygiene), and most were unaware of the periodic water shortages. But the lack of general cleanliness tempted many women to grab a mop and bucket and commence to swabbing tobacco stains from the floors or scrubbing handprints off the walls. One visitor, appalled at the quality of the evening meal, put on an apron and proceeded to instruct the cooks on how to properly boil fresh greens. The indignant woman left the kitchen only when escorted out by Commandant Coleman.

Of more serious concern was the poor health of the men residing in the Home.

"It has been demonstrated that the Home is to be a great infirmary," Florence Barlow wrote to Kentucky UDC members in *The Lost Cause*. "Three-fourths of those who have been received have been unable to do anything for themselves." Bennett Young was also frustrated by the quality of care, but financial constraints allowed no immediate solution. "The truth is, instead of a Home, we have a great infirmary," he admitted to the board members. We must, he said, do something "to give these sick men at least the ordinary comforts that sick people are entitled to have."[15]

The earliest arrivals at the Home were in many cases the most infirm; they were the ones most debilitated by tuberculosis, most crippled from stroke or lost limbs, most blinded by cataracts. Several upstairs rooms had been set aside as sick rooms, but there was no on-site professional medical care. Due to the expense, Commandant Coleman was reluctant to call for a doctor or send the men to a hospital except in the direst of circumstances, so the healthy inmates would carry the sick and dying from their beds each morning to chairs or daybeds in the warmer downstairs sitting rooms.

On June 3, 1903, the birthday of Confederate president Jefferson Davis, a delegation of women—including Kentucky UDC president Mrs. James M. Arnold—arrived at the Home for a solemn ceremony, the conferring of the Southern Cross of Honor on ninety-two inmates. The Cross of Honor had been created by the UDC that year for living veterans, to recognize their "valorous service to the Southern Confederacy." In dress uniform, those inmates who were ambulatory received their brass Cross of Honor pins in a ceremony held under the trees on the lawn of the Home. The UDC delegation then entered the Home, going room to room to pin the award on the blankets of those too ill to attend the outdoor event.

That afternoon the leadership of Kentucky's United Daughters of the Confederacy came face to face with conditions at the Kentucky Confederate Home, and they found the situation too dreadful to ignore. ("Perhaps the most pathetic service ever rendered by the chapter," one woman described it.) By all reports, the Home was going from bad to worse.[16]

The women of the UDC had been content to do their daughterly duty as ministering angels to the sick old veterans, but it was past time to have a say in how the ministering was done and who was ministered to.

It was time for a woman's touch.

One woman in particular recognized that there was a fundamental difference in how the men of the UCV and the women of the UDC perceived their roles in the operation, management, and organization of the Home. She had bumped into that attitude before.

Almost a year earlier Henrietta Morgan Duke had negotiated —reasonably, she believed—with Bennett Young and Harry P. McDonald for the establishment of a woman's advisory board at the Home in exchange for $1,000 the board of trustees desperately needed to complete the purchase of the Pewee Valley property. Young backed out of the transaction at the last minute, apparently preferring to risk bankruptcy than give the Daughters a say in how the Home should be run. Had Young not reneged on the deal, the UDC would even now be helping to assure healthy meals, provide tender medical care, and maintain cleanliness. Instead, the all-male board seemed determined to turn the Kentucky Confederate Home into an overcrowded, disreputable boarding house, while ignoring some of the niceties that made for a respectable place to live.

Henrietta Duke made no public expression of resentment toward Young or the board of trustees for denying the women a role in managing the Home. (To take personal offense would have been unseemly for the wife and sister of beloved Confederate generals.) A woman as well-schooled in high society as Henrietta Morgan Duke could communicate far more clearly with a raised eyebrow, a knowing smile, or between the lines of chatty letters to other UDC chapter members throughout Kentucky. "Is it right and fair, in your opinion," she asked, that women be deprived of having a say in the operation of the Home?[17] Henrietta Duke thought it was not.

Mary Bascom of Owingsville agreed. It was an issue she had discussed with her husband, and they agreed that the presence of women living in the Home would exert a healthy influence on the men there. "The Daughters had better band together" and buy land adjacent to the Home, she wrote her cousin, who was a member of another UDC chapter. "Put the wives of indigent Confederates on it and keep it as UDC property."

Mary Bascom expressed a concern noted by women in other UDC chapters: the wives of married men who had been admitted to the Home were left to fend for themselves or live off the charity of others. If there were a place for wives in Pewee Valley, she argued, those women could help care for their husbands and also by their presence reduce ungentlemanly behavior by unmarried inmates.

Mary Bascom was a small-town woman who lacked the elegance and subtlety of Henrietta Duke. She was as plain-spoken and direct as her stockman husband, and she had no problem expressing dissatisfaction with Bennett Young: "There has been no provision made for the wives," she said, "although General Bennett H. Young promised last winter that should be embodied in the bill that passed the last legislature. So I think the veterans will not do anything for us." She urged her cousin to "bring this to the attention of your chapter, and see what they have to say about the matter."[18]

After the Cross of Honor ceremony at the Home, UDC chapters around the state began to agitate for greater involvement of women in the Home. Some felt that a management or oversight role was the most effective solution; others thought that opening the Home to women residents was the best course.

Henrietta Morgan Duke and Mary Bascom would contribute to the compromise that resulted in The Motion.

The women believed that their large cash donations and active service entitled them to a say in the management of the Home; the men of the board felt that efficient management was men's business, best handled by men. Even so, Bennett Young had to admit that things weren't going well.

Board members were taking a beating in Kentucky's ex-Confederate community over their stewardship of the Home. It was embarrassing enough to hear from friends in the UCV camps, but they also had to answer to wives who had heard of the problems through their UDC chapters. Worse still, friendly newspaper publishers were beginning to spread the word that things weren't right at the Kentucky Confederate Home. Everyone was looking to Bennett Young for answers, and on September 2 he responded with a private letter to the board of trustees.[19]

"It is now certain that the nature and character of the Confederate Home has been entirely misconceived by those who originated it," he admitted. "It was believed at the time that it would be a home; instead it is practically an infirmary." He acknowledged that medical care for the inmates wasn't all it should be: "There ought to be a physician in the Home, and there ought to be two trained nurses constantly on service. These things, of course, cannot be secured now."

To ease overcrowding and the dearth of available sickbeds, Young recommended that the board act to rent the house on an adjoining property to house the sick.

He lamented the increasing discipline problems: "There has been quite a large amount of drinking. Numerous inmates of the Home have been found in a drunken condition, not only on the streets of Louisville but in Pewee Valley and the Home itself."

"We have all probably been carried away by sentimental notions as to what was due Confederate soldiers," he said to the board members. Even so, Young assured them, the general public continued to support the Home and the good work it was intended to accomplish.

To prove his point, he described a woman from Cincinnati, a former Kentuckian, who wanted to provide new bookcases, armchairs, lamps, a sofa, and carpeting for the inmate library. Biscoe Hindman, a well-to-do insurance man, had offered to pay for a monument to Confederate dead on the grounds of the Home. And Dr. Dudley Reynolds, a Louisville optician and Union army veteran, was treating the vision problems of inmates at no cost.

"The people of Kentucky have responded nobly to the call made upon them," Young reassured the board of trustees. "While there has been some criticism and some friction as a result of these contributions, yet without them the work of this board would have been impossible."

Uncharacteristically, Young neither took responsibility for nor offered a solution to the problems at the Kentucky Confederate Home. Instead, he seemed to express a willingness to tender his resignation if the board asked for it.

"All these matters are merely suggestive on the part of the president," he told the members, referring to himself in the third person. "He lays them before the board for its action and for the expression of its judgment in all things."

For the time being, the judgment of the board was to continue accepting applications and hope for the best.

The judgment of the delegates to the seventh annual state convention of the United Daughters of the Confederacy meeting in Owensboro, however, was to act on The Motion.

The second day of the Kentucky UDC annual meeting began with a continuation of chapter reports, committee reports, and memorial tributes read by well-mannered women in large hats. Shortly before lunch, state president Arnold asked if any new business was to be brought before the convention.

Mary Bascom, representing the Bath County chapter, rose to her feet. She had written the words of The Motion in her slanted scrawl on the paper she had in her hand, but she had no difficulty reading it aloud to the women assembled.

"We hereby move that a committee be formed to . . ."

Mary Bascom, Henrietta Morgan Duke, and other women representing UDC chapters from across the state had decided it was time for women to take a more active role in the management of the Kentucky Confederate Home. The motion presented that morning in Owensboro called for a committee to be "composed of Daughters from different sections of the state" to meet at once with Governor Beckham, asking him to appoint an auxiliary board of trustees, a board consisting of women who would have sole responsibility for the health care, food, and entertainment needs of the inmates of the Kentucky Confederate Home. The same statewide committee would meet with state assemblymen, urging them to require that the Home be opened to aged wives and widows of veterans, who would live in cottages paid for by the UDC.[20]

It was an ambitious plan, and one that would be considered a slap in the face of Bennett Young, the Home board members, and Kentucky's UCV leadership. It was indicative of the bad relations between the UDC and these groups that the women chose not to discuss their concerns with Young and the board, opting instead to go directly to the governor. The women knew their actions would be seen as nothing short of a declaration of revolution. For those women whose husbands served on the Home's board of trustees or as UCV camp officers, this was an act of outright defiance.

The Motion passed unanimously.[21]

It was obvious by October 1903 that conditions in the Kentucky Confederate Home were getting worse, not better. About the time Bennett Young received word of the women's actions in Owensboro —just thirteen months after the Home opened—160 inmates were "cramped for room and for comfortable arrangements" in a facility meant for no more than 100. The rented house had eased overcrowding hardly at all, but at least there were more infirmary beds for the sickest of the inmates.

Young met with his old friend Harry P. McDonald, who was still a state legislator, and with Henry George, a respected ex-Confederate and Democratic state senator from Graves County, to discuss the problems at the Home.

They all agreed Young would have to return to the state capitol for help.

Chapter 8

The Knight and the Icemaker

Andrew Jackson Lovely and Otway Bradfute Norvell shared Room 52 on the third floor of the Kentucky Confederate Home. Approximately fifteen feet wide by twenty feet long, their room had a washstand and chest of drawers built into one corner of the room and a small closet in another. On warm days, the room was sunny and well ventilated. The east-facing window at one end of the room overlooked the laundry building at the rear of the Home; on the opposite wall, a door and transom opened to the hallway.

Furnishings in the small room were necessarily spare. Muslin curtains framed the window, and except for a few framed prints, the papered walls were bare.[1]

Room 52 was intended to be a sickroom, and both men had their own single iron bed. (In most rooms, two men shared a double bed.) Norvell was partially paralyzed, and he remained in bed on those days when other inmates were unable to carry him downstairs to the library or one of the sitting rooms. A steward visited Room 52 twice a day to feed and clean him. Lovely was able-bodied, but his mind was cloudy: sometimes he was lucid and engaging, other times disoriented and fearful. A matron locked the door each night to prevent Lovely from wandering the hallways and losing himself.

Room 52 was one of the rooms visited by the delegation of women from the United Daughters of the Confederacy on Jefferson Davis's birthday in June 1903; Norvell and Lovely were among those who received Cross of Honor awards.[2]

Indignant over conditions of overcrowding and poor health care, the women of Kentucky's UDC chapters selected a committee to call on Governor Beckham and key state legislators to ask for a formal management role in the affairs of the Home. In high dudgeon, the committee of women departed for Frankfort, intending to wrest a measure of control from Bennett Young and the Home's board of trustees.

They never stood a chance.

Bennett Young was all too aware of the problems at the Home, and he was sure they stemmed more from lack of money than lack of management. "The state appropriation will have to be increased to $175," he stated flatly to the board of trustees late in 1903.[3] The time for donations and volunteers was past. Only the state treasury was sufficient to cover the monthly operating costs and, with a little arm-twisting, pay for some of the improvements the Home needed so desperately. But if Young was going to lobby for increased funding for the Kentucky Confederate Home, he sure didn't need disgruntled women of the UDC kicking up any dust at the state capitol.

"We are sure that a generous people will, through their legislators, liberally respond to reasonable requests for additional appropriations," he told the trustees. Intending to neutralize the UDC's lobbying effort, Young announced to newspapers that he and the board of trustees would ask the state for more money to help ease overcrowding. "The Home was projected upon the idea that there would never be over eighty inmates," he said, trying to turn lemons into lemonade. "Few realized the tremendous necessity for such an institution."[4]

Trustee Harry P. McDonald, speaking in his role as a state representative, told reporters he intended to introduce a bill that would allow the wives of indigent veterans to reside in the Home.[5] His announcement blocked the wind from the Daughters' sails before they arrived in Frankfort.

The delegation of Daughters found little traction at the state capitol; Young and McDonald had preempted them. The women could express their moral outrage, but without access to the ballot box they had little leverage in Frankfort. State senators and representatives were dismissive, saying that, because the governor was the only one mandated to choose trustees, the women must talk to the governor. The governor's office directed the women to Bennett Young, saying that only the board president had the power to appoint a women's auxiliary.

Even as the women began to realize they were getting a polite runaround, Bennett Young was already drafting legislation and lining up votes.

Having been frustrated in the state capital, state UDC president Mrs. James M. Arnold arrived in Pewee Valley on January 6, 1904, for the Home's regular board of trustees meeting. The board members—except for Bennett Young, absent by necessity or choice—listened without comment as Mrs. Arnold asked that the Daughters be given representation on the Home's board of trustees. When Mrs. Arnold departed, the trustees voted to write her, explaining why they could not comply with her request. Regretfully, they said, they were unable to make arbitrary changes in the Home's legal charter, but if Mrs. Arnold's committee were to speak with state legislators in Frankfort, perhaps . . .

If the women of the UDC expected their actions to infuriate the men, it was Mrs. Arnold who exploded. Fed up with the runaround, she fired off an angry broadside complaining of the men's unfairness in shutting out the women. The UDC chapters "had contributed liberally to the maintenance of the Home," she wrote, and "had also helped to obtain it, and were being urged consistently to spend more money." It was like "taxation without representation," she asserted.[6]

The women still believed that their donations and service entitled them to a say in the management of the Home; the men of the board still felt that efficient management was men's business, best handled by men.

In the end, Kentucky's United Daughters of the Confederacy had to settle for a plan to establish a UDC chapter in Pewee Valley, an outpost located at the very gates of the Kentucky Confederate Home. With a wholehearted recommendation from the state organization, UDC national president Louisa McLeod Smythe authorized sixteen women to associate themselves under the name "Confederate Home Chapter #792 of the United Daughters of the Confederacy."

They described it as a "love feast," the smoker his lodge brothers organized as a going-away party. A hundred members of Rathbone Lodge No. 12, Knights of Pythias, sponsored a royal reception and banquet in Rassenfoss's restaurant in Paris, Kentucky, to wish their brother A. J. Lovely a raucous farewell before he departed for the Kentucky Confederate Home. Clumsy quips, overlong toasts, and maudlin speeches brought tears to the eyes of the seventy-four-year-old Confederate veteran who had earned the love of his community.[7]

There was not much to distinguish Lovely's wartime service. Thirty-three years old and unmarried, he enlisted at Prestonsburg as a private when it became apparent Kentucky wouldn't join the Confederacy. By 1862 he was serving under Colonel E. F. Clay in the Third Kentucky Cavalry as a lieutenant, a commissary officer. His company eventually surrendered in May 1865 in Mt. Sterling, and Lovely returned to Paris.

As unremarkable as his military service may have been, A. J. Lovely and sixteen other Bourbon County veterans made a remarkable choice three years after the war when they organized Lodge No. 12, Knights of Pythias, the first lodge of that order in Kentucky (and perhaps the first in any state of the Old Confederacy).

Of the popular fraternal orders of the time, most had historic roots reaching back centuries. The Order of the Knights of Pythias, however, had been formed in the final years of the Civil War by Union men. Taking their history and rituals from stories of the legendary friendship and loyalty between Damon and Pythias, Pythians believed that any two men, meeting in a spirit of goodwill and making an honest effort to understand each other, can live together in peace and harmony. A public part of the Pythian ritual involved the order's Uniform Rank, an armed militia on horseback that engaged in complex drills and exercises. The Pythian creed of universal peace through understanding in the wake of America's Civil War (combined with opportunities for practicing competitive horseman-ship) must have had powerful appeal for these seventeen Bourbon County veterans.[8]

Lovely lived out the years following the war with little public accomplishment. He lived with his brother's family, farmed a little, kept shop occasionally, ran for mayor when urged, and pitched in from time to time on municipal jobs for which he was suited. He never married, never had children, never accumulated a financial estate.

Instead, Lovely lived his lodge.

He was the kind of member who never missed a meeting, who actively prospected for new members, who memorized every word of his rituals, and who performed the piddling little organizational jobs that other members overlooked. But, more important, Lovely was a man who, in every aspect of his life, during every waking hour, lived the principles of the Order of the Knights of Pythias: friendship, charity, and benevolence.

Lovely held every local and state lodge office to which he could be elected and received every honor that the Knights could bestow. "There was no heart purer than the heart of Andrew Jackson Love-ly," a lodge brother said. Another described Lovely's patience, time after time and year after year, as he instructed initiates in the secrets of the Pythian Knighthood. "His battle cry the Golden Rule; his watchword, 'Love ye, one another.'" He was adored for his good-ness. Without preachiness or judgment, he lived a practical applica-tion of religious and charitable principles throughout his otherwise unremarkable life.[9]

There came a time, however, when he was no longer able to sup-port himself. With the passing of his older brother and sister-in-law, A. J. Lovely found himself with no place to live. At the same time, his lodge brothers may have noticed that their saintly old Knight was becoming more distracted, more forgetful about meet-ings or meals, neglectful of personal hygiene. A little forgetfulness was nothing surprising in a seventy-four-year-old man, but more disturbing might have been an occasional tendency to wander away, becoming hopelessly lost on the lanes he had traveled all his life.

Comrades in the Paris UCV camp and brothers in Lodge No. 12 helped Lovely complete his application for admittance to the new Kentucky Confederate Home, and he was accepted.

By the time he arrived at the Home on November 26, 1902, and was assigned to Room 52, it was apparent there was a fog gathering in A. J. Lovely's brain.

Otway B. Norvell arrived in Room 52 of the Kentucky Confederate Home from Alabama by way of Louisville.

Born in 1840 in Virginia and raised comfortably in northern Kentucky, Otway Norvell studied mechanical engineering at a locomotive works in Baltimore. He was mastering the industrial science of boilers, fluid systems, gases under pressure, and propulsion engines with a vague idea of entering the U.S. Navy.

When secession fever broke out across the South, Norvell joined the Rifle Grays, part of the Eleventh Virginia Infantry, in Lynchburg. At the end of his enlistment period, he returned to Kentucky to join Basil Duke's regiment, the Second Kentucky Cavalry, under General John Hunt Morgan. Norvell was captured during Morgan's Ohio raid and sent north with other enlisted men to Chicago, where he was imprisoned in Camp Douglas for nineteen months. The young engineer was one of the fortunate few to be exchanged during the final months of the war, and in February 1865 he rejoined Basil Duke, who was reorganizing his cavalry. At the time of Lee's surrender, Duke was assigned to escort President Jefferson Davis and the Confederate government southward from Richmond, and Norvell's knowledge of locomotive systems helped speed the last retreat.[10]

Not yet thirty years old at the end of the war, Otway Norvell traveled south to Mobile, Alabama, carrying with him a knowledge of man-made ice.

Man-made ice is one of those easy-to-overlook keys to the creation of the industrial New South. Ice provided portable refrigeration, and refrigeration allowed the meat and milk produced in rural areas to be transported to cities, where they could feed the families of men employed in factories or busy port facilities. Northern cities maintained a large industrial workforce using stored ice—ice that was harvested from frozen lakes during winter months—but natural ice was a rarity in the South.

An Indianapolis inventor was developing machinery that could produce large quantities of man-made ice economically, and the equipment was being proven in Louisville, Paducah, and Atlanta. The process involved boilers, fluid systems, and gases under pressure, just the sort of complicated mechanical engineering Norvell understood. The equipment produced quarter-ton slabs of ice—and huge profits.

Installing similar equipment, Norvell opened Mobile's first artificial ice plant in 1870. By then, the young entrepreneur had married Ida Pillans, daughter of a civil engineer who was making money hand over fist helping rebuild Mobile after the war, and the couple lived with her parents as the ice business boomed. After several years, Otway and Ida moved to Birmingham to open an ice plant in the city that was becoming the South's iron manufacturing center.

A medical text published in 1884, the year of Norvell's stroke, classified "a stroke of paralysis" as an illness of passion, a condition caused by the welling-up of great emotion, such as fear, excitement, or anger. Almost overnight, the active man found himself "entirely paralyzed, having only the partial use of his left arm, and had to be propped by pillows when writing." Doctors advised total bed rest in a darkened room, devoid of any loud noise or stimulation.[11]

Norvell rested in his Birmingham bedroom for three years, he and Ida living off the proceeds of the sale of his Birmingham and Mobile ice factories. In 1886 he applied for admittance to the Lee Camp Soldiers Home in Richmond, Virginia. "I believe under favorable circumstances I will recover my health," Norvell told the admissions committee in a letter accompanying his application. His certainty that his health would be restored (and a strong recommendation from Basil Duke, his former commander) earned Norvell a bed in Virginia's new Confederate home.[12]

Five years of convalescence in Richmond brought no improvement, and he returned to Birmingham and his wife's care. To keep his mind active, Norvell found work reviewing the financial books of some Birmingham businesses. He kept up an active correspondence with his wartime comrades in Kentucky and traveled occasionally to Louisville to consult with doctors at the medical school there.[13]

By the time Norvell applied for admittance to the Kentucky Confederate Home in 1902, he had been an invalid for two decades. His muscles had atrophied, and he was prey to pneumonia and bloody bedsores. Loyal Ida was losing the strength to care for him.

Otway Norvell was one of the first veterans accepted into the Kentucky Confederate Home, and he arrived on November 1, 1902. Before assigning him to Room 52, Superintendent Ford noted on a chart that Norvell's mental condition was good, but his physical condition was "ex[tremely] feeble." A. J. Lovely joined Norvell in Room 52 several weeks later, and the old Knight's mental condition was assessed as "poor."[14]

The two men in Room 52 needed special care, care that was increasingly hard to come by as the Home battled financial and overcrowding issues in 1903. The eager women of the new Confederate Home chapter of the United Daughters of the Confederacy could provide some assistance, but the men needed regular medical care and access to a fully equipped medical facility.

In short, they needed an infirmary.

In February 1904 state representative Harry P. McDonald and state senator Henry George introduced a bill that would amend the original Confederate Home legislation. The bill raised the annual per capita payment significantly, from $125 to $175, and the alternative minimum annual payment to $20,000.[15]

As Harry McDonald had promised, the bill contained a section that *might* allow the wives of ex-Confederates who were living in the Home to take up residence there. The board of trustees *might*, at their discretion, erect cottages on the grounds of the Home in which married inmates *might* be allowed to live in company with their wives. (It is debatable whether the ex-Confederates actually meant this provision to work, or whether it was included as a sop to the UDC.)[16]

The bill passed the Senate without dissent and the House with only four votes against, but McDonald never had a chance to cast his vote. The Honorable Harry P. McDonald, Democrat and trustee of the Kentucky Confederate Home, was stricken with pneumonia and died four days later.

There was some good news to offset the loss, however. Young and McDonald had hoped to get $20,000 earmarked in the current appropriations bill to build an infirmary for the Home, but state senator Henry George, lobbying fellow legislators to honor their beloved colleague Harry McDonald, secured the $20,000 and squeezed out an extra $36,000. George's deal making meant that the Kentucky Confederate Home could afford a modern infirmary, an assured water supply, an overhaul of the sewerage system, and improvements to the main building—and have a small cushion besides.

Harry P. McDonald was buried in the Confederate lot at Louisville's Cave Hill Cemetery, just forty yards from Sergeant Billy Beasley's gravesite. An honor guard of inmates from the Kentucky Confederate Home and the Confederate Glee Club joined Bennett Young, Basil Duke, W. B. Haldeman, John Castleman, Thomas D. Osborne, John Leathers, and dozens more as Kentucky's business, social, and political elite—Confederate veterans all—escorted McDonald's body to its final resting place.

Within days of the funeral, Bennett Young nominated Louisville manufacturers' representative Andrew M. Sea to fill McDonald's role as board secretary and member of the executive committee. And he began interviewing architects who could design an infirmary and oversee improvements to the Kentucky Confederate Home.[17]

"Only a short time ago the Confederate Home at Pewee Valley was established and was quickly filled with old veterans," the *Adair County News* noted, "but they are fast passing away. There is scarcely a week but from one to three deaths are reported from this institution."[18]

The Confederate generation was dying off.

Forty thousand Confederate veterans returned to Kentucky at the end of the Civil War; twelve thousand were recorded living in the state in 1890. By 1920 only slightly more than a thousand would remain. Time was closing in on the veterans. Even boys who had been teenagers when they enlisted in 1861 were, by the beginning of the twentieth century, approaching their sixth decade.[19]

"In the little more than two months that the Home has been open, four of its inmates have died," noted one state UCV officer in January 1903. "Two other veterans, whose applications for admission had been favorably acted upon, died before they reached the Home."[20]

From the beginning, Kentucky's Confederate veteran camps took it upon themselves to "pay a decent respect to the remains and to the memory of those [comrades] who die." Whether state legislator or the owner of a cigar stand, every ex-Confederate was due the honor of a send-off by other veterans and a place to lie in eternity if he needed it.

Thomas Jefferson Vaughn and John B. Patton each needed such a place.

Vaughn was a mining man, a Virginian living near Prestonsburg in Floyd County. He was a strapping seventy-seven-year-old with an ill temper, no family, and a hacking cough from advanced lung disease when he arrived at the Home in early November 1902, the fifteenth inmate to sign the Home Register. He passed away during the night of January 16, 1903.

At eighty-three years, John Patton had outlived his family and he was too ill to travel alone, so comrades from the UCV camp in Cynthiana accompanied him to the Home in January 1903. The superintendent noted that Patton's physical condition was "bad" and his mental acuity only "fair." The old man was sent directly to the Louisville hospital due to "general debility," and he died there during the first week of February.

Death was no stranger in the Kentucky Confederate Home, but the deceased's remains were usually shipped back to their hometowns for burial in country cemeteries or family plots. There was no place, however, for Vaughn and Patton in Prestonsburg or Cynthiana, no churchyard or burying ground waiting for them. Hometown comrades and clergy would accept the remains, of course, but was there really any need to ship them across the state? Couldn't the Home bury them in Pewee Valley?

Pewee Valley had a chartered public cemetery, ten acres of cleared land that had been shaped into eight large sections and planted with ornamental shade trees. It was located just a mile south of the Home at the end of Maple Avenue, a quiet residential lane spotted here and there with dogwood, rosebud, and crimson rambler. Shortly before the Home opened (and knowing there was no money to spare), Bennett Young asked the Louisville veterans camp to investigate the purchase of a section in the Pewee Valley cemetery as a burial lot for the Home's inmates. Young didn't anticipate that the men of the Louisville camp would approach Henrietta Morgan Duke.

"[We] have upon [our] own motion," James Bowles of the Louisville UCV camp wrote Young, "made an effort to induce the ladies of the Albert Sidney Johnston Chapter, Daughters of the Confederacy, to buy one acre of ground in the Pewee Valley cemetery to be used as a burial place for veterans of the Home." Bowles was certain the women would come up with the money "if certain assurances were given by your honorable Board."[21]

Once again, Henrietta Duke wasn't willing to open her chapter's purse without some guarantees. She wanted her chapter to have exclusive responsibility for "adorning, and beautifying and decorating" the lot, including the understanding that they might erect an ornamental gateway or monument that included the name of the chapter. To be sure no one reneged on the deal, she wanted the cemetery deed made out in the name of her Albert Sidney Johnston UDC chapter.

Bennett Young wasn't about to travel that road again. On the day they received the proposal, Young and the board of trustees responded, saying that, on second thought, they "did not believe in localizing this plan." No single chapter or camp should be responsible for buying the section. Instead, responsibility should be shared "by all the sons and daughters of Confederates throughout the state." Thanks, but no thanks.[22]

Meanwhile, the board spent money it could barely afford to buy individual burial plots for T. J. Vaughn and J. B. Patton in Section III of the Pewee Valley cemetery, hoping to recover the cost from veterans in Prestonsburg and Cynthiana.

But the problem wasn't going away. The deaths of three inmates—Robert E. Meade of Carrollton, S. R. B. Nichols of Hopkinsville, and Timothy Burns of Louisville—during the summer of 1903 raised the same questions. Was there really any need to ship them home? Couldn't the Home bury them in Pewee Valley? Once again, the Home bought individual plots and buried the men in Section III of the Pewee Valley cemetery.

Passage of the new appropriation for the Kentucky Confederate Home in February 1904 finally allowed the board of trustees to buy Section III—enough space for up to 400 plots—for use as a Confederate burying ground. The directors of Pewee Valley Cemetery Company permitted burials there to commence prior to formal completion of the purchase in July. Section III would thereafter be known as the Confederate Cemetery at Pewee Valley.

By February 1904 Commandant Coleman had removed A. J. Lovely and Otway Norvell from Room 52. The Home was too crowded, the need for special care too great, to permit a two-man sick room.

Coleman converted the parlors and sitting rooms on the south end of the third and fourth floors into a makeshift clinic. Living four, five, or even six to a room, men temporarily incapacitated by illness lay side by side with those (like Otway Norvell) who were permanently bedridden. The large rooms—now crowded wards—made it easier to nurse the sick, feed them, and bathe them, but the dearth of good ventilation and sufficient heat (not to mention the likelihood of cross-contamination) made for an arrangement that was more conducive to dying than healing.

Even as assemblymen in Frankfort were voting funds for a Home infirmary, twenty men were confined in the Home's makeshift hospital rooms. By the summer of 1904, Norvell was sharing the space with thirty-nine others.

There was no place in the crowded clinic for A. J. Lovely. The old Knight was generally able-bodied and required no regular medical care, but the fog in his brain was becoming thicker, and the Home didn't have enough spare rooms to lock away confused old men.

On June 30, 1903, his hometown newspaper noted, "The many friends of Mr. A. J. Lovely will regret to hear that he has been adjudged insane at Pewee Valley, where he was in the Confederate Home, and sent to Lakeland, the asylum near Anchorage."[23]

Lakeland Asylum, a state institution located five miles from the Home, was an expedient destination for men whose scattered minds made them difficult to care for. Commandant Coleman didn't have the space, staff, or expertise, and in 1903 alone he helped commit eight inmates. With a fully staffed infirmary, perhaps, A. J. Lovely and the other men might be able to return to Pewee Valley.

"The Board of Trustees feel that the infirmary is an absolute and pressing demand," *The Lost Cause* informed Kentucky's UDC members shortly after the state appropriation was passed, "and the architect is being urged with all possible speed to complete the provisions for an infirmary."[24]

Throughout the summer of 1904 Bennett Young and the board met regularly with C. J. Clarke of Clarke & Loomis, the Louisville architectural firm that had been hired to design the infirmary and oversee other improvements. Clarke presented drawings for a combination infirmary-dormitory, a single building with a surgical suite, forty-eight hospital rooms, four treatment rooms, nursing offices, a sitting room, and an airy central solarium. Clarke's design also included twenty residence rooms, two parlors, and a library. The estimated cost to build and furnish the facility was $28,500.[25]

Wells and rooftop cisterns had proven insufficient to the increasing water needs of the Home, so the board voted to construct an impoundment pond, a concrete-lined reservoir the size of a football field. The $10,000 cost of the reservoir was matched by another $10,000 necessary to acquire the properties on which the pond and infirmary would be sited. Another $3,000 would be required to replace and enlarge the outmoded septic system.

Fire prevention was another concern. Pewee Valley had no standing fire department, and the Home was a four-story wooden building crammed with decrepit old men. Andrew Sea noted that "if the building were burned, the loss to the Confederates of Kentucky would be well nigh irreparable." (Only later did he remind the board of the "probability that if the buildings burn, some of the older and most infirm inmates would certainly be burned with them.") An adequate fire protection system would run about $3,600.[26]

At a special meeting on July 9, 1904, the board of trustees approved these projects, in a single afternoon spending all but $2,400 of the state's $56,000 appropriation. The board urged the architect to complete the projects by the end of October, in time for the second anniversary of the opening of the Home.

Florence Barlow, editor of *The Lost Cause*, was asked why there had been no money earmarked for constructing cottages on the property, cottages that might have been used to house the inmates with their wives. "So many calls are made upon the trustees for improvements at the Home, that this matter, we are informed, has not been taken up at all," she wrote to Kentucky's UDC chapters.[27]

According to a story told by Bennett Young, one of the old veterans in the Home was dying, and he was asked where he wanted to be buried. "Just put me over with the other boys in the cemetery here," the old man answered, motioning toward the Pewee Valley cemetery. The story inspired a Louisville businessman to pay for a monument in memory of the ex-Confederates who died at the Home.

Biscoe Hindman was the son of General Tom Hindman, a Confederate who distinguished himself at Shiloh, Chickamauga, and elsewhere. The younger Hindman was also an early member and former commander-in-chief of an organization formed just six years before, the Sons of Confederate Veterans (SCV). As an organization, the UCV would die with the last Confederate veteran; its offspring heritage organization, the SCV, was intended to live for generations while celebrating the Lost Cause virtues of the ex-Confederates.

Hindman was the exclusive general agent in Kentucky and Tennessee for a large insurance company. Flush with cash, he offered

Bennett Young carte blanche to select a monument for the new Confederate Cemetery at Pewee Valley.

The monument eventually chosen was a symmetrical shaft of white bronze, twelve feet high and four feet square at the base. A well-attended dedication ceremony on June 18, 1904, followed the familiar template for monument dedications: prayers, music, and plenty of Lost Cause oratory. Biscoe Hindman spoke, Bennett Young was the featured orator, and Lieutenant Governor W. P. Thorne accepted the monument and cemetery plot on behalf of the Commonwealth of Kentucky. Members of the new Confederate Home chapter of the Daughters of the Confederacy sat on the speaker's platform.

To one observer, the most memorable sight at the ceremony was the solemn presence of scores of inmates from the Kentucky Confederate Home. The old men, dressed in their freshly laundered gray Home uniforms, had formed up in column at the Home and marched silently up dusty Maple Avenue a mile to the cemetery. Throughout the ceremony, they stood in double line, sixty-, seventy-, eighty-year-old men standing at attention, bareheaded in the summer heat. It was only after the closing prayer that the old men broke ranks for a dipper of water and some rest in the shade.[28]

It was about this time that a tradition began, a tradition that would last more than a quarter century. Every inmate who was to be interred in the Confederate Cemetery would receive an honor escort from his fellow inmates. Regardless of the weather, the old men of the Kentucky Confederate Home would don their freshly laundered gray uniforms, form up in column behind a color-bearer, and march silently up Maple Avenue a mile to the cemetery alongside the remains of their comrade. They would remain silent and bareheaded in double line throughout the burial ceremony, breaking only after the closing prayer for a sip of water, a bit of rest, and a raucous walk back down Maple Avenue to the Home.[29]

Well into the twentieth century, residents of Maple Avenue would come out of their homes and stand on their front porches to see the solemn procession of old Confederates accompany another veteran to his final resting place. Then, after a quarter hour or so, they would step outside again to watch the boisterous old men on their walk back to the Home, yipping and yawping like schoolboys, full of the giddy and guilty exhilaration of having outlived another comrade.

The inmates lined up for a different type of march on Friday, November 11, 1904, for the dedication of the Kentucky Confederate Home's new infirmary. More than a hundred old vets, dressed in summer Home uniforms, greeted officers of the state UCV organization at the Pewee Valley depot and escorted them to the Home.

A crowd of nearly 2,000 arrived that morning for the ceremonies, and many availed themselves of the opportunity to tour the old resort hotel and the new Infirmary Building. At Young's urging, the board had spent the remainder of the state's appropriation for improvements to the original building. The two lower floors had been recarpeted, repapered, and repainted, and the smell of fresh paint replaced the smells of old cooking and leaking sewage. A new coal boiler in the basement doubled the heating capacity, and an electrical plant was providing light and power to the Infirmary Building (although the main building had not yet been wired). Kirker-Bender fire escapes—tall spiral escape slides—stood at each end of the building, and Babcock chemical fire extinguishers near each staircase on every floor had replaced the sand-filled leather fire buckets. The fire buckets now hung inside a red-painted shed behind the infirmary, alongside two forty-gallon wheeled fire carts and eight fire ladders.[30]

At noon, the crowd gathered in front of a speaker's platform for the dedicatory ceremonies. After an opening prayer and brief remarks by minor politicians, Bennett Young stepped to the rostrum for the ceremonial presentation of the building to the Commonwealth of Kentucky.

The ex-Confederates had expected Governor Beckham to attend the dedication and accept the Home, but last-minute business in Frankfort kept him away. Young adjusted his remarks accordingly, but was interrupted mid-speech when Lieutenant Governor Thorne pushed his way through the crowd, mounted the platform, and elbowed a stunned Bennett Young away from the podium. Thorne made a few remarks thanking the ex-Confederates for improvements to the Home, then launched into a disjointed defense of his controversial executive pardon.

There was later speculation that Thorne was drunk that afternoon, but there was no question that he was political poison. Several weeks earlier, with Governor Beckham out of state, Thorne had pardoned a man from his hometown who had been convicted of the rape and murder of his own daughter. The details of the man's crime and trial had been reported across the state and were so repulsive that Thorne's pardon—apparently granted to repay a political favor—was unthinkable.

Boos and hisses broke out among the crowd, and women on the platform fled as men surged toward Thorne, threatening to beat him to a pulp. Not wanting to wrestle Kentucky's lieutenant governor away from the rostrum, Bennett Young sat down, but only after turning his chair to face away from Thorne. When Thorne concluded his rambling harangue, he signaled to the band to strike up "My Old Kentucky Home." Band members placed their instruments on the ground and crossed their arms.

The celebration collapsed in confusion and disgust, but the dedication was only ceremonial, after all. The Home that had opened two years before could then accommodate fewer than a hundred inmates comfortably; now it could shelter twice that number. Sick and injured inmates now had a reasonable expectation of medical care in an infirmary that might help heal them. And the main building, sorely taxed by the earlier flood of inmates, had been freshened and improved.[31]

Otway B. Norvell was one of the first to move to a private room in the new infirmary. Unfortunately, that building, too, was soon overcrowded.

"It has been shown that even this infirmary will not care for those absolutely dependent upon its appliances for comfort," Bennett Young admitted less than a year after it was completed.[32]

Even so, a well-equipped infirmary with a staff of four nurses and a full-time physician was eminently preferable to Room 52, a drafty third-floor sleeping room. Completion of the new Infirmary Building probably prolonged Norvell's life by a few months, but the paralyzed icemaker died of pneumonia on July 2, 1905. At his wife's request, he was buried in Cave Hill Cemetery in Louisville, where he was described as "a brave soldier, a silent sufferer, a fond husband, a guileless Christian."

A. J. Lovely never made it back to Pewee Valley from Lakeland Asylum; his mind had clouded so completely as to remove any hope of recovery. Lodge brothers, comrades, and friends from Paris organized monthly trips to visit him until he died on September 30, 1906. They returned his body to Paris to lie in state at the Knights of Pythias Hall before burial services by ex-Confederates in the Paris cemetery. A year later, Rathbone Lodge No. 12 unveiled a monument dedicated to Lovely's memory, saying that "no grave on earth [was] deep enough to conceal the blameless knighthood of such a man."[33]

With the encouragement and blessing of its citizens, the Commonwealth of Kentucky provided $57,000 to help make the Kentucky Confederate Home a more respectable place for its aging and invalid Confederate veterans. But every improvement made to the Home created a fresh spurt of applications for admittance.

For the remainder of its first decade of operation the Home would remain crowded, and its directors would have to deal with the particular problems of managing the care of two hundred or more needful (and sometimes troublesome) old men.

Chapter 9

The Railroad Man and the Barber

William S. Gray deserved his Saturday night toots. He had worked day labor for the railroad most of his life, Monday morning to Saturday afternoon. For Gray, Saturday night was the workingman's night for a little carousing, a little drinking, and a little howling at the moon. It made no matter to him that he lived under the rules of the Kentucky Confederate Home.

On Sunday morning, October 9, 1904, Gray staggered downstairs to the dining hall for breakfast, still drunk from the night before. He was loud and boisterous, and the other diners tried to ignore him. When George Wood leaned across the table to shush him, Gray drew his knife and threatened to cut Wood's throat.

A later inspection of Gray's room uncovered a stash of whiskey hidden in the top of his closet.[1]

Visitors to the Kentucky Confederate Home often described the luxury of the facility and referred to the dignity, nobility, grace, and charm of the old inmates. If the physical conditions there were less than what the United Daughters of the Confederacy expected during the first year of operation, things improved markedly as a result of the state's increase of the per capita payment to $175 and as effects of the 1904 special appropriation were felt.

By March 1905 more than 220 inmates were living in the Home and infirmary (with 27 more on temporary furlough or hospitalized in Louisville), and applications for admission continued to flood the board of trustees. For old men past their working age, or men who

141

lived off the uncertain grace of relatives and friends, the Home was a sweet retreat that clothed, fed, and healed them.

Tom Fain was a seventy-one-year-old widower when he came to the Home in 1904 from Ashland. Shortly after he arrived in Pewee Valley, Fain gloated to the editor of his hometown newspaper about the weight he had gained, thanks to the excellent meals and pleasant surroundings. The inmates have plenty to eat and wear, Fain told the newspaperman, and little to do but eat, drink, and lie around in the shade.[2]

Peter Snapp was born in Germany seventy years before he came to Pewee Valley from Owensboro in 1903. He arrived at the Home near dead from consumption, but care, food, and warmth helped him recover. Snapp's only brother died, leaving him $75, and the inmate chose to donate a part of the windfall to the Kentucky Confederate Home. "He took $25 for his own and insisted that he wanted to give $50 for the Home, as the Home was his best friend," marveled treasurer Fayette Hewitt.[3]

Pleasant as it may have been to inmates who had never dreamed of living in such luxurious surroundings, the Home was also an institution populated by old men who needed an increasing amount of medical care. Added funding and the new infirmary allowed the Home to treat ex-Confederates who might not otherwise have been able to afford it.

Within months of the Home's opening, in early 1903 the board of trustees voted to hire Dr. R. B. Pryor of Louisville as full-time physician. On January 5, 1905, they established a medical advisory committee to oversee medical care and sanitary conditions at the Home. (One of the first actions of the advisory committee was to ban smoking in the infirmary.)[4]

Sixty-three-year-old Charles E. Bellican owned a printing company in Louisville until he turned it over to his nephews and entered the Home in 1903. By 1905 persistent cataracts clouded his eyes to such a degree that he was virtually blind. Dr. Pryor arranged for Dr. Dudley Reynolds to remove Bellican's cataracts in the Home's new surgical suite.

Reverend A. N. White was a traveling minister from south of

Lexington until his hip crumbled, the eventual result of a Union bullet lodged in the bone for more than thirty years. He entered the Home confined to his bed, too disabled to use crutches, but the Home provided White a new wood and wicker rolling chair.

There were some rough patches during the first eighteen months, but by mid-1904 most inmates were finding the Kentucky Confederate Home the comfortable, respectable place that had been promised them.

Even with the new infirmary and improvements to the Home, women of the UDC were still keeping a sharp eye on conditions there. Mrs. C. C. Leer, representing the Richard Hawes chapter in Paris, scheduled an overnight visit to Pewee Valley to check on the welfare of Bourbon County veterans residing in the Home.

Alice Leer arrived in Pewee Valley with her brother, Home trustee H. H. Ewing of Owingsville, who was there to attend a board meeting. She was a lifelong Bourbon County resident, and her remembrance of the war years there led her to become a charter member of the United Daughters of the Confederacy chapter. Leaving the depot and walking to the Home, her first impression was of its elegant grounds and buildings.[5]

"We were welcomed by a friend of my childhood, he having recognized us as we approached the Home," she wrote. The Bourbon County inmate escorted Leer and Ewing into one of the downstairs parlors.

Commandant Coleman wasn't above a little stagecraft for visits like this, and coincidence or not, four other veterans with ties to Bourbon County were waiting in the parlor. "Soon each ex-Bourbon's hand was extended, whilst the eye expressed a thrilling pathos as of the meeting of a friend, mother, sister."

Mrs. Leer chatted with the old men for a while before being taken on a tour of the Home.

The lobby stairwell led upward to a spacious foyer on the second floor. Thirty men lived in thirteen rooms on the second floor north of the foyer, but this was the most desirable floor, with small suites and sitting rooms opening onto the sunny verandahs. Commandant

Coleman, the Home's matron, the bookkeeper, and the stewardess had rooms south of the foyer. The smallest room, a linen room, contained stacks of freshly laundered towels and bedding. Two rooms on the second floor were reserved for visitors and guests, and Mrs. Leer was probably given Room 19, the "General John S. Williams" room, named and decorated by the daughter of the late general.

On the third floor, fifty men lived in twenty-five rooms. These were smaller rooms, without the regular presence of Commandant Coleman, the matron, or visiting dignitaries in the hallways.

The fourth floor was prized by men who wanted to hear the sound of rain on a roof at night and by a few mischief-makers who wanted as much distance as possible between themselves and Home authorities. The rooms, several with barrel ceilings and most with dormer windows, were clean and orderly.

"We were shown from the first to the fourth floor," Alice Leer reported to other UDC chapters, "and I am proud to say we found every department in perfect order." Mrs. Leer and her brother took their evening meal at Commandant Coleman's table in the dining room, and she spoke of her "great pleasure to see the gray-haired veterans seated at a bounteous table." She couldn't help but recall, however, "the many times that I had seen the stalwart Southern soldier cold and hungry."

After supper, the Bourbon County contingent retired to the parlor for more conversation. Alice Leer likely shared with John Marshall, Thomas Cummins, and John Nesbitt the latest news and gossip about their relatives back home. Isaac Mundy may have told her that he had recently joined the Episcopal church just across the tracks and road from the Home. They certainly would have discussed the recent death of John Hourigan, the burial of John B. Patton in the new Confederate Cemetery at Pewee Valley, and the broken mind of sweet old A. J. Lovely, who was still residing at Lakeland Asylum.

Eventually, Mrs. Leer sat at the piano to play some old tunes. She was accompanied by fiddler Trimble Arnold, "an ex-Bourbon whose reputation as a violinist is renowned." They closed the evening with a half-dozen choruses of "Dixie," and other inmates crowded into the parlor to sing along and cheer. "My memory swept back forty years ago when just budding into womanhood, I so proudly played that old tune, so often surrounded by Confederate soldiers."

The matron, Mrs. Girand, then announced that lights would be extinguished at nine o'clock.

In her report to UDC chapters, eventually published in *The Lost Cause*, Alice Leer was effusive in her praise of the Kentucky Confederate Home. "It affords me pleasure," she wrote, "to know these comforts are being enjoyed by these blameless martyrs who have reached the evening of life, while the shadows of night are crowding on the pathway to the tomb."

Tom Fain, Peter Snapp, Charles Bellican, and the Reverend A. N. White—all men who showed sincere appreciation for the benefits of the Home—may have been among the inmates who crowded the parlor the evening Mrs. C. C. Leer and Trim Arnold played "Dixie" well into the night. "It stirred my soul to its utmost depths upon glancing over this body of soldiers," Mrs. Leer wrote of that evening. She felt herself surrounded by aging, yet noble, Johnny Rebs, all marching bravely through their final years toward a Final Bivouac.

Sincere though her emotion may have been, Alice Leer was viewing the Home and its inmates through Lost Cause goggles.

The Home was, to be certain, a well-appointed, safe, clean place of refuge for men who had run out of options. But these were old men living away from their lifelong home and relatives, each man with his share of deafness, missing teeth, hemorrhoids, phantom pain from amputated limbs, irritating habits, meanness, and outright craziness.

Generally, the inmates were ordinary old men, more than two hundred of them living in close confines, day after day, with a lot of time on their hands and little to fill the hours. What made them different from others of their age was that the men of the Kentucky Confederate Home had spent four years in a civil war that was bloodier, uglier, deadlier, and more personal than any other conflict in American history.

The nightmare of combat and fear of imminent death can haunt a soldier long after he leaves the battlefield.

Doctors in the wake of the First World War noticed that some men couldn't shake their paralyzing fear, even after being removed from the sound of the guns. They named the condition "battlefield neurosis," or "shell shock." Hospitals treating veterans of the Second World War established wards for soldiers suffering from what doctors then called "battle fatigue." Only near the end of the twentieth century, in the aftermath of still another war, did doctors define the condition and give it a new name: "post-traumatic stress disorder."

Some are more susceptible than others, but for even the bravest soldier the emotional effects of a horrific experience like combat may extend far beyond the battlefield. The veteran might relive frightening moments over and over in his mind; might have trouble concentrating or sleeping; might become numb to relationships with spouse or family; might become unreasonably aggressive or combative. Without treatment, the veteran might come to rely on alcohol, drugs, or suicide to end the unremitting pain.

The inmates of the Kentucky Confederate Home didn't have a name for it, but many must have suffered from post-traumatic stress disorder. Episodes of drunkenness, violence, and even suicide were all too common. The men of the Home were old men of differing temperament and background, of course, but some still carried psychological wounds from their wartime experiences of decades before.

Some could demonstrate a touching kindness to a comrade; others might attempt murder for a stolen pouch of tobacco.[6]

J. P. Muncy's outburst may have been sparked by something as mundane as a missing pair of socks. Or an overcooked pork chop. Or a careless remark by a hard-working woman tired from a day of seeing after the needs of two hundred crabby old men.

Whatever the reason, it caused one of Alice Leer's "blameless martyrs" to explode.

J. P. Muncy arrived in the Home from McCracken County in October 1903 and quickly developed a reputation as a hothead and troublemaker. On January 5, 1904, responding to some real or imagined slight, Muncy laid into the Home's portly matron, Mrs. F. N. Girand, with every bit of blue language and spittle-flying rage a former riverman could muster. He never touched the woman, but Muncy ended the encounter with threats against the matron.

When Muncy heard that Commandant Coleman preferred charges against him for "filthy, indecent and slanderous language," he urged his fellow inmates to boycott morning roll call in a show of solidarity. Most other inmates, however, had no interest in standing with Muncy, especially when Coleman tacked on an additional charge of insubordination.

Drunkenness was by far the most common discipline problem for Commandant Coleman and the board of trustees. Despite the requirement for references and a medical screening with each application, some lifelong alcoholics were admitted to the Home. Not a few took up alcohol as a way to ease the boredom of living there.

Section 3 of "The Rules and Regulations for the Government of the Kentucky Confederate Home" strictly prohibited the use or possession of alcohol anywhere in the Home. Experience at other Confederate veterans' homes demonstrated that availability of strong drink among men with little else to fill their time could escalate into bad language, arguments, destruction of property, or violence. (Worse yet might be the image these "blameless martyrs" would present to the ladies of the UDC if they were allowed to stagger around the Home like drunkards in a saloon.)

James H. Mocabee was caught red-handed.

Born in 1840 in Scotland, Mocabee came to the United States as a boy. He was an enthusiastic enlistee at the outbreak of the war, entered the Confederate army in April 1861, and served four years with the Fourth Tennessee Cavalry.

In April 1904, eight months after Mocabee entered the Home

from Paducah, fellow inmate (and night guard) Ed O'Brien heard Mocabee's distinctive Scots burr echoing down a hallway after lights-out. O'Brien summoned Commandant Coleman, and the two men entered the old veteran's room. There they found Mocabee, drunk as a laird, in the act of passing whiskey bottles to several other inmates.

Commandant Coleman charged the Scotsman with smuggling whiskey into the Home, soliciting other inmates for money to purchase whiskey, and imbibing his own wares.

The Home wasn't a prison, and inmates who valued a taste (or a quart) of a spirituous beverage could obtain it easily enough. ("Friends, in mistaken kindness are disposed now and then to give the inmates liquor," Bennett Young noted.) Month after month, Commandant Coleman would bring inmates up on charges for "drunk and disorderly conduct," "continuous drunkenness," or being "beastly drunk" on the premises.[7]

Coleman was able to tolerate an otherwise well-behaved inmate like E. J. Sanders, who went on the occasional tear but did so without causing a commotion. During his initial crackdown in March 1903, Commandant Coleman cited Sanders for being drunk and disorderly in his room. Sanders expressed contrition and accepted a reprimand. A year later Sanders was caught again, and he was again properly remorseful on accepting his reprimand. Sanders would be charged with drunkenness five more times in the next six years, each time appropriately repentant as he accepted his reprimand.

Joe Slemmons, on the other hand, was a loud and public drunk from the minute he walked in the door on November 27, 1903. On the one-year anniversary of his arrival at the Home, the Barren County native showed up drunk at Sunday prayer services. Coleman charged him with being "drunk and disorderly," then added a recommendation to the board of trustees: "In view of the many times [he] has been seen intoxicated at the Home, I respectfully urge his dismissal."

There was no tolerance for drunken behavior that spilled outside the gates of the Home and threatened to besmirch the public image of a noble and worthy Johnny Reb.

Alfred N. Peyton's drunken two-day binge on the streets of downtown Louisville got him removed from the Home. "This man's repeated sprees are a stinging menace to the good morals of the Home," Commandant Coleman wrote, "and I recommend he be suspended ninety days."

Coleman developed a sort of ranking system to catalog the seriousness of incidents involving alcohol. Quiet drunk E. J. Sanders might be "unsteady on his feet," while the disruptive Joe Slemmons was "drunk and disorderly." Worst of all, however, was the offense of being "beastly drunk," a condition that usually involved drunken threats or harm to women.

One of the "beastly drunks" was H. C. Melbourne, who missed roll call on May 3, 1904. He was spotted later that morning, asleep on the porch of a neighboring Pewee Valley home. A Home employee coaxed Melbourne away from the premises and back to his room, where he was confined to quarters. Later in the morning, Melbourne—still drunk—left the Home and returned to the nearby residence. He was back on the same porch, pounding on the front door and demanding entry while the women of the household cowered inside. Melbourne was later suspended from the Home for ninety days, and never returned.[8]

Whether fueled by alcohol or escalating from minor personal grievances, violence between inmates was another issue for Coleman to deal with. Unless one party was clearly at fault (and there was no grievous harm done), the solution was generally to restrict each party to a separate wing of the Home and require them to take meals in their rooms.

But even relatively minor events could whip up a fury.

J. A. Burdette came to the Home in March 1903. He had been a barber in Louisville, so he knew how to make friends by putting other men at ease. He was well liked. When he felt like it, Burdette cut the hair or trimmed the beards of other inmates, and they paid him a nickel here or a dime there for a haircut (and the conversation that went with it).

On January 8, 1904, Burdette sought out Commandant Coleman to report that someone had stolen two silver dollars from a coin purse that he kept in his room. Burdette steadfastly refused to name a suspect, not wanting to stain the reputation of an innocent man. Instead, he provided a list of witnesses who he said might be in possession of facts that would determine the guilty party.

For the next week, suspicions, allegations, and anger ricocheted around the Home, all relating to guilty knowledge of Burdette's silver dollars. Before he could investigate the theft, Coleman had to write up charges against seven inmates for "fistfights, fighting and otherwise disturbing the peace and quiet" of the Home. Commandant Coleman eventually asked the board's executive committee to investigate, but Burdette's silver dollars were never recovered.

Serious violence was rare, but it could come with sheer and terrifying unpredictability.

No one actually accused John B. McCreary of stealing the pouch of tobacco, but heads turned in his direction when the issue came up in conversation. To end the gossip once and for all, McCreary rose before five o'clock one morning and, with a fire axe taken from a hallway bracket, crept to the room of Ed O'Brien. O'Brien was still asleep when the fire axe glanced off the head of his iron bed, cutting him on the cheek. O'Brien suffered two more chops to his head and arm before other inmates subdued McCreary and rushed O'Brien to the infirmary. McCreary didn't wait to be disciplined before making his getaway from the Home. Three days later he wrote the commandant from another city, saying he regretted the affair and would be leaving that evening for Texas.[9]

Ex-Confederates living in the Home had witnessed their share of military discipline during wartime. A miscreant might have his head shaved or be required to wear a sign describing his offense. Kentucky veterans told of men locked in wooden stocks for days and described the "barrel shirt," where a culprit would have to give up all clothing and wear nothing but a rough wooden barrel. An entire division might be called out to the parade grounds to witness the execution of a comrade convicted of being absent without leave.[10]

Commandant Coleman had none of those punishments at his disposal, of course. Instead, "The Rules and Regulations for the

Government of the Kentucky Confederate Home" described a specific process by which discipline would be administered to inmates. Regardless of the offense—from profanity to assault with a fire axe—the commandant was required to file charges with the board of trustees, describing the offense, citing specifications, and listing witnesses. Meeting monthly, a committee of the board would hold a court-martial for each of the accused, calling witnesses, determining guilt, and meting out punishment. "There is no punishment except reprimand, suspension, and dismissal," Bennett Young explained to Governor Beckham.[11]

Whenever possible, trustees would reprimand the misbehaving old veteran, asking only that he express remorse and promise never to repeat the offense. Easygoing E. J. Sanders became expert at expressing contrition for his episodes of drunkenness, and even the more disruptive Joe Slemmons was allowed multiple opportunities to express his regrets. J. P. Muncy, the foul-mouthed riverman, had his charges of "filthy, indecent and slanderous language" dismissed when he wrote a letter of apology to Mrs. Girand, the Home's matron.

"After reprimand comes suspension," Young explained. "This has been found at times to be cruel, and it produces hardships which would touch the heart of any humane individual."

Repeat offenders faced a thirty-, sixty-, or ninety-day suspension from the Home. For men unable to earn their own living (and without any other resources), suspension could mean begging for food and shelter while waiting for the calendar pages to turn and the Home's doors to reopen to them.

In August 1904, the Pewee Valley Depot stationmaster sent word to Commandant Coleman that an inmate was near death at the rail station. Inmate T. B. Patterson was on suspension for drunkenness and insubordination, but he had no other place to go. Patterson was starving and dehydrated when Coleman and Dr. Pryor retrieved him from the depot. Dr. Pryor recommended that Patterson's suspension be indefinitely suspended.[12]

James H. Mocabee, the bootlegging Scotsman, discovered during his ninety-day suspension that he preferred living outside the discipline of the Home. He asked for an indefinite furlough and settled in nearby LaGrange. There he raised vegetables and regularly brought beets, beans, and radishes to his old comrades until his death ten years later.[13]

Dismissal was the final punishment, reserved for incorrigibles and those whose offenses were outrageous enough to threaten public support of the Home. An inmate dismissed from the Kentucky Confederate Home would, following the verdict of the trustees, be stripped of his Home uniform and given civilian clothes, $1.00 in cash, a lunch basket, and a rail ticket returning him to the community from which he first made application to the Home.[14]

"The age of these men makes this still more disagreeable and unpleasant," said Bennett Young.

Commandant Coleman recommended dismissal for H. C. Melbourne after the incident on the Pewee Valley porch. The trustees, however, voted to give the eighty-one-year-old veteran one more chance. "For repeated drunkenness and for entering a private citizen's house in a maudlin condition," Melbourne was sentenced to a sixty-day suspension. He never returned to the Home.

"If there is no restraint," Young explained, "it would be impossible for those who obey the rules and are willing to observe the law to live quietly or comfortably in the Home."[15]

Almost lost among the stacks of disciplinary charges and specifications that Commandant Coleman prepared each month was the charge against inmate Joe Pike.

Sixty-seven-year-old Joe B. Pike was one of the Home's earliest residents, having been recommended by John Leathers's Louisville camp. He had no reputation as a troublemaker. But on a July afternoon in 1904, according to Coleman's uncharacteristically terse report, Pike stated in front of another inmate "that Coleman and Mrs. Girand were stealing everything they could lay their hands on." Coleman's charge of "malicious slandering" against Pike was forwarded to the board of trustees for action on August 9.

The trustees might have generally disregarded the Pike matter had it not been for the Lawson letters. In the week previous, four of the trustees had received letters from Alexander Lawson, Home steward and respected ex-Confederate, alleging theft, mismanagement, neglect, and favoritism in the Home.[16]

In the early months of operation, when the Home's financial situation was the darkest, Bennett Young enlisted Alexander Lawson as an independent financial agent. Lawson raised a decent amount of money for the Home, earned a decent commission, and in the process made the acquaintance of Kentucky's prominent ex-Confederates and UDC members. A year later, the board offered Lawson regular employment as steward of the Home. As such, he was responsible for implementing some efficiencies in the purchase of supplies and management of the kitchen.

If the trustees thought that adding Lawson to the staff of the Home might ease Commandant Coleman's administrative burden, they couldn't have been more mistaken. The two men were like tigers in a cage, with Lawson critical of Coleman's management and Coleman suspicious of Lawson's motives. By the summer of 1904, it was obvious the pairing wasn't working. "In view of the friction existing in the management" and "with a view of harmonizing matters," the board voted on July 9 to end Lawson's employment. Bennett Young received letters from the commanders of the Paris and Boone County UCV camps in support of Lawson, but expressing their support of Young and the rest of the board.[17]

At the August 9 board meeting—the meeting at which the charges against Joe Pike were presented—the Home's board of trustees named a special committee, chaired by Fayette Hewitt, to investigate the charges of theft against the commandant and the matron.

From a public relations standpoint, the allegations couldn't have come at a worse time. The General Assembly had voted $56,000 for improvements, and construction of the new infirmary was well underway. The state's increase of its per capita funding from $125 to $175 was intended to pay for better care of Kentucky's blameless martyrs, not to be siphoned off by crooked bureaucrats.

Hewitt's investigation moved quickly. He reported that he could find no evidence of theft, and he implied that Lawson's charges were

motivated by his termination. The charges of favoritism and neglect, Hewitt said, were "largely due to the selfish and exacting na-
tures" of the old men in the Home. "We would suggest that many of
these complaints might be obviated by a little tact on the part of our
superintendent," Hewitt said of Coleman.[18]

Coleman felt vindicated, but Bennett Young wasn't so sure. Three
months later the board received more charges of mismanagement and
neglect.

A Freemason living in the Home wrote a desperate—and anonymous—letter to Kentucky's Masonic Grand Master, describing the
recent death due to neglect of another Mason in the Home. Not
sure how to proceed, the Grand Master forwarded the letter to John
Leathers, who delivered it to Andrew Sea, secretary of the Home's
board. "In my opinion we have the best Confederate Home in the
United States," Leathers assured Sea, but the letter "contains serious reflections on the Home" and should be investigated.[19]

Andrew Sea wasn't able to get the issue in front of the board of
trustees before another shoe dropped.

Inmate Ed Browder, a likeable old coot from Fulton County and
the brother of trustee R. A. Browder, wrote a chatty and generally
well-meaning letter to the editor of the *Fulton Commercial* about living conditions in the Home. The newspaper editor chose to build a
story around Browder's innocent gripes about overcrowding, poor
food, lack of heat, and other management issues.[20]

Bennett Young tried to get ahead of the damage by appointing a
standing inspection committee, but the newspapers that had given
the Kentucky Confederate Home so much favorable ink were now
looking for a little muck to rake. In February 1905 the Oldham
County Board of Health announced an investigation into sanitary
conditions at the Home, which set off a spate of anonymous letters
from inmates to their hometown newspapers about conditions real
and imagined. Coleman, for his part, cracked down even harder,
failing to heed Fayette Hewitt's suggestion that a little tact might be
more appropriate.[21]

Newspapers received more fodder for speculation and gossip in
July 1905 with the sordid death of trustee R. E. Duncan of Hawes-

ville. Judge Duncan checked himself into the Home's infirmary for what was later described to be treatment of a drug habit. At bedtime he took a heavy dose of morphine—supplied, most likely, by Dr. Pryor—then closed the door to his room and slit his wrists. A night nurse found him almost completely bled out, but the dying man was still hacking away at his own throat with a small knife.[22]

Alexander Lawson, meanwhile, continued his feud with Commandant Coleman by recycling stories of misfeasance in the Home.[23]

In December 1905, intending to blunt the criticism, Young wrote the governor "demanding a full, complete, impartial and rigid examination calling for the closest scrutiny of everything the Board of Trustees has done." The board also approved the hiring of an outside accounting firm to prepare "a detailed statement of all receipts and expenditures of the Home from its opening" to the current date.[24]

The Kentucky Senate appointed a committee of five to investigate the Home, but, with state senator Henry George chairing the committee, there was little doubt as to its findings. Days before the final report was completed and published, George provided his succinct assurance to Young: "It will be favorable."[25]

The audit was favorable, too, detailing every dollar expended and every dollar received, right down to the single dollar donated by grocer John L. Stout of Bowling Green.

"It is most gratifying to the board," Young wrote of the Senate report, "that after an investigation prompted by malice, that such a splendid testimonial has been given to the conduct of those entrusted with the management of the institution."

By the end of 1905 the Kentucky Confederate Home was operating on a financial footing more solid than at any other time since it opened. The new infirmary, dormitory, and renovated main building were all fully occupied, but the needy and decrepit ex-Confederates were receiving the best care they had known in their lives.

The place was respectable again.

In his 1905 "Annual Report of the Kentucky Confederate Home," Bennett Young acknowledged that some of the disciplinary problems and operational complaints were inherent in the nature of the institution. "It would be unreasonable to expect that there would be no complaints," he said. "Many of these [inmates], removed from all that is near and dear to them, with no employment, sick and despondent, where placed together in such large numbers, naturally meet things which result in misunderstandings."[26]

Three weeks after pulling a knife on George Wood at breakfast, William S. Gray went on another of his Saturday night toots. When a drunken Gray was asked to leave the Sunday worship service for shouting out profanities, he threatened the deacon with his blade.

That evening, Commandant William O. Coleman wrote up charges and specifications against the old railroad man, recommending that he be expelled from the Home "as his continual bad behavior is intolerable." Gray was confined to his room, and a seventy-four-year-old "guard" was posted at the door until a court-martial could be called.

The rhetoric of respect for Gray, Patterson, Mocabee, Peyton, Slemmons, and other veterans of the Lost Cause too often exceeded the reality of their lives. The old men of the Kentucky Confederate Home were old men living elbow to elbow with one another, some still suffering from wounds of a war long past. The Home was a respectable place, providing shelter, clothing, food, and care, but it required that the men live up to standards never required of them in civilian life.

Some thrived in the environment, while others resisted to the point of expulsion.

Chapter 10

---·••·---

The Socialite and the Editor

According to the story told later, Confederate veteran Charles W. Russell contacted Bennett Young sometime during the summer of 1905 about a New York socialite who was visiting Louisville. The visitor was Mrs. L. Z. Duke, a wealthy widow and native Kentuckian, who desired to pay a call on the Kentucky Confederate Home. Russell was careful to explain that she was not directly related to General Basil and Henrietta Morgan Duke of Kentucky; it was rumored that her late husband was one of the Carolina tobacco Dukes. The New York woman had money, and it was thought she might be persuaded to donate some of it to the Home.

By the time Young arranged to call on Mrs. Duke at the Galt House, however, she had departed for New York. Young wooed her with a series of flattering letters, inviting her to return soon for a tour of the Home.

Mrs. Duke was unable to schedule a return trip to Kentucky until June 1906. Young asked Florence Barlow, former editor of *The Lost Cause* and newly elected president of the Confederate Home chapter of the UDC, to meet Mrs. Duke in Louisville and escort her to Pewee Valley.

Mrs. L. Z. Duke was a small woman, standing barely over five feet tall, and she dressed for the short trip in a shirtwaist and skirt that made her look younger than her sixty-five years. She was quick with a firm handshake that spoke of her free and generous nature and a sprightliness that promised excitement and adventure. Nature stopped short of making Mrs. Duke beautiful: her blue-gray eyes were set too far apart, and a flattened nose looked as though it might be more at home on a retired prizefighter. But she had a warm, open smile that beckoned men and women to her.

If Mrs. L. Z. Duke was not the reserved and aloof New York socialite that Florence Barlow was expecting to meet that day, then Florence Barlow was certainly not the shallow small-town club-woman that Mrs. Duke may have expected.

Miss Barlow—she was an unapologetic spinster—had recently celebrated her fifty-first birthday with the sale of her interest in *The Lost Cause*, and she radiated a competence and an enthusiasm that earned the trust of businessmen and moneyed women used to hiring social secretaries and planners. Even at middle age she retained a youthful prettiness, and she styled her hair and wore her dresses in the latest styles, but without a hint of flashiness or brass. (She avoided haute couture, however, not wanting to give the impression of competing in any way with corporate wives or potential patronesses.) She could converse knowledgeably on almost any subject, but always with a subtle respect for the social status of her conversational partner.

By the time the editor and the socialite arrived in Pewee Valley on that June morning in 1906, the two women were on their way to becoming fast friends.[1]

Clocks moved slowly at the Kentucky Confederate Home; the days were long, and there was little to fill them.

A day at the Home began for inmates at 6:00 A.M. with a cannon shot, a blank charge fired from a field artillery piece that had been donated to the Home and placed on the front lawn. Eighty-year-old Lorenzo D. Holloway, the first inmate to arrive at the Home and the first to sign the register, was the self-appointed color guard. At sunrise on dry days Holloway climbed to an access hatch on the fourth floor and raised the U.S. flag—forty-six white stars united on a blue field—over the Home.

By six-thirty, the men would fall in for morning roll call. Rules required that all inmates wear a standard uniform—pants, vest, coat during winter, and hat outdoors—and present themselves for inspection each day. After all the inmates were accounted for, the men were dismissed for breakfast mess.

A typical breakfast might consist of sliced ham, fried potatoes, coffee, biscuits, oleomargarine, and perhaps fruit preserves. (There weren't enough hens in the area to provide eggs for 250 men every day. Most of the eggs purchased by the Home were used for cakes or other desserts.)[2]

Weather permitting, inmates might stroll the grounds after breakfast or find a chair on one of the galleries, but the rules prohibited them from leaving the Home's grounds without the commandant's permission.

Dinner, served at midday, was the heaviest meal of the day, better suited to an active farmer than a sedentary seventy-year-old. Sliced roasts of beef or mutton, seasonal vegetables, potatoes, and bread would be served family style from big platters, brought to the tables by dining stewards. Friday was usually a day for fish—filets of bullhead cat, drum, or some other river fish poached in milk.

Afternoons stretched out as empty as the mornings. Some inmates returned to their rooms for naps; others loitered in the library or one of the parlors. This was the time to break out the checkerboards or deal a game of Seven-Up.

Dinner, served at 5:00 P.M., was a light meal: stewed fruit, rice pudding, or some cold corned beef.

After an evening roll call inmates might once again linger in the downstairs common rooms. A few would retire to their sleeping rooms, but there was no smoking or chewing allowed in bed, no loud noises, no reading in bed by lamp or candle. The day ended at 9:00 P.M. with all lights extinguished and a night guard posted at the front door.

Amusement was in short supply during the earliest years of the Home. There was a well-stocked library, and a piano with box after box of sheet music. But the inmates were not, in the main, books-and-music men. Instead, they created their own diversions.

Whittling was a common hobby, and a cedar telephone pole left on the roadside near the Home provided a bonanza for inmates Elbert Smith and J. J. Hurly. Smith and Hurley dragged the pole back to the Home and chopped it into manageable pieces. The men carved hundreds of souvenirs: whittled figurines, balls-in-cages, and other cedarwood knickknacks that they marked with their names and sold to visitors. ("I'm selling these to raise money to have my teeth filled," Hurly told one visitor, who observed that Hurly's purse was filled by the end of the day.) Inmate T. J. Haynes of Fulton County was another penknife entrepreneur. He carved custom walking sticks out of found hardwood and sold them, sometimes clearing as much as $20 a day.[3]

Gardening was another popular leisure activity for the able-bodied. It was common in springtime for inmates to stake out a patch of ground for their own gardens, and their fresh vegetables usually ended up on the Home's dining tables. The Louisville Parks Commission (chaired by ex-Confederate John B. Castleman) donated bulbs, shrubs, and trees to the Home. "[Lexington inmate P. A.] Davidson takes charge of the planting and arrangement of them," a visitor noted.[4]

Lorenzo Holloway scoured donated magazines for puzzle contests and subscription sales offers. He often donated his prizes—a set of glassware or a monogrammed, hand-painted china service—to the Home. His cataract surgery a success, Charles E. Bellican, the former printer from Louisville, created a sort of free-form art using thousands of stamps, paper bows, and cutout pictures. He decorated the walls of his room with his fantastical creations and gave them to children who visited the Home.[5]

Overall, however, there was little activity to fill the hours. Visitors broke the tiresome sameness of the days, but visiting hours were limited to six hours a day, three days a week, and many inmates had no friends or relatives to visit them.

There was no large public room in the Home for entertainment events. Funerals and religious services—always well-attended breaks in the daily routine—were held in the main lobby. (Due to lack of space, inmates were forced to stand, and the presiding clergyman conducted the service from a perch on the stairway.)[6]

"These old men need entertainments," Young wrote in his 1905

annual report. "Some kind of amusement is essential to the happiness of the inmates." He envisioned "free lectures and concerts,
which could be arranged, if only there was a place in which they
could meet."

Even as he wrote this, Young had an idea of what was needed and
how to go about getting it.

At its first meeting of 1906, the board of trustees authorized Bennett Young to draft a bill for the legislature—a bill requesting still
another special appropriation for improvements at the Home. Top-
ping the list of improvements was a chapel for worship.

"Many ministers of the Gospel have offered to come and preach
every Sabbath, if the proper place could be assured," Young noted.
"There is no place where there could be an assembly in the Home,
and, if half the inmates should attend the church in Pewee Valley, it
would be crowded."

What self-respecting legislator could vote against a chapel for
Christian worship?

Bundled with the request for chapel money was a request for
monies to improve the Home's sewage and water systems. These had
been built with funds appropriated just two years before, but neither
was working up to spec, and the Home was again dealing with the
conjoined problems of too little water and too much sewage.

Young found it necessary to remind legislators that "improvements which are made on the property only enhance its value to the
Commonwealth of Kentucky." Because the deeds to all the properties
were in the name of the Commonwealth, the state "will then have
property largely increased in value" once the last ex-Confederates
died off.

The request for a house of worship died in the Senate, however,
and Young was forced to bide his time on the chapel plans while he
and the board dealt with other administrative matters.

The Kentucky Confederate Home's regular income was growing
due to a swelling inmate population and the increased per capita allowance, but the board of trustees was fielding more demands—

some proper, some petty—on its budget. No one was trying to steal the bacon, but too many people were trying to cut off a slice for breakfast.

When money was tight, Commandant William O. Coleman had detailed inmates to perform tasks around the Home, but with the Home on a better financial footing, the inmates wanted to be paid for their services. Inmate Henry Fry presented a bill to Fayette Hewitt for $5.00, his monthly charge for picking up mail at the Pewee Valley post office and carrying it back to the Home. The bill was returned to Fry unpaid, with the advice that Fry should continue carrying the mail if he expected to enjoy free bed and board at the Home. Likewise refused was the bill from Levi Prewitt, who wanted to be paid for his "volunteer" services in the Infirmary Building. Finis Renshaw petitioned the board of trustees for $5.00 a month to buy a patent medicine he had seen advertised, a concoction he felt sure would cure him of all ills. Bennett Young none too gently bounced the request to Dr. Pryor, and though Renshaw would live another fifteen years, nothing more was heard of his miracle cure.[7]

But the biggest claim on the budget came on March 2, 1906, from Commandant Coleman himself.

In a letter handed to Bennett Young moments before the executive committee meeting convened, Coleman threatened to resign immediately "unless my salary is increased to $1,200 per annum." Like Coleman himself, the letter was curt and undiplomatic: "The salary I have been receiving, of $900 per year, is wholly inadequate for the very arduous services required of me."[8]

Young was inclined to accept Coleman's resignation on the spot, but the executive committee voted to delay the matter until the entire board of trustees held its quarterly meeting two weeks later.

Coleman felt justified asking for a raise. He had taken over management of the financially strapped Home from Salem Ford three years earlier and had instituted the draconian measures necessary to keep its doors open. He had followed the board's instructions to the letter while dealing with the disrespect of an increasingly unruly and surly population of old men. With the new infirmary and a larger staff to manage, the former sheriff of Trimble County felt his current annual salary of $900 was no longer commensurate with the work and responsibilities.

Young, for his part, may have been justified in thinking that Coleman was at the root of the problems that had plagued the Home throughout 1905. The commandant had been too rigid, perhaps, with no sense of empathy or compassion. ("Many of these complaints might be obviated by a little tact on the part of our superintendent," according to the committee that had investigated the problems.) His dealings with other employees were often rocky ("In view of the friction existing in the management . . ."), and there were unresolved complaints about his personal integrity ("stealing everything they could lay their hands on"). Young had considered replacing Coleman the previous year, but backed off when one of the candidates for the job went public with the employment offer.[9]

In the end, Coleman shot himself in the foot when he provided a copy of his ultimatum to the *Louisville Courier-Journal*. When a story about Coleman's salary and demands appeared in the newspaper, a half-dozen qualified applicants presented themselves to the board for consideration.[10]

On March 14, 1906, the Confederate Home board of trustees voted unanimously to accept Coleman's resignation and to offer the position of commandant to state senator Henry George at an annual salary of $1,200 (and free lodging in the Home).[11]

Henry George's appointment may have been an expression of gratitude for legislative work performed on behalf of the Home; but George was a boyishly good-natured man in his fifties and a welcome replacement for the ill-humored Coleman. "His selection will prove a popular one throughout the state," a newspaper editor predicted.[12] Henry George, equipped with a natural enthusiasm and politician's gregariousness, shared Bennett Young's belief that "some kind of amusement is essential to the happiness of the inmates" at the Kentucky Confederate Home.

Florence Barlow and Mrs. L. Z. Duke would help Henry George provide those amusements.

Florence Barlow was a career businesswoman at a time when few women had professional occupations outside the home; she was a socially active single woman at a time when most spinsters felt themselves lucky to be keeping house for a brother's family. But above all, she was a true Daughter of the Confederacy.[13]

Born in Lexington in 1854, Florence Dudley Barlow was the daughter and granddaughter of inventors, a father-son team of creative and gifted craftsmen. The elder Barlow is said to have invented the first steam locomotive and demonstrated it (with passenger car attached) in Lexington in 1826. By the 1840s father and son had created and patented a mechanical planetarium, a massive clockworks contraption that demonstrated relative movements of the planets of the solar system and all the known moons. The inventors built a foundry in Lexington, and their families lived well off the proceeds of planetariums sold to universities and collectors.

In the years before the Civil War, Florence's father, Milton, turned his attention to weaponry. In 1855 Milton patented a forty-foot-long breech-loading rifled cannon designed to lob an explosive shell further, and with greater accuracy, than any cannon in existence. Using a Federal grant as seed money, he was well on his way to constructing the prototype when Union troops arrived in Lexington in 1861 to confiscate the weapon.

Concerned that Milton Barlow's designs might be used by the Confederacy, Federal soldiers entered his shop to seize the drawings, molds, castings, tools, and every piece of machinery. When Barlow resisted, he was imprisoned. Seven-year-old Florence Barlow's first memory of war was watching her father led away in manacles by armed men in blue uniforms. Her memory of that event, she told an acquaintance fifty years later, was "as vivid as if it happened yesterday."[14]

Milton Barlow eventually escaped from the Federal jail and, with no opportunity to tell his family good-bye, rode southward to join General Abraham Buford. Commissioned a captain in the Confederate army, he spent the war in a staff position as Chief of Ordnance.

Impoverished after the war, the family moved to Madison, Kentucky, where the former inventor and foundry owner found work as a miller. As a child, Florence Barlow had enjoyed pretty dresses and needlepoint and art lessons; in Madison she earned money teaching wealthy women how to paint decorative china.

"I determined to cultivate gumption," she said later, "and bring into use all the intelligence I could command."

Gumption led Florence in 1890 to Middlesborough, then a southeastern Kentucky coal mining boomtown. She had heard of fortunes being made in land speculation and, with no experience, traveled there alone to open a real estate office. She was the only woman in the business; within a week every banker, attorney, surveyor, and insurance man in town was sending referrals to her.

Her gumption had given Barlow her start, but she was a quick study, and her natural intelligence allowed her to capitalize on her sales successes. An officer of a large building and loan association arrived in Middlesborough, looking to establish an agency there. Barlow wanted to represent the company, but had to admit she knew little about how the business worked. She asked for a stack of company literature and an appointment for later that day.

"After I had read the matter put into my hands and heard him talk 'building loan' for an hour," she said, "I was able to talk 'building loan' intelligently."

The company appointed her its agent, and she papered the town with posters reading "$200,000 to Loan by Miss Barlow!" Business boomed.

The real estate and building loan boom stalled when a fire leveled the town. As soon as the telegraph station reopened, Florence Barlow was wiring building materials firms all over the country, seeking to be appointed their commissioned sales agent in Middlesborough.

On the fly, she learned a new career as the town rebuilt. "I did splendidly," she said, "selling thousands of brick, mantels and grates, many carloads of sand, and a number of iron fronts."

Though she was dealing with contractors and workmen at their job sites, she never failed to wear feminine attire. "I never forgot I was a lady bred and born, and others always remembered it."

Barlow left Middlesborough with a healthy bank balance just before bust followed boom in 1893. She had learned to cultivate important people with her personal charm, self-confidence, winsome manner, and a sincere interest in their business. It wasn't long before she was employed as business manager of the *Lexington Observer*.

Barlow's return to Lexington, her childhood home, rekindled memories of the war years. Her father was dead, never having recovered his creative spirit, and she found herself curious about the events that had so affected her family.

"The war was very little talked about," she wrote an acquaintance after Milton Barlow's death. "Then it was too late for me to get much valuable and interesting information from him, to my great sorrow."[15] She began corresponding with prominent Kentucky veterans, men with whom her father might have served, asking about their experiences in war and their knowledge of her father. In short order, a comrade of her father's, General Basil W. Duke, employed her in Louisville to help him edit and operate *The Southern Magazine*, a literary journal.

Through Basil Duke (and as a result of her self-promotional correspondence), Florence Barlow became known to Kentucky's influential ex-Confederates as a woman who could meet business challenges. Bennett Young retained her when he needed someone to scout out public speaking opportunities; John Leathers referred her to the principals of a New York life insurance company, who hired her to open and operate their Kentucky offices.

By the turn of the century Barlow was employed by Henrietta Morgan Duke as associate editor and business manager of *The Lost Cause*, a regional news magazine for Kentucky UDC members. She subsequently purchased the magazine and edited it for four years, further cementing her relations with ex-Confederates and their loved ones. Barlow had only recently sold *The Lost Cause* in 1905 when she met Mrs. L. Z. Duke of New York City at the Louisville depot for the ride to Pewee Valley.

A coach carried Florence Barlow and Mrs. L. Z. Duke the short distance from the Pewee Valley depot to the Kentucky Confederate Home. Bennett Young, new commandant Henry George, and a contingent of uniformed inmates greeted the two women at the door.

Mrs. Duke's tour of the Home and her overnight stay would doubtless have included a walk around the grounds and several meals in the dining hall. She likely visited the new infirmary and perhaps joined in a song or two by the parlor piano. But what made this visit different from others was the immediate and genuine affection that blossomed between the inmates and the petite New York socialite with the soft Kentucky accent.

Later accounts likened it to love at first sight.

Mrs. Duke demonstrated the elegance of society in her manner and dress, but there was a Kentucky naturalness about her that invited familiarity. Without a trace of coquetry, she had a directness that flattered the men and reminded them of their rooster days. In her presence, the old inmates became like smitten boys lining up to carry her schoolbooks or share their dessert with her. And the feelings were reciprocated.

She shared her tragic personal history with the men of the Home: the death of her beloved older brother on the battlefield at Shiloh, an early marriage to a wealthy industrialist that took her away from Kentucky, the death of her infant child, and the sudden loss of her husband while the grief-stricken couple was recuperating in Europe. She could not compare her trials to those of the valorous ex-Confederates, she said, but she tried to meet adversity like a true daughter of the Southland. She was a grandniece of gallant Confederate general John B. Hood, and she was an active member of the New York chapter of the UDC.[16]

At an appropriate moment before her departure from Pewee Valley, when Mrs. Duke asked how she might help brighten the lives of the veterans, Young and Barlow described the need for an assembly hall, a place that might contribute more to the inmates' pleasure than anything else she could do. Soon after Mrs. Duke's visit, on September 6, 1906, Young announced to his board of trustees a donation of $2,200 from Mrs. L. Z. Duke of New York. The money—the largest single cash gift in the history of the Home—would be used to erect the L. Z. Duke Hall on the grounds of the Kentucky Confederate Home.[17]

In exchange for the money to build his assembly hall, Bennett

Young was willing to validate the phony personal history of the so-cialite from New York.

According to best evidence, Mrs. L. Z. Duke was actually Sarah Elizabeth Howe from eastern Kentucky. Daughter of a dirt-poor subscription schoolteacher, she was a convicted prostitute and had owned several brothels in Dallas, Texas.[18]

"Lizzie" Howe was born in 1844 in Greenup County, Kentucky, the youngest of six children. The family moved to Missouri in the 1850s. Lizzie was barely sixteen years old when she married Missouri farmer Joshua Thomas, according to a legal document filed years later by an abandoned daughter of the young couple. After two or three more marriages she appeared in 1874 in Dallas, Texas, using the name Lizzie Handley, and purchased property for a bordello.

Settled barely two decades earlier, Dallas in the 1870s was still a rough-and-tumble town on the edge of the western frontier. Prairie farmers, cotton growers, and loggers came to Dallas to bank some of their money and spend the rest on entertainment. Lizzie Hand-ley's entertainment business boomed. Within a decade she owned two ornate residences, each located on prime property in the boom-ing town and each operating with up to fifteen women "boarders." (For tax purposes the properties were listed as residences, but Lizzie and her girls could be frank with the census-taker. When asked their occupation, they all answered, "prostitute." Newspapers had no compunction about referring to Lizzie as "proprietress of a bawdy house.")

From time to time, when Lizzie was charged with running a "disorderly house," she closed her doors for a few days, paid her fine, then put her girls back to work. Lizzie lived well, and she plowed her profits into the purchase of more Dallas real estate.

Among the sporting men of Dallas, Lizzie was a charmer. The nature of her business required her to treat men well, to feed their self-confidence while managing them like smitten schoolboys. Her free and generous nature so captivated at least one city official that he made her arrest records disappear. On Christmas Day she would deliver boxes of cigars to prisoners in the city jail (for which the prisoners desired "to return their heartfelt thanks," according to one newspaper).

By the 1890s, however, Dallas was striving for respectability. The arrival of major rail lines and schemes to open the Trinity River for navigation to the Gulf of Mexico convinced city boosters that the Texas town could become a metropolis and a polite home for wealthy families. A corps of fire-breathing local ministers, the Salvation Army, and other social reformers joined forces to clean up the "Reservation," the name given several square blocks of open bars, pool halls, sporting clubs, and Lizzie Handley's bordellos. Her residences suffered several fires of suspicious origin. The state legislature and Dallas city government passed strict new laws meting out harsher penalties to owners of disorderly houses, and reform-minded judges were throwing the book at any such proprietors who were brought before the bar.

Lizzie Handley—now calling herself Lizzie Duke—began selling off her Dallas properties and then departed for an extended vacation in Europe. By 1891 she had liquidated Dallas real estate worth more than $120,000 and had resettled in New York in the guise of a wealthy widow and investor.

A resident of Manhattan in 1900, she was calling herself "Elizabeth Z. Duke" and had shaved ten years off her age. She began trading in (apparently legitimate) residential properties and making short-term business loans as she completed the sale of her Dallas holdings.[19] Though she no longer delivered cigars to men in jail, she became active in the Woman's Society for the Prevention of Crime, and—as L. Zebbeon Duke—applied for membership in the New York City chapter of the United Daughters of the Confederacy.

When Sarah Elizabeth Howe, daughter of a dirt-poor Greenup County schoolteacher, returned to Kentucky to visit the Kentucky Confederate Home, it was as Mrs. L. Z. Duke, wealthy New York socialite.[20]

Bennett Young wasted no time banking Mrs. Duke's $2,200 contribution and commissioning an architect to design the assembly hall. The building was completed well before the planned dedication of the hall in October 1907, a date chosen to coincide with the state-wide reunion of UCV camps and the fifth anniversary of the opening of the Kentucky Confederate Home.

In designing the hall, the architect didn't stray far from Young's original desire for a house of worship; the assembly hall resembled a country church building. It was a large, open, rectangular building with a stage and proscenium on one end and a slightly canted balcony overhanging wide front doors on the other. The walls on the long sides were lined with tall windows; balcony windows and four small dormers added more interior light. A Federal-style covered front porch provided shelter for those entering through the main doors. The modern building was piped for running water and wired for electricity, and it could seat a crowd of 300.

The assembly hall was sited in a line with the original hotel entrance and front doors of the infirmary, and a broad sidewalk created a promenade that connected the three buildings.

The day was bright and warm, but fewer than 2,000 people showed up in Pewee Valley on October 31, 1907, for the dedication of the assembly hall. Visitors strolled the grounds and explored the main building and infirmary. Most inmates basked in the attention of the crowd, and several sold their crafts. The boys' band of Louisville's School of Reform entertained attendees with vocal and instrumental music. As UCV members arrived at the Home for their annual reunion and business meeting, they were directed to the dining room, where the cooks laid out platters of sandwiches, big cucumber pickles, salads, and a selection of cakes.

After lunch, the crowd gathered around the front porch of the new assembly hall, waiting for the ceremony to begin. At 1:00 P.M., the doors of the new hall flew open, and Mrs. L. Z. Duke herself—on the arm of Bennett Young—stepped out of the building and invited the crowd to enter the new L. Z. Duke Hall. She stood on the front porch, graciously receiving each visitor, as the crowd filled the hall to overflowing.

Among the visitors that day were General and Mrs. Simon Bolivar Buckner and the widow of General Ben Hardin Helm. Henrietta Morgan Duke was in attendance, but the state UDC organization had no formal role in the festivities. Florence Barlow attended, of course; she was there as an employee of the Kentucky Confederate Home. Young had hired her as full-time bookkeeper to assist Commandant Henry George with his administrative details. She had also taken it on herself to begin publication of the *Confederate Home Messenger*, a newsletter "published monthly in the interest of the Confederate Home."

The crowd followed Bennett Young as he escorted the petite and demure Mrs. Duke to a seat on the stage. Young presented her to the crowd, and she was bathed in wave after wave of applause as several in the audience took the stage to speak of her generous gift and the love she so obviously felt for the aging men of the Lost Cause. Virginia Parr Sale, daughter of now-dead Captain Daniel Parr, the boat captain whose gift of Louisville property had sparked the establishment of the home five years before, presented Mrs. Duke with a bunch of red and white roses, tied with ribbon the colors of the Confederate flag.

"Deeply moved by this outburst of sentiment," the *Messenger* reported, a teary Mrs. Duke stood to acknowledge the honors paid her. She spoke briefly of the great joy she derived from doing something special for the inmates of the Home.

After several speeches and the election of UCV Kentucky Division officers, Chaplain J. H. Deering closed the meeting with a prayer, praising the good works and exemplary life of Mrs. L. Z. Duke.[21]

It's hard to believe that Bennett Young was ignorant of Lizzie Duke's sooty past. He was too smart and too well connected not to know more about the Home's largest single cash donor than just the color of her money.

Young was an experienced corporate attorney, a skillful litigator, and a savvy politician. He certainly must have routinely advised his clients that acceptance of large amounts of cash from a source not thoroughly investigated could, all too often, result in embarrassment.[22] Some of Mrs. Duke's claims—that she was the grandniece of General John Bell Hood and the granddaughter of Revolutionary patriot Richard Montgomery—could have been proven false with just a few discreet inquiries of the Greenup County clerk. (Charles W. Russell, the Greenup County native who allegedly first told Young about Mrs. Duke's interest in the Home, must have heard rumors of the Howe family daughter who had fallen into sin.) And a closer look at some of Lizzie Duke's New York real estate transactions would probably have led back to Texas, where her business activities seemed to be an open secret.

As commander of the Kentucky Division of the UCV and well-known orator at UCV events nationwide, Bennett Young had plenty of sources who would have known, could have checked, or might have volunteered information about Lizzie Duke's professional career. Of Lizzie Duke's thousands of customers during two decades in Dallas, certainly some were Confederate veterans who recognized her picture and name when they appeared in *Confederate Veteran* along with an account of the assembly hall's dedication.

If Bennett Young knew about Mrs. L. Z. Duke's past, others in Kentucky's UCV command and on the Home's board of trustees must have, too. Young was too smart a politician not to share the information (and the responsibility) for accepting such a large and public donation from a woman of the demimonde.

It's likely that the shady background of New York socialite Mrs. L. Zebbeon Duke was an open secret in Kentucky. Lizzie Duke's visits to Kentucky were limited to quiet stays at the Home or the residences of a few select friends; there's no mention of her attendance at social events or gatherings honoring her visits. Kentucky newspaper editors, normally lavish in their coverage of special events at the Home, were uncharacteristically silent about the dedication of L. Z. Duke Hall. Newspapers that did note the dedication failed to identify the donor of the new hall by name.

Florence Barlow seems to be the only person in Kentucky who wasn't aware of Mrs. Duke's past. Or maybe she didn't care. *Confederate Home Messenger* venerated the New York donor, and its editor regularly published news of the socialite's visits and her letters to Pewee Valley.[23]

The morning following the dedication, Mrs. Duke met the inmates informally in the new L. Z. Duke Hall. The elegant woman moved among the old men, sharing a quick story with one, touching the elbow of another, all with a natural Kentucky openness that radiated approachability and a directness that flattered the men. She gave a short talk, expressing her joy at their happiness and comfort, and then joined the inmates in singing new words to the tune of "Give Me That Old-Time Religion":

> We are old time Confederates,
> We are old time Confederates,
> A band of Southern Brothers
> Who fought for Liberty.

The inmates formed into columns and escorted the petite woman down the driveway to the Pewee Valley rail station for her departure. They stood, waving, on the platform as her train departed to the sound of their God-bless-yous and not a few Rebel yells.

The old men adored their benefactress. Maybe they couldn't put their finger on what it was, exactly; but there was something about Mrs. L. Z. Duke that reminded the men of the Kentucky Confederate Home of their rooster days.

The dedication of L. Z. Duke Hall marked the start of a new era for the Home. The appointment of new commandant Henry George, the generous gift of Lizzie Duke, and the infusion of Florence Barlow's gumption and intelligence helped make the Kentucky Confederate Home a gentler, kinder place for both the residents and those who cared for them.

Chapter 11

The Fiddlers and the Indian Agent

The audience knew to wait for the handshake.

Colonel J. A. Patee and his Old Soldier Fiddlers were performing their feature act on the stage of L. Z. Duke Hall. This was the full thirty-five-minute act, the one that topped the bill on vaudeville stages in Trenton, Little Rock, and Billings, not the ten-minute opener for the larger legitimate houses in Chicago, Philadelphia, or New Orleans.

At Florence Barlow's suggestion, Virginia Parr Sale and her husband had arranged with John Patee to bring his act to Pewee Valley in February 1911 for a special morning show during his weeklong booking in Louisville. Eager inmates of the Kentucky Confederate Home filled most of the seats in Duke Hall, while Pewee Valley neighbors and some out-of-town visitors crowded in behind. Commandant Henry George sat surrounded by the inmates, as delighted with the show as any in the audience.

The Old Soldier Fiddlers was a five-man traveling novelty act that appeared on vaudeville stages small and large from coast to coast. The performers—Civil War veterans whose age ranged from sixty-six to seventy-six—performed antebellum tunes and old camp songs from North and South. Colonel Patee, wearing a formal black suit that showed off his showman's coif of glowing white hair, sat center stage. To his left were the "Two Sons of Dixie" in their gray uniforms; to his right were the "Two Boys in Blue" in Union army uniforms. Left and right, they alternated playing regional favorites on the fiddle, with spoons or bones clapping out jaunty rhythms.

("Goober Peas" was a favorite, with Commandant George and the inmates clapping along and shouting, "Peas! Peas! Peas! Peas!" during the chorus.)

But Colonel Patee and the Old Soldier Fiddlers provided more than just a musical specialty act.

Their tunes were interspersed with cornpone jokes and humorous banter between the men in blue and the men in gray, each taunting the other about their musical skills, the quality of their songs, and the general superiority of their section of the country. Henry George's loud, honking laughter echoed around the hall. He and the inmates cheered their Confederate comrades on stage, especially during the rube sketches, when the Sons of Dixie showed up the Boys in Blue as the thin-blooded cold fish that they were. (The Sons always got the best of the exchanges when the act performed in Southern states; the Boys won out on Northern stages.)

Near the end of the act, as the jibes became more pointed, a seemingly irritated John Patee stood to admonish his players and deliver a short speech: We fought a bitter war many years ago, he said, but we are brothers now. He urged the shamefaced fiddlers to approach one another with the open hand of friendship. We are Americans all, he intoned.

Blue and Gray then stepped together on stage for hearty handshakes that marked the emotional finale of the act. As the crowd broke into enthusiastic applause for brotherhood, reconciliation, and America, the men in gray picked up their fiddles to play "Dixie" while the men in blue waded into the audience at Duke Hall to shake the hands of the old ex-Confederate inmates. The applause, cheers, and Rebel yells continued until every hand was shaken.[1]

The members of Old Soldier Fiddlers were veteran performers who put on a great show. And no one enjoyed a great show more than Commandant Henry George.

Henry George was a boyish man, fifty-nine years old when he replaced William O. Coleman as commandant of the Kentucky Confederate Home in 1906, and he set out to make the Home a more pleasant place for veterans and staff alike. Like the successful retail merchant he had once been, Henry George was no stay-in-the-office manager; Florence Barlow could handle the bulk of the correspondence and reports. Instead, George preferred to spend his time with the inmates, lingering with them over cups of coffee in the dining hall or sharing a lengthy chin-wag around the parlor stove. His youthful enthusiasm, his involvement with inmates, his softer approach to discipline, and a full calendar of activities and entertainments transformed the Home for almost a decade.

A casual man without airs, Commandant George was constantly rumpled, with a physique that would frustrate the most skillful tailor. His globular potbelly meant that he rarely fastened the bottom buttons of his vest, and the ends of his string necktie were never even. He had a full head of hair that was the yellow-tinged white of a mature magnolia blossom. (Despite the best efforts of his wife to brush it back, a runaway curl was always falling over his forehead.) He wore a goatee and shaggy mustache that covered his mouth and changed color depending on what soup was served at the last meal. George's nose was often red, not from drink, but from regularly blowing it into the huge, crumpled handkerchief he kept stuffed into a coat pocket. His wide-open blue eyes were the eyes of a boy, constantly amazed and amused by the wondrous world around him. Inmate John F. Hart described the new commandant as "a kindly, unpretentious gentleman, ever on the *qui vive* for our comfort and popular with all the inmates."[2]

Henry George listened appreciatively to the humorous tales told by the old men of the Home, and he would reward the storyteller with a honking laugh at the punch line. When asked, however, he had some interesting stories of his own to tell.

At the age of fourteen, with both parents dead and nothing else to do, Henry George lied about his age and enlisted in the Confederate army in 1861. He was an impulsive soldier, but he made it through the war with only minor wounds and then returned to Graves County. The restless young veteran went to work in a dry goods store and found he could sell a muzzle to a dog through sheer enthusiasm alone. At age twenty-five, he opened his own store in Wingo, the county seat.[3]

The Wingo store was an immediate success. Attorneys, judges, and citizens in town for court day would gather around George's stove and swap stories. The young man's willingness to listen and his boyish enthusiasm (even as he was selling them things they didn't know they needed) was enough to keep them coming back. In 1876 Graves County Democrats sent him to Frankfort as state representative.

Henry George thrived in the political environment. His disarming appearance and genial good nature allowed him to sell other legislators on his bills as easily as he sold canned goods and nails at his store in Wingo. He served two terms as state representative and a term as state senator before being appointed by President Grover Cleveland to the Colorado River Indian agency in 1888.

Located on the Colorado River ninety miles north of Yuma, Arizona, the Colorado River Indian Reservation was established in 1865 for the "Indians of said river and its tributaries." The job of Indian agent was largely administrative and organizational; the agent doled out blankets, beeves, and discipline to the Mohave, Chemehuevi, Hopi, and Navajo natives who lived on the reservation. While other agents treated their charges like troublesome freeloaders, Henry George listened to them. He lingered over pots of coffee with them and listened to their legends; he sat around campfires and listened to their problems. He shared his own stories with them—Bible stories, mostly—and shared his enthusiasm with his laughter.[4]

After three years, frustrated by the graft-ridden system, George resigned and returned to Graves County, where he promptly regained his old seat in the Senate. For several years, George served as warden of the Kentucky State Penitentiary in Frankfort, and under his beneficent management the institution became self-sustaining, the prisoners making and growing enough to offset the cost of housing them. Returning to his Senate seat, Henry George helped shepherd the Kentucky Confederate Home's $56,000 appropriation through the legislature after Harry P. McDonald's sudden death.[5]

When Bennett Young needed a compassionate man with solid institutional credentials to replace the autocratic William O. Coleman as commandant of the Home, Henry George fit the bill. The former Indian agent accepted the job with the undisguised glee of a small boy at a Fourth of July parade.

The Kentucky Confederate Home was, by the end of 1907, the brightest jewel in a necklace of Confederate veterans' homes draped across the South and the border states.

Confederate veterans in various states had acted largely independent of one another as they planned, financed, built, and opened soldiers' homes in Louisiana, Virginia, Texas, Maryland, Arkansas, North Carolina, Missouri, Tennessee, Florida, Georgia, Alabama, and Mississippi. (South Carolina would open a home in 1909, Oklahoma in 1911, and California in 1929.) Each state group was aware of the successes and disappointments of the others (and could learn from them), but each state faced different challenges in attempting to rally the optimum combination of active Confederate veterans groups, a sympathetic public, and generous state legislators. As a result, each state home differed in its financial footing, operational structure, and physical setting.[6]

The Kentucky Confederate Home opened in Pewee Valley twelve months after the first statewide organizational meeting of Kentucky's ex-Confederates, an accelerated schedule due in no small part to Bennett Young's lobbying expertise and Governor J. C. W. Beckham's desire to please the ex-Confederate electorate. Other states experienced a more protracted schedule. Georgia's veterans built a home in 1891, and then asked their state legislature for operational funding. The state turned down the funding request, and the building remained unoccupied for a decade until it burned in 1901. The Georgia veterans finally received support from the legislature and opened a rebuilt home in 1902, a month after the Pewee Valley dedication. Alabama delayed any serious effort to build a home until 1901, largely because the state's Reconstruction constitution mandated that a tenth of all state revenues go toward Confederate pensions. The state eventually passed an appropriation to support the home in 1903.

All the homes dealt with overcrowding and budget shortfalls from time to time, but Kentucky's legislature rarely denied a timely appropriation request for funds to maintain or improve the Pewee Valley facility. The superintendent of the Oklahoma Confederate Home, by contrast, would complain that his state's appropriation was insufficient. "It became necessary to use hallways for sleeping rooms in some instances," he said. And the manager of the Texas home had to house inmates in a stable until the state legislature finally provided funds for remodeling. Several of the homes had to suspend admissions because of overcrowding; there is no evidence that the Kentucky trustees were ever forced to delay admitting qualified veterans due to lack of space.[7]

An inmate of the Kentucky Confederate Home could swing in a hammock all day long, if he chose; able-bodied inmates of some other Confederate soldiers' homes were required to work for their keep. None of the homes expected to be truly self-supporting, but the Virginia, Texas, Arkansas, Louisiana, and North Carolina homes (among others) required inmates to find employment on the grounds, work that might include growing supplies for the home, clearing land for building, doing carpentry tasks, or performing laundry duty.

The homes that supported active farms—Arkansas, Alabama, and Florida, for example—were often located in rural areas, accessible to family and visitors only after a rough ride down rutted lanes. The Georgia, Louisiana, Tennessee, and Texas homes were built in large cities, close to urban distractions and temptations. The Kentucky Confederate Home's location in the silk-stocking exurban village of Pewee Valley was near the population center of the state and easy to reach by roadway and rail.[8]

The Virginia, Florida, and Alabama homes were organized on the cottage plan, with small cabins or barracks that were often difficult to heat or plumb. Arkansas, Tennessee, and Georgia built institutional (though attractive) central buildings that were more like a combination dormitory and rest home. Inmates in Kentucky lived in what had been a posh resort hotel, an elegant structure built for the comfort of its guests. "As we entered the spacious grounds we were almost startled by the impression that we were approaching a delightful summer resort," a visitor from Tennessee wrote. A Florida veteran who had visited his own state's home said of the Kentucky Confederate Home, "If the inmates are not happy, the surroundings are not at fault."[9]

The appointment of Henry George and the opening of L. Z. Duke Hall in 1907 transformed life in the Home in several ways, ushering in an eight-year period marked by more comfort, graciousness, and affability than the Home's inmates and managers had experienced in its early years of operation.

"There are now at present in the Home more men than were ever there at one time," the *Confederate Home Messenger* noted in October 1907. Almost 400 men had been admitted to the Home since its inception, and the board of trustees was approving more applications every month. "The question arises, where will they find quarters?"

More than 250 inmates were living in the Home in 1907 (with several dozen more on temporary furlough at any one time), but with the opening of L. Z. Duke Hall the Home seemed less crowded. Though the hall provided no additional living space, the new building gave veterans more elbow room, a place for their religious services, holiday gatherings, and other assemblies.

Before the hall was built, occasional Protestant religious services were held in the main building, with a few old inmates standing in the lobby while a visiting preacher delivered his message from a perch on the stairway. But the 300-seat Duke Hall allowed for formal services (and more of them).

The Reverend Alexander N. White, Confederate veteran and itinerant Baptist minister, was accepted as an inmate of the Home shortly after it opened in 1902. The wheelchair-bound preacher guided his comrades down the path to salvation whether they wanted to travel it or not. He rarely missed an opportunity to share the Gospel with another inmate; he was a cheerful presence at sickbeds and a comforting figure at deathbeds. Time after time, Home management warned White for being too meddlesome, but enough of the inmates welcomed his religious ardor that the cheerful minister was undeterred.

With the opening of Duke Hall (and with Henry George's tacit approval), White took it upon himself to organize regular religious services, scheduling visiting ministers for Sunday afternoons, song services on Wednesdays, and revival evangelists whenever he could snag them.

"The veterans at the Home are having religious services of a superior quality every Sunday afternoon," the *Confederate Home Messenger* reported. "Pastors as a rule give the best they have on these occasions."[10]

Preachers with congregations in LaGrange, Middletown, and Prospect rotated regular Sunday service assignments at Pewee Valley. Dr. Peyton Hoge, however, had a hometown advantage. He had been called to the pulpit of Pewee Valley Presbyterian Church about the time the assembly hall was dedicated, and he signed up to preach at the Home on the third Sunday of each month. In 1908 Hoge and another Presbyterian minister held a weeklong revival in L. Z. Duke Hall that drew crowds of inmates and Pewee Valley residents. Other denominations also served residents of the Home. The rector at St. James Episcopal Church regularly administered communion to Anglican inmates or any others who desired to partake. Members of the nearby St. Aloysius Catholic Church arranged to transport Catholic inmates to Mass, and the Salvation Army announced its intention to hold band concerts and preaching on the Home's lawn.[11]

As religious activity flourished in the Home, problems with drunkenness and bad behavior seemed to decrease. The *Confederate Home Messenger* noted that several inmates had chosen to affiliate with local churches. "It is hoped that more will be impressed with their need of a Savior," the paper added drily.[12]

L. Z. Duke Hall provided a venue well suited to the programs and entertainments that Henry George and Florence Barlow were more than happy to arrange, amusements that helped reduce some of the tensions and discipline problems that had festered during the Home's earliest years.

Suddenly, calendar pages had more entries and clocks seemed to run faster for idle inmates.

One of the first entertainments held in the hall was a lecture by Louisville attorney William B. Fleming, a state assembly member and acquaintance of Henry George. Fleming brought his electric stereopticon to the Home for a lantern show illustrating the rise and fall of Napoleon Bonaparte. "The rare and beautiful pictures which he presented are taken from fine paintings, statuary and points of interest in the life of Napoleon and Josephine," an attendee reported.[13]

Music lover Andrew Broaddus, owner of a freight company, was invited to bring his Victor Talking Machine and a collection of recordings to the Home for a special concert. Commercial music recording was still in its infancy, and these Civil War veterans marveled at the voice of famed tenor Enrico Caruso wafting from the wooden box that sat onstage at Duke Hall. "But it was when the clear, beautiful notes of a cornet rang out 'Dixie' that the veterans almost stood on their feet in rapture," according to the *Confederate Home Messenger*. "They almost imagined themselves again on the field of battle."[14]

Florence Barlow, too, was active in filling the calendar with amusements for the inmates; her bookkeeping responsibilities left plenty of time to line up lecturers and performers to appear in Duke Hall. Singers, ventriloquists, elocutionists, magicians, folklorists, bird callers, and dialecticians: all of them responded to Barlow's polite invitation to appear onstage at Duke Hall before an audience of Confederate veterans.

She wasn't shy about encouraging some of the Home's suppliers to provide entertainments for the inmates, either. The Ballard Flour Mills of Louisville arranged for a demonstration of motion pictures in front of a packed audience in Duke Hall, another display of twentieth-century technology that likely astounded the old vets.[15] (Later, in 1909, the board of trustees contacted the electric railway company asking permission to tap its lines to obtain sufficient power to install a movie projector in Duke Hall.)

But the acts that excited the inmates most were the vaudeville acts.

"My Dear Miss Barlow," vaudevillian Polk Miller wrote in the confident, expansive hand of a lifelong showman, "I write to tell you that the long cherished hope that I might go to Pewee Valley to entertain those dear old comrades in the Home is soon to be realized."[16]

Miller was a Confederate veteran from Virginia, a banjo virtuoso and dialect storyteller. He and his "Old South Quartette" traveled the country nine months a year, booked into a circuit of vaudeville theaters a week at a time, usually playing three shows a day, six days a week. Second-tier acts like Miller's could prove their value to a city's theater manager (and assure future bookings) by generating local publicity. A free performance for "those dear old comrades in the Home" would be certain to add press clippings to his scrapbook.

Miller was no second-tier act to the veterans when he played to a standing-room-only audience of inmates, family, and friends at L. Z. Duke Hall in January 1911. "More veterans were present than ever before on any similar occasion," according to Florence Barlow, to witness Polk Miller's two-hour show of yarns, jokes, and old-time music.[17]

Another favorite performer at the Home was "Captain Jack, the Poet Scout." Jack Crawford was a bigger-than-life Western showman, a contemporary (and minor competitor) of Buffalo Bill Cody. The Poet Scout's performance consisted of a recitation of his cowboy poems, interspersed with stories of the Wild West and (largely fictional) incidents from his life. "Captain Jack gave the veterans one of the most unique and delightful entertainments they have had," Florence Barlow reported.[18]

Inmates had the best seats—front and center—in L. Z. Duke Hall to see nationally known performers like Captain Jack, Polk Miller, and the Old Soldier Fiddlers. But these shows, and other entertainments arranged by Barlow and George, drew increasingly large numbers of Pewee Valley residents. Perhaps the greatest benefit of Lizzie Duke's gift of an assembly hall was the increasing involvement of neighbors in the daily life of the Home. Duke Hall served to open wide the institutional gates of the Kentucky Confederate Home to the residents of Pewee Valley.

In 1902, when trustees announced that the new Kentucky Confederate veterans' home would be established in Pewee Valley, local homeowners threw a fit. They threatened lawsuits to prevent having a state institution plopped in the midst of their quaint village.

At first, the Home was everything the quiet community feared: boisterous crowds jamming the area for ceremonial events, bad smells from an overworked sewage system, and drunken inmates passed out on local porches.

But five years later, by the time L. Z. Duke Hall was dedicated, those problems had largely disappeared. (It didn't hurt that the Home was a good economic neighbor, providing wages for up to twenty local residents and regular income for the coal distributor, the harness shop, the funeral home, and other local tradesmen.)[19]

Commandant George and Florence Barlow reached out to their Pewee Valley neighbors, inviting clubs and organizations to use Duke Hall for meetings, concerts, and dances. "The hall is at all times open to any one who will come to amuse or entertain the veterans," Florence Barlow wrote in the *Confederate Home Messenger*.

Mrs. Mary Craig Lawton, who kept a summer house near the Confederate Home, conducted drama classes for Pewee Valley youngsters. Barlow invited her to present the drama club's play for the community in L. Z. Duke Hall. Nannie Barbee, known for her dialect performances before clubs and organizations in Louisville, drew a large crowd of Pewee Valley residents for her impersonations when she came to Duke Hall for a show. Oldham County's Masonic lodge used the hall to stage its fundraising musicales. After cataloging the Home's donated books and shelving them in the hall balcony, Barlow opened a lending library for Pewee Valley residents. The young single women of Pewee Valley held their leap-year dance in Duke Hall, and local churches united to hold a common Sunday night prayer service there.[20]

Duke Hall thus became Pewee Valley's assembly room, theater, lecture hall, music room, movie house, party room, library, and chapel. At the same time, the Kentucky Confederate Home became an integral part of community life in Pewee Valley.

Children played on the Home's rolling lawn, and residents used the Home's drives and pathways to pass from one part of the village

John Boyd, Addie Graves, and a crowd of two thousand
Lost Cause adherents dedicated this statue in Lexington
Cemetery on Confederate Decoration Day, June 10, 1893.
A more melancholy memorial erected twenty years earlier
by the Ladies Memorial and Monument Association stands
in the background. (KUKAV-PA62M49-061, Lyle Family
Photographic Collection, PA62M49, Special Collections
and Digital Programs, University of Kentucky)

Confederate raider and Louisville attorney Bennett H. Young used his political skills, personal relationships, and inexhaustible energy to drive the creation of a Confederate home in Kentucky. He served as president of the Home's board of trustees for almost two decades. (Courtesy of the Kentucky Historical Society, accession #2000PH12.Young)

J. C. W. Beckham was a thirty-year-old public school principal when he became governor of Kentucky. The Boy Governor desperately needed the support of Kentucky's ex-Confederates to win reelection. (From *The Battle for Governor in Kentucky: Photographs of the Conflict* by Carl Dailey, 1900; courtesy of the Kentucky Historical Society)

Henrietta Morgan Duke, sister of legendary general John Hunt Morgan and wife of General Basil Duke, was the founding president of Kentucky's largest UDC chapter. Even Bennett Young was no match for this formidable woman. (PA96M3: KUKAV-PA96M3-152, Hunt-Morgan House Deposit photographs, University of Kentucky Archives)

OFFICE OF
SECRETARY
OF THE BOARD OF TRUSTEES
OF THE
"KENTUCKY CONFEDERATE HOME"

LOUISVILLE, KY. *Sept 17th* 1914

Mr John J. Jones

Winchester Ky

Dear Sir:

It affords me great pleasure to inform you that your application for admission to the "Kentucky Confederate Home" was favorably passed upon by the Executive Committee at their meeting held on *Sept 16th 1914.*

The home is now open for your reception at any time you may desire to enter, and you are hereby requested to present this letter to the Commandant, Col. Henry George, at the home in Pewee Valley, Kentucky, as your authority for admission.

Yours very truly,

Andrew M. Sea

Secretary.

(*Above*) The board of trustees reviewed every application and voted on whether to admit the veteran to the Home. Accepted veterans received formal letters from the secretary. (Courtesy of Susan Reedy)

(*Left*) Salem H. Ford, first superintendent of the Kentucky Confederate Home, was popular with inmates and employees but lasted fewer than five months on the job. (Salem Ford MSS A F 711a; courtesy of the Filson Historical Society, Louisville, Kentucky)

Inmates relax in the library of the Kentucky Confederate Home. The mismatched furniture was donated piecemeal by Kentucky UDC chapters. (Courtesy of the Kentucky Historical Society, accession #1987PH01.0364)

Commandant William O. Coleman (with black beard, standing left) required the inmates to wear formal uniforms to all meals in the dining hall of the Kentucky Confederate Home. (Courtesy of the Kentucky Historical Society, accession #1987PH01.0359)

(*Above*) Four distinguished visitors relax in the down-stairs parlor of the Kentucky Confederate Home. Left to right: trustee Charles L. Daughtry (who would later serve as commandant), Commandant William O. Coleman, former U.S. senator J. C. S. Blackburn, and Kentucky prison warden Eph Lillard. (Courtesy of the Kentucky Historical Society, accession #1987PH01.0358)

(*Right*) Wearing ribbons like this one, the women of the UDC escorted out-of-state visitors around the Home during the national United Confederate Veterans reunion held in Louisville in 1905. (From the United Daughters of the Confederacy Records, 1855–1999; courtesy of the Kentucky Historical Society)

RECEPTION COMMITTEE
—
KENTUCKY CONFEDERATE HOME

JUNE 15, 1905

(*Right*) New York socialite Mrs. L. Z. Duke was elegant in manner and dress, but there was a Kentucky naturalness about her that flattered the old men and reminded them of their rooster days. (From *Confederate Veteran*, courtesy of Jim Wheat)

Inmates gather for a photograph in front of the new L. Z. Duke Hall. Lizzie Duke, who donated money to build the entertainment hall for "her boys," built her fortune on Texas real estate and prostitution. (Courtesy of the Kentucky Historical Society, accession #1987PH01.0368)

John Pattee's Old Soldier Fiddlers was one of the touring vaudeville acts that played for veterans in Duke Hall at the Kentucky Confederate Home. (Courtesy of Linda Walcroft)

Commandant Henry George (standing, second from right) at a reunion in Graves County. He delighted in hearing the stories of other Confederate veterans. (KUKAV-PA65M158-05, Guide to the Confederate Veterans Reunion Photographic Collection, PA65M158, Special Collections and Digital Programs, University of Kentucky)

Tourists posing with the cannon on the lawn of the Kentucky Confederate Home. The cannon is probably a veteran of the Spanish-American War. (Courtesy of the Kentucky Historical Society, accession #1987PH01.0366)

The Kentucky Confederate Home was a tourist destination for veterans, history buffs, and even families on vacation. Many visitors bought picture postcards of the facility. (Author's collection)

Postcard of the Kentucky Confederate Home. (Courtesy of the Notre Dame Archives)

Inmates, visiting Confederate veterans, UDC members, Pewee Valley neighbors, and children gather on the lawn of the Kentucky Confederate Home, perhaps for one of the UDC's Cross of Honor ceremonies. (Courtesy of the Kentucky Historical Society, accession #1987PH01.0367)

True Daughter Charlotte Woodbury was one of the first women to take a formal management role in the operation of the Home when she was appointed to the Women's Advisory Board. Commandant Daughtry resented her meddling, but she devoted much of her life to the care of Confederate veterans. (ULPA 1994.18.4672, Herald Post Collection, 1994.18. Special Collections, University of Louisville)

Confederate Home.

Pewee Valley, Ky. *March 30th 1914*

Leave of Absence is hereby granted to *Jno. Y.*

Jones an inmate of the Confederate Home,

for *30* days, to take effect from *March 30th 1914*

Approved: *Henry George* Commandant.

President.

Any inmate who wished to leave the Home for an overnight stay was required to obtain permission from the commandant and a signed furlough slip. (Courtesy of Susan Reedy)

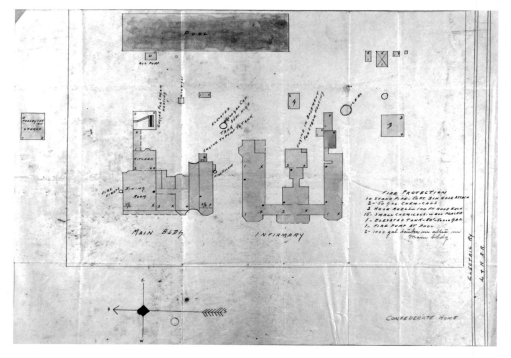

Insurance schematic showing the location of hoses, pumps, standpipes, extinguishers, and other firefighting equipment at the Home. On the evening of March 25, 1920, when a disastrous fire swept through the facility, much of the equipment was missing or inoperative. (Courtesy of the Kentucky Historical Society)

After a career that was "neither particularly conspicuous nor obscure," Baptist preacher Dr. Alexander N. White entered the Home in 1903 and lived there until it closed thirty-two years later. (ULPA 1994.18.0358, Herald Post Collection, 1994.18. Special Collections, University of Louisville)

Charlotte Woodbury (left), pictured with Governor and Mrs. "Happy" Chandler. Despite her political connections, she was unable to prevent the closing of the Kentucky Confederate Home. (ULPA 1994.18.1550, Herald Post Collection, 1994.18. Special Collections, University of Louisville)

to another. The Home regularly loaned chairs, tables, and cookware to local organizations for their own events, and fire equipment from the Home often responded to fires in the surrounding community. Bennett Young and the Home's trustees voted money to help maintain streets in the township.

Despite the early fears of vocal Pewee Valley homeowners, the Home and its hundreds of old veterans eventually became, as one resident described it, "just part of our neighborhood."[21]

As Duke Hall helped open the gates of the Home to the local community, so did it open the Home to the camps and chapters of Kentucky's UCV and UDC. To the delight and benefit of the inmates—men whose presence in the Home was due to their long-ago military service—L. Z. Duke Hall became a sort of Lost Cause clubhouse.

At its annual meeting on the day the hall was dedicated in 1907, the Kentucky Division of the United Confederate Veterans voted to hold all future state reunions among the inmates on the grounds of the Kentucky Confederate Home.[22] Reunion day came every autumn, when hundreds of veterans from UCV camps from around the state (along with their families and friends) descended on Pewee Valley for a day of reminiscing, tale-telling, food, music, a short business meeting, and plenty of Lost Cause oratory. Henry George saw to it that the Home looked its best: floors scrubbed, yard raked, and kitchen spick-and-span. Florence Barlow decorated Duke Hall with photos, flags, fresh greenery, and colorful bunting hung across the stage.

Other Confederate veterans' groups chose to meet in Duke Hall. The Orphan Brigade and Morgan's Men, as well as several other statewide veterans groups, held reunions at the Kentucky Confederate Home in the eight years after Duke Hall was completed.

At these events, the inmates were hosts as well as guests of honor. Dressed in fresh uniforms, they would meet arriving trains and escort visitors back to the Home. They welcomed guests and showed off the Home's grounds. Proud inmates posed for snapshots, bragged on the quality of food served in the kitchen, and told tall tales about the luxury and ease surrounding them. The old men of the Kentucky Confederate Home, lacking the society of relatives and friends, basked in the elegance of the respectable place in which they were fortunate enough to live.

"It was a happy thought to hold these reunions at the Home," Barlow mused. "It increases the interest in the institution, and at the same time brings pleasure and joy to those who are gathered here."[23]

Ex-Confederates who visited the Home began including their inmate comrades in activities outside the confines of the institution. Louisville's UCV camp paid for eighteen Orphan Brigade inmates to attend the brigade reunion there, and the state organization paid travel expenses for thirty inmates to attend the national UCV reunion in Little Rock in 1911.[24] Confederate veteran and political boss John "Colonel Johnny" Whallen invited inmates and Home employees for an outing at White City, an amusement park on the banks of the Ohio River near Louisville. Colonel Johnny arranged for private railcars to transport 115 inmates from Pewee Valley to the park, where they were met by a band and jugs of lemonade. The inmates were given the freedom of the park, where they could get on the thrill rides, peek into the sideshows, and marvel at the dancing elephant.[25]

Bennett Young had managed to avoid giving a formal oversight role to the Daughters of the Confederacy, but Florence Barlow opened the gates of the Home to any chapter that wanted to honor the inmates. Barlow's duties in the Home allowed her enough free time to serve as an energetic president of the Confederate Home chapter of the UDC. Representing the Confederate Home chapter and the Home itself, she solicited other UDC chapters to hold celebrations at Christmas, Thanksgiving, Lee's birthday, and Fourth of July in the new hall.

At Christmastime the UDC women hung presents on Christmas trees in the infirmary and the main building, then distributed them to inmates on Christmas morning. "We all got a small present: apples, oranges, candy, some gloves, handkerchiefs," inmate T. W. Duncan wrote his family. "I got a neck warmer. All the old fellows here were well pleased."[26]

Barlow enlisted other chapters to produce gala events for the residents. For a springtime Strawberry Festival, visiting UDC members set out thirty decorated tables on the Home's lawn and hung the trees with Japanese lanterns. Chapter members brought twenty-five cakes, twenty gallons of ice cream, and twenty-five gallons of fresh strawberries for the old men. A band and vocalist performed as the women delivered plate after plate of cake and berries to the inmates ("We were absolutely choked with strawberries," one veteran said later).[27]

The Albert Sidney Johnston Chapter of the UDC hosted the inmates at the annual Jeffersonian Barbeque at the Kentucky State Fair. A hundred uniformed inmates a day, along with their chaperones, boarded private railcars for the trip to the fairgrounds for the two-day barbeque. Singly, the veterans had no problem roaming the grounds to visit the speakers' stands or the racecourse. As a group, however, the inmates drew so much attention from the crowd of 20,000 Kentuckians that the UDC women had to rope off a section of their booth to protect the old men from the throng of well-wishers and the curious. Amazed at their celebrity, the veterans pocketed gifts of tobacco, coins, and baked goods before boarding the trains for their return to Pewee Valley.[28]

An affable Henry George and the industrious Florence Barlow used L. Z. Duke Hall to throw open the institutional gates of the Kentucky Confederate Home. They wove the Home into the religious and social fabric of Pewee Valley village life; they knitted the daily lives of Home inmates into the larger communities of the state's Confederate veterans camps and UDC chapters.

And with the open doors came visitors—plenty of visitors.

In its earliest days, the Home was not so much a destination for visitors as a drop-off point for charitable donations. Inmates' family members and friends came to Pewee Valley, but visiting hours were limited to one day a week for four hours. An overcrowded and smelly institution filled with hundreds of crotchety old men held little attraction for casual tourists, anyway.

Improvements to the main building, construction of the new infirmary, the addition of modern utilities, and the opening of Duke Hall made the Kentucky Confederate Home a more attractive destination for Kentuckians who wanted to see how their tax monies were being spent. The Home attracted an increasing number of Sunday drivers and tourists as well as relatives and friends.

More inmates in the Home meant more callers, and a guest register kept in one of the main parlors recorded increasing numbers of visitors every year. In 1911 the board of trustees altered the rules of the Home to expand visiting hours to three days a week, six hours a day, but Commandant Henry George welcomed callers on any day at any time.

In 1911 the nation marked the fiftieth anniversary of the beginning of its Civil War, and interest in the old veterans blossomed. The increasing use of motorcars (and road improvements) allowed tourists to visit the home for an afternoon, strolling the Home's parklike grounds or studying the wartime flags, firearms, swords, and photos that Florence Barlow had collected and mounted on the walls of Duke Hall. (Barlow arranged to have a series of picture postcards printed—twelve full-color views of the Home—and she sold them to tourists.)[29]

The Kentucky Confederate Home became a living museum of sorts, a twentieth-century repository of animate Lost Cause relics. Parents brought young children to shake the hands of men who had charged the valley of Stones River, ridden with Morgan's Raiders, or dug trenches in defense of Atlanta a half century before. Most inmates were thrilled to interact with tourists, to earn a few dimes posing for snapshots, to sell their wood carvings, or to recount their wartime exploits to a fresh audience. They thrived on the activity and attention.

In 1907 Bennett Young envisioned the Home's assembly hall as a chapel for the inmates' religious services; by 1915 L. Z. Duke Hall was a bustling community entertainment center for inmates, Pewee Valley residents, tourists, and Kentucky's ex-Confederate groups. Florence Barlow and Henry George did their best to keep a full schedule of activities in the hall, but one activity took precedence over all others: any other planned event was delayed, moved, or canceled to accommodate the funeral service of a Kentucky Confederate Home inmate.

Inmate John F. Hart reported to a friend in April 1908 that only four fellow inmates had passed away since the first of the year. "This is a remarkable showing," he wrote, "when it is remembered that there are nearly three hundred inmates whose ages range from 58 to 93 years, and most of them are more or less enfeebled by the weight of time."[30]

Despite improved medical care, better food, and a more cheerful environment, death was the inevitable outcome for every inmate. Ex-Confederates had pledged to "pay a decent respect to the remains and to the memory" of comrades who die, and Duke Hall became the Home's funeral parlor.

Local undertaker Milton A. Stoess supervised construction of a portable framework on which a coffin could rest during funeral services. The catafalque and black draperies were stored under the stage of Duke Hall, ready for use on short notice.

When T. J. Haynes, the inmate who carved and sold hardwood canes to Home visitors, died suddenly of heart failure in January 1910, his coffin lay in state on Stoess's bier, draped with a Confederate flag. Inmate comrades sat with him overnight in L. Z. Duke Hall until relatives could arrive from Fulton County and escort his body home for burial.

Death comes one at a time in small towns, and even Pewee Valley residents gathered at Duke Hall to mourn inmates who passed away at the Home. "Everyone in town went to the funerals," one resident recalled. "We had seen these men at the Home and around town. It was just respectful that we went to their funerals."[31]

Sixty-seven-year-old inmate Robert G. McCorkle had been an active member of Anchorage Presbyterian Church before entering the Home, and as long as he was able, he rode the electric car to Anchorage on Sunday to attend services there. Before he passed away in December 1909, he asked that his funeral service be held in Duke Hall among his comrades. McCorkle's flag-draped coffin rested on the bier at the front of the hall beneath portraits of Robert

E. Lee, Stonewall Jackson, John Hunt Morgan, and Mrs. L. Z. Duke as the pastor from Anchorage Presbyterian Church conducted the funeral service. The choir from McCorkle's church stood in the balcony, and a hundred uniformed inmates sat downstairs in neat rows before McCorkle's remains while Pewee Valley neighbors and a crowd of mourners from Anchorage and Louisville filled the side and rear seats.[32]

At the end of the service, the old inmates of the Kentucky Confederate Home formed up in columns outside Duke Hall and accompanied McCorkle's casket as they marched silently for a mile up Maple Street to the Confederate Cemetery. They remained silent and bareheaded in double line at the cemetery, breaking only after the closing prayer for a dipper of water, a bit of rest, and a high-spirited cakewalk down Maple Street to the Home.

The years following the opening of L. Z. Duke Hall were the Home's apple-pie years.

Henry George and Florence Barlow delighted in providing for the happiness of the men under their care. The Home was full to the point of being crowded, but the religious services, special entertainments, community events, and direct involvement with activities of the UCV and the UDC made it seem less so. For a while, the Home met the highest expectations of the men and women who organized it, built it, and operated it.

"I don't know what I would have done if it had not been for this Home," the Travelin' Tree Man wrote to his sister. "'Tis a Godsend to me."[33]

The Tree Man was admitted to the Home in December 1913.

The seventy-nine-year-old veteran's real name, the one recorded in the family Bible, was Taliaferro Walton Duncan. He signed his papers as "T. W. Duncan" and never used his first name, pronounced "Tolliver" in the Southern manner. Family and friends called him "Tol." For more than thirty years before arriving in Pewee Valley, he walked the lanes, avenues, paths, and pig trails from farmhouse to farmhouse, zigzagging across northern Kentucky to sell his fruit trees. People in twelve counties knew him as the Travelin' Tree Man.

From March to September the Tree Man called on country farms and cabins, taking orders for the apple, cherry, peach, pear, persimmon, and pawpaw varieties best suited to that part of the state. He took a small deposit and arranged for later delivery from a big Ohio grower. At planting time, Tol Duncan would arrive with the trees, shovel in hand and full of advice about spacing, pruning, watering, and controlling disease and rodents. The Travelin' Tree Man never married, never kept a regular house. He lived outdoors mostly, on the road or off the kindness of his customers.

By the time he came to the Home, the Travelin' Tree Man was worn out by a lifetime of labor without much money to show for it. "I am real weak. I give out doing nothing," he wrote in one of his first letters from Pewee Valley. But the rest of the letters he wrote to relatives during the year he lived there marvel at the unexpected luxuries.

"We old fellows here do not know when it is cold," he wrote during his first winter. "We don't have to go outdoors for anything. House is kept warm all the time with heaters."

He described the thrill of being fitted with his new Home uniform: "If I had to buy it, it would cost me about $14. I am real proud of it. I know it will last me a long time."

"I wish you could be here to see the beautiful roses and the other flowers that are blooming now," Tol Duncan told his sister. "This Home is an earthly Paradise."

Tol Duncan and the other inmates of the Confederate Home would enjoy that earthly paradise until tighter budgets and a looming world conflict once again closed the gates of the Home to the outside world.

Chapter 12

The Farmer and the Daughter

At the February 1919 meeting of the board of trustees, for the first time in the history of the Kentucky Confederate Home, three women representing the United Daughters of the Confederacy—Mrs. John L. Woodbury of Louisville, Mrs. Russell Mann of Paris, and Mrs. George R. Mastin of Lexington—sat with Home trustees at the boardroom table. If some trustees expected the officers of their new Ladies Advisory Committee to make trivial recommendations that could be easily sloughed off, Charlotte Osborne Woodbury would set them straight with her first report.

Midway through the meeting, Mrs. Woodbury was asked to speak.

After a sweet expression of gratitude for the privilege of attending the meeting, she reported that her committee had inspected the Home on several occasions in the previous month and found everything in perfect order, except for . . . just a few minor things.

"There was a shortage of linens," she said. The Kentucky UDC chapters have been notified, she added, and they were holding linen showers for the Home. New linens were already on their way to Pewee Valley.[1]

With new linen tended to, Woodbury added that there were "interior decorations and other necessary things" that needed maintenance, and she produced a list for new commandant Charles L. Daughtry. Unused to taking orders from women, Daughtry accepted the list without a word. To show how appreciative the women were for the honor of serving the board, Mrs. Woodbury continued, the Daughters would gladly inspect the Home every month. The women would compile monthly lists of problems relating to nutrition, sanitation, and health care, then notify the commandant so he might correct them.

Before relinquishing the floor, Charlotte Woodbury sweetly asked the board secretary to correct the minutes of the meeting. Board members were referring to her committee as the *"Ladies* Advisory Committee" when it had actually been voted into existence as the *"Women's* Advisory Committee."[2]

"I have been forced to suspend painting and other repairs on the building," Commandant Henry George reported to the board of trustees on July 31, 1915.

The Kentucky Confederate Home was a very different facility in 1915 than it was when it opened in 1902. In addition to the original old resort hotel, by 1915 there were also the sixty-room infirmary, Duke Hall, a three-story laundry building, several small outbuildings, and a cottage used to segregate inmates with tuberculosis. Someplace always needed painting, papering, patching, or plastering, and now there was not enough money to pay for repairs and maintenance.

By 1915 the Kentucky Confederate Home was experiencing a cash squeeze.

The Home had always operated at full capacity. Whatever it took—doubling or tripling men in rooms, building an infirmary, encouraging longer furloughs—there was always room for another needy ex-Confederate. More veterans entered the Home each year than left it—until 1914.

"You will observe there were six deaths more during the year than were admitted," Henry George told the trustees at the end of that year. The inmate population was beginning its inevitable decline.[3]

By 1914 the Kentucky Confederate Home supported a hefty overhead. More than half the cost of operating the Home—about $26,000—was spent on salaries, fuel, lighting, and other items of fixed expense necessary to keep the facility operating.

Aside from special appropriations, the Home depended for its income on the mandated annual payment: $175 per inmate residing in the Home. Fewer inmates meant less income. If the number of inmates continued to decline (which it certainly would) and the board of trustees was unable to slash the overhead expense, there would be less money available for food, clothing, drugs, laundry, repairs, and maintenance.

At first the trustees took no drastic action—perhaps waiting to see if the downward trend would continue—but they instructed Commandant Henry George to defer all but necessary repairs. They hired an engineer to look after the facility, a skilled and patient man from Anchorage named Alexander S. McFarlan; but McFarlan had his hands full making sure the heating, lighting, and water systems were operable. There was little time left over for renovation or maintenance.[4]

Bennett Young went to Frankfort to work his lobbying magic on the legislators once more. He informed them that the inmate population had turned the corner and was now decreasing, and asked that the sum of $42,000 per annum (or $3,500 per month) be appropriated regardless of the number of inmates. This amount was based on an average of the amount expended by the Home for the past three years.[5]

Young's proposal was extraordinary. Every other state-run institution in Kentucky—from prison to asylum—received funding based on its resident population; Young was asking the legislature to fund the Kentucky Confederate Home as its population dwindled to its last, single inmate.

Young was well aware of what he was requesting. The amount he was seeking, he said, was "absolutely essential to the very existence of the Home."

The Senate passed the appropriation bill just in time, for the Kentucky UDC chapters had been closing their purses to the Home and turning their attention elsewhere.

For fifty years, Kentuckians could refer among themselves to "The

War" knowing it was understood that they were talking about the War Between the States. But by 1916, with fighting in Europe and the possibility of American involvement, public attention shifted from America's past armed conflict to the coming war "Over There."

Kentucky women of the United Daughters of the Confederacy preserved a memory of wartime: human loss, economic hardship, terrifying vulnerability. The Paducah chapter endorsed an appeal by the National Peace Association, urging President Woodrow Wilson to cooperate with other neutral nations to end the conflict in Europe. Wilson promised peace even as America prepared for global war.[6]

As American involvement became inevitable, UDC chapters turned their attention and efforts to war relief and overseas charities.[7]

"Our work has been principally for the Red Cross," the Springfield chapter president reported in 1917. In Williamsburg, members met weekly, "making hospital garments and knitting the various supplies and articles needed for our fighting men." Another chapter collected and packed 1,359 garments—sweaters, socks, mufflers, wristlets, and bedshirts—for Belgian relief, "filling nine large packing cases." The same chapter contributed $1,300 to the local Red Cross chapter in one month alone, at the same time buying $250 in Liberty Bonds.[8]

"Much interest of individual members of the Kentucky Confederate Home chapter has been drawn into the work for the world-wide war," Florence Barlow reported.[9] In the spirit of patriotism, she could hardly refuse when a Red Cross unit asked to take over L. Z. Duke Hall to roll bandages, make surgical dressings, and assemble first-aid kits. "We have felt it would be out of place in these strenuous times to give entertainments for any purpose other than war relief," she said.[10]

The inmates would enjoy no more vaudeville shows, strawberry festivals, or musicales in Duke Hall for the duration.

During the Civil War, commissary officers called it "chasing the pig." It happened time after time during the war: two opposing armies, hundreds of thousands of men facing each other across a valley, waiting to go into battle. There were only so many hogs in the vicinity suitable for butchering into bacon and chops. The commissary officer who did the best job of "chasing the pig" had the better-fed army, and a better-fed army often meant greater success on the battlefield.

In 1917 the U.S. Army was chasing the pig with greenbacks, buying pork, flour, sugar, coffee, and other staples on the open market to feed hundreds of thousands of doughboys bivouacked at Camp Zachary Taylor in Louisville and nearby Camp Henry Knox. The Kentucky Confederate Home's grocery purveyor charged 16 cents a pound for bacon in 1913; by 1917 Army quartermasters had bid the price up to 30 cents a pound. A barrel of sugar that cost $17 in 1913 was going for $33 in 1917. Flour, laundry soap, brooms, and quinine tablets: all now double in price. After fifty years, the old Confederates were once again competing with the U.S. Army for provisions.[11]

A year earlier, Bennett Young lobbied for—and won—a fixed annual appropriation for the Home. Now, prices were rising faster than the inmates were dying. Young, John Leathers, William Milton, and Andrew Sea met in executive session at Leathers's Louisville office on August 29, 1917. Soaring grocery prices, along with higher overhead expense and decreased UDC support, were squeezing the Home in a financial vise, and the trustees had to find a way to ease the pressure.

They cut employee and management salaries by 10 percent. The executive committee voted to notify the state auditor that they would be selling off some dead trees on the property to a lumberman for $80, and they directed Commandant George to move all inmates out of the fourth floor of the main building, then cut off all light, heat, and access to that area. They authorized a contract for $1,000 to retrofit the furnace and reduce the amount of coal necessary to heat the buildings.

The committee's final action of the day, however, was more dramatic and more personal. "It was moved and carried that on the 9th of September only two meals per day be served for the present."[12]

The ex-Confederates had lost the pig chase.

The public first became aware of the two-meals-a-day plan a month later, when ex-Confederates and Daughters in Lexington called "an indignation meeting" to protest the reduction in rations. The Lexington Daughters painted a word picture of old men starving to death by the wagonload and threatened to appeal to legislators in Frankfort; a representative of the UCV camp announced their intention to ask for Bennett Young's resignation from the Home's board.[13]

Newspapers demanded answers: "If the old soldiers of Lexington know anything against the management, let them speak up. If those in charge have anything to say, let them say it. Let there be no hiding behind rhetorical statements."[14]

Sensing a dogfight, a *Louisville Herald* reporter phoned the Home and spoke to an unidentified inmate. The inmate acknowledged that the dining hall had cut back to two meals a day. The reporter then pressed to find whether the reduction in rations was causing a hardship. "I can't say as to that," the inmate hedged.[15]

Newspaper editors questioned the wisdom of the menu reduction. They accepted the financial difficulties that confronted the institution, but if "the food is inadequate to meet the demands of the body, some means should be found to effect a change immediately."[16]

Young did what any good attorney with an unpopular case might do: he piled up the facts that helped his case, then wrapped them in the flag. He and the board of trustees released a twenty-page statement to newspaper editors, complete with charts and affidavits, justifying the change.

The statement included a list of twenty-five "articles essential to living in the Home" and a comparison of the current prices and prices five years before. A two-meals-a-day menu was accompanied by the rhetorical question: "Do fifty percent of the people of this state . . . fare any better day by day than these aged soldiers?" The statement listed the European countries with "meatless days" and the American states observing "wheatless days," then asserted, "The Confederate Home has none." Dr. Rowan Pryor and four other physicians on his medical advisory board opined that the inmates were not being hurt by the reduction in rations.

Finally, Young added patriotism to his argument. "The old soldier inmates of the Home would do their bit in helping win the present world war by cutting out one meal a day," he said. "They would comply as far as possible with the appeal being made by President Wilson and Food Administrator Hoover for the conservation of foodstuffs for the duration of the war."[17]

Young had a point: the inmates of the Home—with their two meals a day, gas lighting, steam heat, telephone, and indoor bathrooms—were probably living better than many other Kentuckians. Almost overnight, public interest turned back to the war, and the issue died away.[18]

The death of Henry George's wife dragged away his ebullient spirit like a creature carrying off its kill. Martha Galloway George, his wife of forty-five years and the mother of his three children, died of breast cancer in 1916.

Henry George spent ten years as commandant of the Kentucky Confederate Home, the longest continuous employment he had ever enjoyed. He earned $1,200 a year, a comfortable salary for the time, and he and Martha made their home in a suite of rooms in the Home. He had his own table in the dining room for meals, and the Home matron made sure their rooms were clean and their laundry was done to perfection.

For a man who had navigated the treacherous shoals of elective politics for most of his life, his berth at the Home was a delight. Florence Barlow handled most of the paperwork; Henry George could spend time sharing stories with inmates and guests. He found time to dabble in local politics and write a book, a detailed history of four Kentucky Confederate regiments.[19]

But Martha's death dealt the good-natured man a blow he just couldn't shake off. "He pays but little attention to his duties," an inmate wrote, "his having lost his wife, becoming despondent from it."[20]

Fiercely loyal to her employer and friend, Florence Barlow stepped in to do much of his work ("Miss Barlow is virtually the superintendent," according to a visitor).[21] She and Henry George were of like minds about bringing joy and humor to the Home, but there was no more loud, honking laughter from the commandant.

During the financial problems, the closing of Duke Hall, and the two-meals-a-day controversy, Henry George lost weight and the color in his cheeks. Just before Thanksgiving 1917, thin and wan, he presented himself to the resident physician complaining of chest pains. Dr. Pryor sent him immediately to a hospital in Louisville.

Several days later, while convalescing at his son's home in Louisville, George sent a letter of resignation to Bennett Young. His health required that he should give up, at least for the present, his duties and responsibilities at the Kentucky Confederate Home.

The board was divided about how to treat George's resignation. Some trustees felt he really wasn't up to the job anymore; others wanted to give him time to recover from his physical and emotional problems. John Leathers came up with a compromise at their meeting on December 4, proposing that George be "granted an indefinite leave of absence with hope that in the near future he may be able to resume his duties." In the meantime, trustee Andrew M. Sea would become acting commandant, visiting the Home daily and discharging the duties of the commandant.[22]

It was a sound plan for about eighteen hours, until seventy-seven-year-old Sea, on a train to Pewee Valley the next morning to assume his duties, dropped dead of a heart attack.

Immediately on news of Sea's death, Bennett Young telegraphed another trustee, Charles L. Daughtry, at his farm in Bowling Green, asking him to take charge of the Home right away. Daughtry arrived the following day.

Charles Lawrence Daughtry was a smart man. He was efficient. He was a planner. Active in the Bowling Green UCV camp, he was

named to the Home's board of trustees in 1904 and reappointed after each term.

Daughtry's military record is a little sketchy (and he later took
pains to smooth over some of the wrinkles). He was fifteen years
old, living with his widowed mother near Gallatin, Tennessee,
when Union troops occupied the town. With some vague plan to
join the Confederate troops, he and another boy stole two Yankee
horses, "intending to go to the country for a short while." The boys
spent several weeks hiding in the woods around Gallatin, dodging
Union patrols, before falling in with a crew of out-of-uniform marauders. He eventually enlisted in John Hunt Morgan's Ninth Tennessee Cavalry and may have ridden on the Ohio raid. Either with
the marauders or with Morgan's raiders, Daughtry was captured
and sent to a prison camp under the name Charles Douglass. He
was exchanged in time to join General Basil Duke's retreat from
Richmond.[23]

After the war Daughtry and his mother moved north to the high
rolling hills near Bowling Green, where he took up farming. Daughtry was an early adherent of what came to be called "scientific
farming"—rotating and checkerboarding grain crops, experiment-
ing with seed types, cutting furrows to precise depths—and his high
yields made him a success. His success made him a self-proclaimed
expert.

Daughtry was short, barely over five feet tall, with all the inten-
sity of a man who never learned how to relax. He wore short-cropped
hair on his round head, and a fastidiously trimmed beard accentu-
ated his high cheekbones. He was assiduously self-educated, and he
could declaim on topics as diverse as water management or streetcar
operation. There was no problem that couldn't be solved, it seemed,
if only the listener would adopt Daughtry's solution.

During the 1903 harvest season, Daughtry left his wife, Mattie
Rose, alone on their Bowling Green farm while he attended to some
out-of-town business. No sooner had he left than the hired harvest
laborers struck, asking for more money before they would bring in
the wheat crop. Mattie Rose, described as "a club and society wom-

an," sent the workers on their way, changed into work clothes, and cut twenty acres of wheat before her husband returned. She knew how Charles Daughtry could be when things didn't go according to his plans.[24]

Over the years, Bennett Young had used Daughtry's self-assurance to investigate problematic situations at the Home. If a woman from the UDC reported that a Home matron had been rude, Daughtry would hold hearings and investigate; if a furnace were malfunctioning, Daughtry would build a case against the manufacturer. His reports were concise, conclusive, compulsively neat, and perfectly spelled.

When Young asked him to come to Pewee Valley to take over the Home, Charles Daughtry knew there were problems there and knew he had the solutions. He didn't need to be likable; he just needed to be smart, efficient, and tough.

Daughtry had three weeks to inspect the Home, inmates, and employees before his first board meeting as commandant on January 5, 1918. The problems facing the Home, he reported to the board members, were greater than he expected.

The Home itself was in deplorable condition—roofs were leaking, paper was peeling from the walls, and dry rot was ruining the floor beams. Too much maintenance had been deferred for too long, and the place was in danger of collapsing on the old men.

Discipline was nonexistent. Daughtry blamed Henry George for laxness, but it was more likely that the inmates were restive after being denied the use of Duke Hall and crowded together again as parts of the main building were shut down.

The employees were in revolt. After twelve years of Henry George's easygoing temperament, Florence Barlow and head matron Lela Henley weren't ready to accept Daughtry's more autocratic management style. Even more critically, engineer Alexander McFarlan had received another job offer, and without a raise he would be forced to leave. (The board quickly voted the talented man an extra $20 a month.)[25]

Daughtry drew up a plan for what needed to be taken care of, but Bennett Young had a bigger project to discuss. He needed Daughtry's toughness to help reverse the financial outlook at the Home. Despite deferring needed maintenance and reducing the number of meals, the Home was still operating at a deficit. Young and Daughtry would travel to Frankfort the following week in a plea to win yet another increase in the Home's appropriation. They would ask legislators to increase the Home's annual payment from $42,000 to a whopping $60,000.[26]

Incredibly, they succeeded.

After the state legislature passed the increased appropriation, Daughtry made ready to work on the maintenance, inmate, and employee problems he had identified. Before the acting commandant could pick up a hammer, however, Henry George wrote the board of trustees announcing his intention to return to work.

It was apparent to others that Henry George wasn't ready to return to work; he just needed someplace to go. The once-vigorous man was still frail and distracted. He wasn't happy living with his son in Louisville, and after twelve years in Pewee Valley he had no home or friends left in Graves County. As much as Bennett Young liked Henry George, Young knew that Charles Daughtry was the man who could whip things back into shape. So Young recommended a compassionate solution that would have unfortunate consequences for the Home.

The board wrote Henry George "to congratulate him on the improved condition of his health and express the appreciation of the board for the good and faithful services rendered in the past." The board requested that he remain on leave of absence, but "continue to occupy his room at the Home" and "to stay at the Home as much as he possibly can."[27]

Daughtry was thus forced to deal with the problems of the Home under the nose of the man who, in Daughtry's opinion, was responsible for the problems. And, because Henry George would continue to occupy the commandant's suite in the Kentucky Confederate Home, Daughtry was unable to move his wife to Pewee Valley.

Things were definitely not going according to plan for Acting Commandant Charles L. Daughtry.

On January 9, 1918, President Woodrow Wilson, a Democrat and a Southerner, announced his support of the Nineteenth Amendment to the U.S. Constitution, granting women the right to vote. The National Women's Party waged a vigorous campaign against anti-suffrage senators, and it was apparent after the fall elections that Congress would pass the constitutional amendment.

A month later, Bennett Young acquiesced to increasing political pressure by the Kentucky UDC and allowed them a formal voice in the management of the Kentucky Confederate Home.

The women of the UDC had been unwavering supporters of the Home from the time of its conception two decades earlier. They had given freely of their money, time, and hearts to foster a place of comfort, kindness, piety, and respect for the "blameless martyrs" who lived there. Time after time, however, the men of the UCV and the board of trustees had thwarted the women's desire for more oversight of the Home's management. Efficient management was men's business, they believed, best handled by men.

But times were changing. The Nineteenth Amendment (and changes in Kentucky statutes) gave women a voice at the ballot box and more equal standing in courts of law. At the same time, the men of the UCV and the Home trustees were aging, perhaps growing tired of their role as sole head of the ex-Confederate household. At the Kentucky Confederate Home—and at Confederate soldiers' homes elsewhere—the 1920s marked a time of greater administrative involvement by women.[28]

On December 27, 1918, John Leathers put before the board of trustees a proposal to establish an advisory committee of women; William A. Milton seconded the motion. Bennett Young said nothing, perhaps because he was eager to leave on a much-needed vacation to Florida.

The board approved a committee of seven women to advise on domestic issues of the Home. The committee was to recommend to the board such actions "as they deem wise and proper for the comfort and care of the inmates." Members of the committee would elect officers and send a representative to future board meetings. (The board also expressed hope that the committee would encourage UDC chapters to return their attention to the care and maintenance of the Home.)[29]

The Kentucky UDC president recommended a slate of seven women for the Women's Advisory Committee, all officers of the Covington, Paducah, Nicholasville, Lawrenceburg, Paris, Lexington, and Louisville chapters. When the seven women met, they elected as their president and spokesman the Daughter from Louisville, social activist Mrs. John L. Woodbury.

Years later—long after the mothers, wives, and sisters of Confederate veterans had passed away—women such as Charlotte Osborne Woodbury would be recognized as True Daughters. They were the biological daughters of Confederate veterans, true to the principles of the Lost Cause for which their fathers had fought.

Charlotte Osborne Woodbury was the biological daughter of Thomas Osborne, veteran of the Sixth Kentucky Infantry and part of the Orphan Brigade. And she was true to much more than her father's Lost Cause.

Thomas Osborne was a devout Baptist who demonstrated his faith through lifelong charity and progressive social work. His primary career was as a newspaperman—most notably as the *Louisville Courier-Journal*'s religion editor—and he founded *Baptist World*, the weekly political organ of that denomination, while an officer of the Baptist Conference of North America. Closer to home, his dedication was as much to the cause as to the denomination. He was active on the boards of the (largely Catholic) All Prayer Foundling Home, the Kentucky Institute for the Blind (with Bennett Young), and the Louisville Industrial School (with John Leathers). Osborne's ardent support of trade unionism likely caused some concern among his conservative friends, but he was convinced that free access to honest labor was a moral right for all men.[30]

Charlotte, Thomas Osborne's oldest daughter, grew up in a household that prized social work as an imperative of Christian belief. Mealtime prayers never failed to mention the needs of others and one's personal obligation to aid the disadvantaged. In the Osborne home, Charlotte learned that compassionate charity was best exhibited face to face, the result of personal involvement. As a child, she accompanied her father to board meetings, reading to a blind child or playing dolls with little girls who had no parents while her own father conducted the business of the institution. She was fifteen years old in 1888 when Thomas Osborne, John Leathers, and others organized Louisville's Confederate Association of Kentucky, and she witnessed how charity could change the lives of people like crippled Billy Beasley and his family.[31]

Charlotte Osborne graduated from Louisville Girls High School and tried her hand as a journalist before marrying John L. Woodbury, a somewhat effeminate up-and-coming corporate attorney in 1899. He spent the early years of their marriage polishing his career; she threw herself into club work; and the couple never got around to having children.

Beautiful though she may have appeared to her father and husband, Charlotte Woodbury wasn't particularly well equipped to skate through life on looks alone. She was a pale, doughy woman of five foot ten, with a manly figure. Her thin brown hair—long or bobbed—never behaved itself, and her face was slightly off kilter, with eye and mouth drooping lower on the left side than the right. But she had a beautiful heart, a determination to further progressive causes, and a deep, rolling voice that could boom like a pipe organ.

As a young married woman, Charlotte Woodbury joined the heritage groups—the UDC and the DAR—and was invited to membership in several of the social clubs.[32] But it was the work on behalf of Kentucky's children that most warmed her heart.

In 1906 she and eight others formed the Kentucky Child Labor Association (KCLA). Urban industrialization in Kentucky was drawing the children of poor families into factories for long hours at minuscule wages, and the KCLA was intended to expose the exploitation of children while lobbying for protective legislation. (Charlotte Woodbury nominated her father as acting president until the group's members could elect officers.)

Kentucky's rural children were at risk, too. Many parents lacked knowledge of basic nutrition and were condemning their children to scurvy, pellagra, beriberi, and other preventable diseases. Through the Kentucky Federation of Women's Clubs, Woodbury organized and ran the annual Baby Health Contest at the Kentucky State Fair. It proved an effective tool for getting healthful recipes and nutritional information into the hands of rural women who came to the fair in Louisville.[33]

She didn't neglect her heritage work, either. Charlotte Woodbury chartered Kentucky's first Children of the Confederacy chapter (and enlisted her father to serve on the board). Louisville Daughters elected her president of their chapter, and in 1911 she began the first of two terms as president of the statewide UDC organization. By 1917 Charlotte Woodbury had begun to make a name for herself with the national Democratic Party organization, and President Wilson appointed her to the Council of National Defense in 1917. News of the two-meal-a-day plan and reports of unsanitary conditions at the Kentucky Confederate Home drew her attention back to the veterans there.[34]

Charlotte Woodbury's brand of social activism echoed that of Bennett Young, and Young probably engineered her appointment to the Women's Advisory Committee in 1918. Woodbury was determined and headstrong in pursuit of a cause, but Young likely felt he could keep a tight rein on the daughter of his old friend Thomas Osborne.

As it turned out, Bennett Young never had a chance.

"As we look over the faces here today and see the changes that another year has wrought, candor compels us to admit that Death is moving with a busy and relentless hand," Bennett Young told a group of veterans at their state reunion. "His assault is slow and gradual, but he is a foe that will prove invincible, and in the end is sure to triumph."[35]

No one was more aware that the Confederate generation was passing away than America's best-known ex-Confederate.

By 1919 Bennett Henderson Young stood at the apex of the national United Confederate Veterans organization. After commanding Kentucky's state organization for a decade (and hosting two successful national reunions in Louisville), in 1910 he was elected commander of the Army of Tennessee Department, overseeing activities of UCV camps in seven states. Two years later he was elected commander-in-chief, head of a national organization consisting of 40,000 active Confederate veterans. Young won reelection for three more terms until his voluntary retirement in 1916. A grateful organization named him honorary commander-in-chief for life, the only UCV member to hold that title. He rarely missed a meeting of the Kentucky Confederate Home board of trustees, but he was America's premier Lost Cause orator, and he crisscrossed the country to speak at dedications, reunions, political rallies, and anniversary celebrations.[36]

At seventy-six years old, Bennett Young had every right to feel tired when he departed for a much-needed Florida vacation in January 1919. ("It is the only time in all of my life that I have ever felt real puny," he wrote a friend shortly before his departure.) Staying in Jacksonville, where he and the Haldeman families were planning a real estate development, he realized just how puny he was feeling.[37]

"Take me back to Kentucky," he told his wife. "The end is near. I want to die back in the old Bluegrass State."

Bennett Young's final hours were as much a breathless adventure as the rest of his life.[38]

On February 22, 1919, when Young's Florida doctor refused him permission to travel, Young called for a taxi to drive him to the railroad station in Jacksonville. "It means no chance, General!" the doctor shouted after him as the cab roared off into the night. At the train station, Young and his wife were joined by friends and another doctor. They found a private stateroom on a northbound express and wired Young's daughter in Atlanta that the train would arrive in that city in several hours.

Meanwhile, newspapers in Kentucky and throughout the South

began posting news of the famed veteran's death race to the Blue-grass State. Reporters waited with Young's daughter on the platform to see if Young was still alive when the train reached Atlanta.

He was, but barely. His grim-faced daughter boarded the private car, and the train sped off for Kentucky.

Telegrams sent during brief stops in Chattanooga and Knoxville provided details to Louisville newspapers and family friends of Young's last dash across the South. "I want to cross the river and bivouac with my gallant comrades who have gone before," he was quoted as saying, but newspapers also warned their readers that Young's "life was ebbing away fast."

When the train pulled into Louisville's Union Station after mid-night, Young was still clinging to life. A private ambulance, with po-lice escort, met him at the station and carried him to his home at 429 West Ormsby Avenue.

Bennett H. Young—Confederate raider, attorney, entrepreneur, writer, railroad man, historian, Sunday School superintendent, au-thor, orator, and primary organizer of the Kentucky Confederate Home—died the following afternoon, on February 23, 1919.[39]

Published articles marking Bennett Young's death made mention of the Kentucky Confederate Home, of course, but only as a single square in the much larger patchwork quilt that was his life. On paper, the Home was governed by the consensus of an appointed board op-erating according to parliamentary procedure. In fact, Bennett Young had run the Kentucky Confederate Home for eighteen years. With equal parts compassion, pragmatism, and prudence—and demon-strating an incredible attention to detail—he had directed the lives and activities of inmates, employees, and trustees.

His death triggered some unexpected changes.

If Commandant Charles L. Daughtry anticipated that he would be asked to fill Young's slot as president of the board of trustees, he was disappointed. The trustees never even nominated him. In-stead, Louisville attorney William A. Milton was elected president of the board, and Milton asked John Leathers to serve as board secretary.[40]

Even before Young's death, bookkeeper Florence Barlow had reached the end of her rope with Commandant Daughtry. She was slavishly dedicated to easygoing former commandant Henry George and the happiness of the inmates, but conflict with the more rigid and humorless Charles Daughtry grew to the point where Barlow angrily resigned (or was discharged) from the position she had held for almost fifteen years. Bennett Young had allowed her to keep her room in the Home until she could find other employment, but with Young's death all promises were left derelict. Over Leathers's and Milton's objections, Daughtry convinced the rest of the trustees to evict Barlow from the Home.[41] Bitter at Daughtry in particular, the aging bookkeeper moved to a friend's Pewee Valley carriage house, where she could stay in touch with her beloved inmates.

Henry George died of a heart attack several months after Young passed away, but Daughtry still didn't bring his wife to live at the Home. Instead, he employed a particularly unqualified woman from Brandenburg, twenty-one-year-old Imogene Nall, as bookkeeper and special assistant, and he installed her in the rooms vacated by Barlow and George ("I think she will have a refining influence on some of the men," Daughtry explained).[42]

Discipline problems among the inmates increased, and longtime employees seethed at the little farmer's high-handed manner, but Daughtry handled both with a firm hand. During his first two years at the Home, Daughtry recommended more inmate expulsions than Henry George had found necessary in twelve years. Meanwhile, long-serving resident physician Dr. Rowan B. Pryor left to enter private practice, and Daughtry also replaced several of the stewards and nurses. Home Matron Lela Henley expressed her objections to these changes in a manner that Daughtry privately considered insubordinate.[43]

In the wake of Bennett Young's death, the board of trustees seemed to become less involved in day-to-day management at the Home. Meeting minutes reflect a tentativeness regarding personnel decisions, a reluctance to question Commandant Daughtry.

Charlotte Woodbury and the Women's Advisory Committee, however, continued to conduct regular inspections of the Home and its inmates. The committee prepared its monthly lists of problems relating to nutrition, sanitation, and health care and held Daughtry accountable for resolving them. "I know I have made some mistakes," Daughtry admitted to the board, "but I insist that the mistakes were of the head and not of the heart."[44]

All these machinations were largely out of the public eye, however. The inmates failed to stir the interest of Kentuckians, who were then more interested in their returning doughboys than in Confederate veterans of a half-century before.

It would take a near tragedy to rekindle sympathy for the 180 inmates remaining at the Kentucky Confederate Home.

Chapter 13

The Trainer and the Undertaker

Inmate George C. Wells of Scott County was no outdoorsman, but he had cleared enough land, fired enough forges, and boiled enough coffee over enough open campfires in his eighty-five years to recognize wood smoke when he smelled it.

It was supper time at the Kentucky Confederate Home on Thursday evening, March 25, 1920, and George Wells was clomping his way toward the dining hall about as fast as an old man with one leg could ambulate. Midway along the second-floor verandah, however, Wells stopped, sniffed the air, and tried to figure out where that smoke was coming from.

Downstairs in the almost-full dining hall, Commandant Daughtry paced between the tables, making sure each of his men was wearing his bib before he signaled the servers to bring out the evening meal of mutton, string beans, sliced tomatoes, and stewed peaches. Daughtry stopped at the back of the hall, lifted his nose in the air, caught a whiff of smoke, and likely thought to have a word with the cook about burning the cornbread. He turned to step toward the kitchen, but his attention was drawn to the one-legged veteran hopping across the lobby toward the open doors of the dining room.

Red-faced and out of breath, George Wells burst into the hall.

The goddam place is burning down and we'd best get ourselves out!

Frowning at the profanity, Commandant Daughtry turned on his toes and quick-marched toward the one-legged man.[1]

Gusty March winds. A forty-year-old frame structure built of lumber now dry as kindling. Wood-burning stoves and flammable fuel

211

oil drums stacked in the basement. One hundred eighty old men—many bedridden—living in close quarters.

It was a recipe for disaster.

Fire protection was never a particularly high priority at the Kentucky Confederate Home; when the trustees discussed the matter, it was more often in terms of possible financial loss than loss of life. The executive committee kept fire insurance in place (as required by the state auditor) and reviewed the coverage from time to time. (Shortly after becoming secretary of the board of trustees in 1919, John Leathers recommended an additional $16,000 coverage be "placed on the Home in order to fully protect all our property.")[2]

A legislative appropriation in 1903 paid to equip the main building with some fire control and rescue equipment, including two 1,000-gallon wheeled water-pumping wagons. The commandant was instructed to post a fire watch each night, and an inmate was assigned to walk the hallways from lights-out until dawn, but there were no regular fire drills or strict rules for fire safety.

During his tenure, Commandant Henry George organized a fire brigade, a team of inmates who were trained to use the pump wagons and respond to any fire emergency at the Home or the surrounding community. The fire brigade proved its worth in 1908 when chimney sparks touched off a fire on the Home's infirmary roof. Like well-drilled infantrymen, the old veterans ran for the fire shed. Within minutes they were pumping water onto the burning roof, and the fire was completely extinguished by the time Crestwood volunteer firemen arrived. It was "a blaze which for a time threatened destruction of the Home, but was gotten under control by hard work on the part of the inmates," a newspaper reported.[3]

There was no fire brigade in 1917 when a small fire, probably caused by faulty wiring, broke out in one of the towers of the main building. Loungers on the lawn saw smoke and sounded the alarm. A hastily organized bucket brigade using water from a fourth-floor standpipe put down the fire before serious damage was done.[4]

Other institutions of the time weren't so lucky.

In 1915 fire consumed a four-story frame building in San Francisco, a Catholic girls' home, and only heroic action by the nuns saved thirty-six of the forty little girls who lived there.

A few years later, in Chicago, an unattended cookstove touched off a fire in an insane asylum, and flames swept through the dormitory before anyone could sound an alarm. Nineteen inmates died in their beds from burns and smoke inhalation.

A former resort hotel in Quebec, converted for use as a hospital, burned to the ground in 1916, despite its location less than two blocks from a metropolitan fire department. Fanned by a strong breeze, flames blew through the long hallways of the wood-frame building, cutting off patients in their rooms or trapping them in hallways. Recovery crews had difficulty separating the bodies of burned men from their twisted metal bedsprings, and hospital officials declared it fortunate that only twenty-five patients died in the hellish inferno.[5]

On March 25, 1920, hell came to visit the Kentucky Confederate Home.

Inmates later swore that a careless black handyman, out for a smoke on a rear porch in the northeast corner of the Home, started the fire. Whether it was the handyman or one of the inmates, it's likely that embers from a hand-rolled cigarette or a smoldering cigar butt or the live coal from a pipe bowl fell through the porch planks to the dry grass below. Lath latticework hid the dead grass from view, and the ember may have glowed there in the straw tufts for a while, fanned by a southerly breeze, as men walked overhead.

The supper bell rang shortly after 5:00 P.M.

When the grass finally ignited, it may have taken several minutes for the fire to touch off the lattice and burn its way up to the porch beams. Like seasoned firewood, the oak beams were dry, untreated, and ready to burn. Still hidden, the fire may have gnawed along the underside of several beams for a time, emitting little smoke, before poking upward to ignite the porch planks.

By the time one-legged George Wells, late to dinner and following his nose to the smoke smell, saw the fire, flames were burning across a fifteen-foot section of porch and were climbing the walls toward the upper floors.

A fire insurance map of the Home buildings and grounds, dating from about 1909, shows a facility equipped to protect itself from conflagration. Ten standpipes, each with fifty feet of two-inch hose attached, are spread throughout the main building and the infirmary, with fifteen Babcock chemical extinguishers mounted near the stairways of both buildings. Fire buckets, ladders, and two small pumpers are in the fire shed, along with two hose reels, each wound with a hundred feet of hose. The schematic shows a fire pump and hose next to a concrete water containment pool 150 feet to the rear of the Home and two 1,000-gallon water tanks in the attic of the main building. Big Kirker-Bender fire escapes—tall, sheet-metal escape slides like giant corkscrews—stand at either end of the building. Behind and between the main building and infirmary is an elevated wooden water tank, 50,000 gallons standing on legs eighty feet above the ground, with sufficient water and pressure to combat the fiercest blaze.

By 1920, however, most of the fire protection was gone.

The spiral escape slides still stood, but where there had been ten standpipes with outlets on each floor in 1909, many had been covered by paper, paneling, or plaster during periodic renovations in the years following. Most of the hoses were gone, too, borrowed for other purposes around the Home. If the chemical extinguishers were still in place, most were likely inoperable; there is no record of them being recharged, replaced, or serviced after 1915. Fire buckets were still stacked in a storage shed, but the wheeled pumpers were gone, cannibalized for parts or donated to the Crestwood Volunteer Fire Department. The concrete containment pool had cracked years before, and any water it held was green, sludgy, and full of debris. The attic and fourth floor of the main building had been sealed off for years, and it is unlikely that the storage tanks—if they still existed—were filled with water. There was no trained fire brigade; eighty-year-old inmates were too infirm to handle any equipment

214

that remained. The nearest fire equipment was at the town of Crestwood, five miles away.

On Thursday evening, March 25, 1920, a hundred old men were crowding into the dining hall for supper. Fifty-nine more, incapacitated due to age or illness, lay in the infirmary waiting for someone to bring their evening meal. Outside, the southerly March wind was stiffening as sunset approached, whipping the flames that were beginning to burn through the porch roof.

Only the elevated wooden water tank, 50,000 gallons standing on legs eighty feet above the ground, promised any protection against a major fire.

"We was playing checkers when George Wells let out that unearthly yell," Rufus Hawkins said. Hawkins, Jeb Jenkins, John Watkins, and others crowded around Wells to learn what the fuss was about.

Commandant Daughtry wasn't about to take the word of a panic-stricken old man that the building was afire, so he left the inmates in the dining hall and ran to see for himself. By then, flames were climbing the outside of the building, and wind was pushing flames into open windows on the second and third floors, setting curtains ablaze. After a quick look, Daughtry ran for his office on the south end of the main building.

The inmates in the dining hall, smelling smoke and beginning to grasp the situation, came to their feet and moved toward the doors. Like ants in a kicked-over mound, they scattered, some to look at the fire, some to the stairways upstairs, and others to doors leading outside.

Engineer Alexander S. McFarlan grabbed several of the dining servers and a half-dozen of the more able-bodied inmates, leading them outside to the old storage shed. He shouted orders to his makeshift crew, and in ten minutes they were spraying the fire with three hoses that McFarlan coupled to pipes on the big water tower.

McFarlan's fire brigade may have slowed progress of the fire outside the building, but the flames were already eating their way through the upper rooms. Dozens of inmates had left the dining hall to return to their rooms—some seeking a place of safety, others to rescue personal belongings—and the doors they opened allowed the wind to carry flames from room to room and down wide hallways. As smoke purled up the stairways, terrified old men ran aimlessly through doorways, in and out of the small upstairs rooms, slapping at hot cinders that fell on their shoulders, hair, and beards. Flame crawled across bedroom walls, feeding off layers of old paper. Strips of burning wallpaper fell to the floors, igniting hemp carpet runners.

Some of the inmates upstairs tried to fight the fire by swatting it with quilts, only to scatter fiery bits of cotton over the territory they were trying to save. Others grabbed for old photographs or special treasures, then tried to hightail it out of the burning building.[6]

Intending to make his escape down one of the spiral escape chutes, one inmate threw his overstuffed valise before him down the slide. The valise jammed the chute at the first corkscrew, rendering the slide useless for escape.[7]

From the northeast corner of the building where the fire started, the fire ate its way steadily southward through parlors, linen closets, and washrooms toward the commandant's office, where Charles L. Daughtry was frantically calling for help.

Smoke swirled around the ceiling of his office and flames drew nearer as Commandant Daughtry used the candlestick telephone on his desk to call for help.

Though Daughtry could ring his neighbors directly, calls outside Pewee Valley had to be placed through the local phone company's switchboard operator; the best operators remained calm and levelheaded in even the direst emergencies. (Several years before, Pewee Valley telephone operator Ida Ochsner, discovering a fire in her own building near the depot, remained at her second-floor switchboard, coolly calling fire departments and notifying neighbors, as smoke and flame boiled up the stairway toward her. Her job complete, Ida docked the plugs, groped her way to an open window, jumped onto a telephone pole, and slid down to safety.)[8] From her window at the exchange, the Pewee Valley operator could see smoke and embers rising from the Home. Unperturbed, she connected Daughtry to the fire departments in Crestwood, Louisville, Middletown, and La Grange. The departments assured him that help was on the way.

Flames reached Daughtry's office near the south end of the building by 6:15, forcing him to evacuate. He tucked the inmate register and a few other papers under his arm, then left the building for the last time.

The Pewee Valley telephone operator continued to place calls to neighbors who might help fight the fire, to local churches, and to City Hospital in Louisville, warning them to expect casualties.

Most of the neighbors didn't need a phone call to alert them: the twilight sky glowed blood-red as a rooster's comb from flames that were punching through the roof of the main building. They arrived by the dozens with buckets to help fight the fire. Engineer McFarlan recruited some to replace the tired inmates on his hose crew; others assisted veterans who were still stumbling out of the burning building with their rescued possessions. Father E. C. McAllister, rector of St. James's Episcopal Church, saw the fire from the front steps of his church and ran to the Home, arriving out of breath to offer whatever comfort he could provide to the living or the dying.

The intense heat of the fire forced the amateur firefighters away from the building as flames moved through the Home from north to south. Paint on the wood siding of the infirmary—forty feet south of the main building—bubbled in the heat.

Fifty-nine bedridden old men lay in the path of the inferno.

John T. Jones had seen his share of stable fires; he had worked around horses all his life. A native of Fayette County, he turned twenty-three years old in time to enlist in the Confederate army as a cavalryman in 1861. He served most of the war as a Morgan Man, returning to the saddle after a Federal bullet shattered his elbow, leaving him unable to extend his left arm completely for the rest of his life. After the war, Jones went to Bourbon County, earning his living as a horse trainer while he and his wife raised eight children.

The big ranches of Texas had a greater need for horse trainers than did postwar Kentucky, however, and Jones moved his family west. He—and later his sons—worked the stock farms of Texas, training native horses as cowboy mounts. Like R. J. Law up in Red River County, P. D. Self near Granbury, or Will Roberson out of Comanche, Confederate veteran John T. Jones spent the last years of the nineteenth century as an itinerant trainer, working a season or two at one ranch, then moving to another. His wife kept a house in Dallas, but when she died in 1904 Jones judged the range life too undependable for an old man and returned to the Bluegrass. He was admitted to the Kentucky Confederate Home in 1914.[9]

On the night of the fire, Jones was on the lawn of the Home when he heard that the infirmary building was in danger of catching fire. Like horses stabled in their stalls, fifty-nine men were trapped in small rooms, unable to make their own escape.

Jones had seen fire rage through a stable, the horses plunging and fighting for their freedom as the smoke rose and the flames neared—these were sights, sounds, and smells impossible to forget.

Eighty-two-year-old former horse trainer John T. Jones ran to the infirmary, intending to rescue as many of his fellow inmates as he could.

Official sunset that day came at 6:16, and by full dark the blaze could be seen for miles around. More residents arrived by the minute, and they could see in the dark that burning embers were floating high and northward on the wind, threatening to ignite neighboring properties. Someone called out that the nearby G. T. Blackley residence was aflame, and men with buckets ran toward that home.

Meanwhile, as inmates and volunteers carried the infirmary patients to safety, Father McAllister walked among the inmates and draped blankets over the shoulders of singed and shivering survivors. He sent some of his parishioners back to their homes to begin preparing food, and he asked a vestryman to open St. James to shelter the injured.

Trees surrounding the Home were bursting into flame from the heat, lighting the grounds like giant torches, as McFarlan directed

218

his hose crew to throw water on the smoking north end of the infirmary building. The brass nozzles on the three hoses were growing too hot to hold, and the tall wooden legs of the big water tower were beginning to smoke.

At seven o'clock, help arrived in the form of local undertaker Milton A. Stoess.

Crestwood's Volunteer Fire Department was the invention of Milton A. Stoess: he organized the department, paid for most of the equipment, garaged the pumpers in a shed behind his house, and wore the Fire Chief's hat. Locals joked that the fire department was a way for Stoess to get first call on victims for his funeral parlor. The joke was funny because everyone in Crestwood knew how untrue it was.

Milton Stoess had grown up in the area, having been born on a Henry County farm in 1869, the son of German immigrant farmers. Near the turn of the century, having apprenticed with a Henry County undertaker, Stoess opened his own funeral parlor in Crestwood, a bustling railroad town five miles from Pewee Valley.

He looked the part of a small-town undertaker—tall, thin, narrow-faced. His frugality with words, which most took as a sign of his compassion and interest, was more likely the result of growing up in a German-speaking household. In time, Stoess acquired a fine funeral carriage, an ornate coffin wagon, a stable of good horses, a silvered lowering device, and plenty of chairs. He became a conscientious civic citizen, helping to organize a private water company, serving as an elder at the Christian Church, and founding the volunteer fire department.

One of the first regular customers of the M. A. Stoess Funeral Home was the Kentucky Confederate Home. Day or night, Stoess would retrieve the body of a deceased inmate for embalming and burial in the Confederate Cemetery or shipment home. Driving his hearse and dressed in black suit and boiled white shirt, Milton Stoess was the subject of some morbid humor when he visited the Home. So it was a surprise, in a night full of surprises, when the cadaverous undertaker arrived at the Home behind the wheel of a makeshift automobile chemical pumper in leather fire hat and denim overalls.

However he was dressed, Stoess and the Crestwood fire company were needed to fight the flames that had begun to lick and twist
across the north wall of the infirmary building.

Along with the automobile chemical pumper, the Crestwood
volunteer crew arrived with two thousand–gallon horse-drawn
hand pumpers. After a hurried consultation, the taciturn fire chief
deployed his volunteers and equipment. He sent one team of hand
pumpers north to help with the fire at the Blackley home; the other
he assigned to the perimeter of the Home grounds to douse grass
fires and windblown embers. With a wary eye on the large water
tank looming above him, he directed the crew of his chemical
pumper toward the infirmary's north wing.

Welcome as the Crestwood equipment might be, the Kentucky
Confederate Home desperately needed more resources if the place
was to survive. As Stoess assigned his equipment to battle stations,
a motorized fire company from Louisville was crawling over dark
country roads toward Pewee Valley.

Fire Captain Fred Stephan of the Louisville Fire Department received Daughtry's alarm at 6:30 P.M. From his station on Louisville's
east side, Captain Stephan assembled a hose-and-chemical wagon, a
ladder truck, and one of Louisville's massive new American LaFrance
motor-driven, motor-pumping fire engines.[10]

Louisville had acquired its first motor-driven fire engine seven
years before (though it would take another decade to retire the last
of the fire horses), and in 1917 the fire department had bought the
first of its three American LaFrance motor-pumper behemoths. The
huge vehicle rode on wood-spoke wheels across an eighteen-foot
wheelbase and carried a thousand feet of two-and-a-half-inch standard fire hose. Its motorized rotary pump could throw 1,400 gallons
of water per minute, and it was a proven lifesaver for urban fires. But
the narrow solid rubber tires and the contraption's sheer size and
weight—more than two tons—slowed the powerful vehicle to a
crawl when it left paved city streets.

Thirty minutes after the first call, the firefighters rolled through
the town of St. Matthews, on the outskirts of Louisville and still not

halfway to Pewee Valley. For the remainder of the run, Captain Stephan, his fire company of nine men, and the much-needed fire equipment would creep along on dark and rutted dirt roads at less than twenty miles per hour.

As best John T. Jones could tell, the infirmary was finally empty of patients. Some of the horse trainer's old comrades were still being carried to shelter at the Episcopal church or Pewee Valley's Masonic Hall; others were stretched out on canvas litters, stunned to insensibility by the disaster unfolding before them and beginning to wonder who failed to make it out safely. Pewee Valley women circulated among the veterans, offering a warm meal or shelter in their homes.

Hundreds of onlookers milled around the Home grounds as Charles Daughtry and his secretary, Imogene Nall, frantically jotted notes and names, trying to compile a list of inmates who had escaped the fire and those who hadn't.

By 7:30 P.M. Milton Stoess had directed A. S. McFarlan to remove his small hoses from the tall water tower and connect them to working standpipes in the south and central wings of the infirmary. Crestwood's chemical pumper had, so far, managed to contain the fire to the north wing of the hospital, but flames jumped to the three-story laundry building behind the infirmary, and it appeared certain that that building would be lost.

There was still no sign of the Louisville fire equipment.

Volunteers were reporting to Stoess that the Blackley house was fully involved and the nearby Hudson residence was burning. Embers were igniting trees in the yard of writer Annie Fellows Johnson, endangering that house as well. A stiff wind still whipped the flames; glowing embers fell to the ground as far as three miles away.

The wooden legs of the large water tower, now surrounded by flame from the main building, infirmary, and laundry, began to blister and smoke.

At 7:45 P.M. onlookers heard the far-off clang of a fire bell and a hand-cranked siren. The Louisville fire company—a crew of professional firefighters with state-of-the-art equipment—was passing through Berrytown, still more than a mile from the Home.

The Louisville fire engines roared at near the pumper's maximum speed toward the Home entrance. Stiffly upright, Captain Stephan sat almost eight feet off the ground in the open cab of the big American LaFrance engine, leading the three-engine caravan.

Firelight reflected red and gold off the shiny engines as they began to turn into the gate at the bottom of the hill, and a cheer arose from the crowd.

The crowd went silent in mid-cheer, however, as the giant American LaFrance motor pumper slid sideways off the gravel driveway during its turn, tipped, then rolled over into a drainage ditch, wheels up and spinning.

Still stunned by the sight of the disabled fire engine, onlookers reacted to Milton Stoess's shouted warning and turned to see the tall water tower, its legs ablaze, crash slowly down onto the infirmary building.

With no pressure, water coming from the fire hoses slowed to a trickle. Then there was no water at all.

John Leathers picked his way unsteadily across the charred ground of the Kentucky Confederate Home, stepping over pieces of debris and half-burned belongings as he surveyed the damage.

It was 10:30 P.M. The moon was up, a thin sliver in the east, and smoldering tree trunks still popped and sizzled like bacon. Moonlight and ash turned the landscape the color of bone as, here and there, wisps of smoke rose from the ground like tiny white hairs on an old man's arm. Some firemen and volunteers hunted for hot spots in the debris; others coiled their hoses and returned their equipment to trucks. It had taken fifty men to right the once-shiny American LaFrance motor pumper and push the two-ton behemoth to the top of the hill; now it was trapped spoke-deep in mud, its red paint scratched and dirtied. A Louisville city work crew would try to dig it out come daylight.[11]

Leathers was tired. The hour was late; he was seventy-two years old and had long since lost the snap and dash he'd had to assist veterans like crippled Billy Beasley thirty-five years before. As then, however, he felt responsible for the care of his old comrades, so John Leathers, secretary of the Home's board of trustees and closest available member of the executive committee, had caught the evening electric car for Pewee Valley as soon as he heard news of the fire.

His first sight of the grounds told the old banker some of the bad news: the Kentucky Confederate Home was effectively destroyed. Of the main building—the elegant old Villa Ridge Inn, built in 1889 as a luxurious getaway for Kentucky's elite—nothing was left but a pile of char. The three-story laundry building, too, had burned to the ground, along with all its equipment. A small boiler house— no great loss, except for the pumps inside—was nothing but a pile of brick. Much of the three-story infirmary was blackened from smoke and soot-stain, and the roof was scorched from falling tree branches, but the greatest damage seemed limited to the north wing. The falling water tank had crushed an area that acted like a firebreak for the endangered hospital, buying enough time for Louisville's arriving hose crew to lay lines and draft water from a nearby pond. Thanks to McFarlan's inmate hose crew, Stoess's chemical pumper, the falling water tower, and the late-arriving Louisville firemen, two wings of the infirmary were relatively unscathed. Only Duke Hall was undamaged—water-soaked, but whole.

Leathers walked the grounds while Commandant Daughtry cross-checked lists for the names of veterans unaccounted for. Daughtry had formed the healthiest of the inmates into rows and ordered them to sit, cross-legged, on the soggy lawn. The men, some clutching a few salvaged possessions, watched bits of flame flicker through the rubble of what had been their home. Gusts of wind ruffled the singed beards and hair of the old veterans. Charlotte Woodbury had arrived from Louisville sometime during the evening. She and the president of the Confederate Home UDC chapter, Mrs. H. J. Stone, passed among the survivors, offering what comfort they could.

The Episcopal and Presbyterian churches were sheltering dozens of men; handfuls more were sleeping in private residences. Several inmates had already departed Pewee Valley with relatives who came to take them away, and more relatives had wired their intention to retrieve their kin. Twenty-six of the more feeble men were transported to Louisville's City Hospital in ambulances provided by the commander at Camp Zachary Taylor, and infirmary nurse Mary McAllen sent word to Daughtry that the inmates were resting comfortably.

By midnight Daughtry had compiled his list of survivors. He checked it twice before reporting to Leathers.

Not a man was missing. Every inmate was accounted for. No deaths. No serious injuries.

One hundred eighty old veterans had again beaten the odds in the roulette of war. Now, as during countless marches and on battlefields more than a half-century before, the old soldiers wondered: *Where will I sleep tonight? What will I eat? Where will I be tomorrow?*

The next day John Leathers and William A. Milton met newspaper reporters to answer questions about the fire.

"Gray and Khaki to Share Camp," the papers reported. Leathers said that insurance would pay to rebuild the Home, and he was attempting to acquire two barracks at Camp Zachary Taylor to house the men temporarily. "The old warriors and their new-found buddies of the First Division will be sharing camp life early next week," he told reporters.[12]

Leathers's announcement was premature on both counts.

Newspaper reporters interviewing the inmates reported that the old veterans had no desire to live among the young soldiers at Camp Taylor; they were anxious to get back together in Pewee Valley.[13]

Within days, Leathers and Milton were forced to backtrack.

"The men seemed to apprehend they might be subjected to military rule," Milton said. "While this is not at all likely, the Executive Committee felt the veterans should be kept where they want to remain."[14]

Leathers also discovered that the insurance proceeds would fall $15,000 short of returning the Home to its previous condition. He expressed the belief that persons "devoted to these few remnants of the South's once-proud armies will contribute privately to swell the fund for reconstructing the institution."[15]

The board of trustees met immediately to sort out insurance claims and organize a rebuilding program. It quickly became apparent that no significant private contributions would materialize, and the trustees were forced to use monies from the state's $5,000 monthly allotment to supplement rebuilding costs. Kentucky's UDC chapters pledged to provide new furnishings, but it was obvious to everyone that the new facility would be more institutional and less residential in appearance.[16]

Construction continued through the spring and summer, as inmates crowded into undamaged infirmary rooms and took meals under giant mess tents erected on the Home grounds.

"We have had a few mild cases of sickness during the month," Commandant Daughtry wrote in July, "probably caused by the heat and eating more new vegetables. Considering the conditions under which we are laboring, I think we are getting along remarkably well."[17]

In October 1920—eighteen years after the Home was dedicated and seven months after the fire that nearly destroyed it—the board of trustees announced that rebuilding was complete. Two wings of the infirmary had been repaired and new laundry and boiler buildings built. A kitchen and dining hall, with dormitory-like rooms above it, replaced the ruins of the old main building. Above the buildings stood a new 10,000-gallon water tank, this time built of steel and iron.[18]

No crowds assembled, no bunting was raised, no bands played to mark completion of the rebuilt Home.

The fire had destroyed something of the essence of the Kentucky Confederate Home, something that the carpenters, masons, plumbers, and painters couldn't rebuild.

The original building—the old Villa Ridge Inn—had resisted entry into the twentieth century. Its wide verandahs, furnished with comfortable rocking chairs and wooden gliders, spoke of the sociability and leisure of nineteenth-century life. The hand-carved millwork and intricate trim were lost remnants of a time before the age of assembly lines and mass production. The old building had been a living museum of sorts, with a cannon shot marking the dawn, a flag ceremony ending the day, and living relics of America's Civil War on hand to talk about the days of '61 to '65.

The fire had destroyed all that.

Rebuilt following the fire in a coarse style favorable to the lowest bidder and subject to the same bureaucratic oversight as every other state-run prison or asylum, the Kentucky Confederate Home had, by the 1920s, become a twentieth-century warehouse for nineteenth-century artifacts.

And some supporters began to question whether the Home should continue to exist at all.

Chapter 14

---·+·---

The Reverend and the Rector

On a day several months before the fire at the Kentucky Confederate Home, the Reverend Dr. Alexander N. White entered the room in which the charges against him were to be read and discussed. Having spent twenty years in his wheelchair, the inmate could maneuver expertly, and he rolled to the edge of the carpet in front of the table where members of the executive committee and his accuser, Commandant Daughtry, sat.

Daughtry handed a copy of the charges against the inmate to board president William A. Milton, who read them to the gathering. The commandant's rage was palpable in the words he had put to paper.

"Charges will be preferred against you for the abuse of management on various occasions," Daughtry had written. "Notably, when you charged that there was graft on the part of the management, which naturally includes the trustees as well as the inmates of the Home."

White listened, unconcerned, an expression of righteous grace on his face. As a minister of the Gospel, Reverend White had preached that a soft answer turneth away wrath.

This day, however, he brought more than a soft answer.

White asked that two men be admitted to the room. The first was his personal attorney, Judge R. T. Crowe; the other was the commonwealth attorney of Oldham County, there to deliver an order from the County Court enjoining the board of trustees from suspending Dr. White from the Home.[1]

That night in his room at the Home, Dr. White slept the sleep of the blameless. He had won the first skirmish of a bitter war of accusations and allegations that would cost public support and threaten the continued existence of the Kentucky Confederate Home.

Even before the shock of the fire and the stress of reconstruction, Commandant Charles L. Daughtry's behavior was becoming noticeably erratic.

Daughtry had accepted the job of commandant, expecting it to be the capstone of his career. Instead, he found himself whipsawed daily by the needs of crabby old men, whiny employees, sour ex-employees, and a board of trustees intent on involving itself in even the smallest decisions. In 1920 alone, Daughtry wrote a long, rambling letter to the trustees, explaining that he fired an infirmary nurse because she didn't act sufficiently grief-stricken at the death of Bennett Young; he also sent the board a list of inmates who were conspiring against him. Among other things, Daughtry resented the implied criticism of Charlotte Woodbury and her monthly list of "suggestions" from the Women's Advisory Committee. His frustration led him at times to lash out in rage at those around him and to engage in petty persecutions that might cost a veteran his place in the Home or an employee his job.[2]

Daughtry's paranoia may have become self-fulfilling; there were plenty of individuals ready to gossip about his actions at the time of the fire.

Pewee Valley resident Mrs. H. J. Stone watched Daughtry confront longtime Matron Lela Henley on the night of the Home fire. Daughtry was almost gleeful that the loss of the Home would cost Henley her job. "He told her there was no place for her, there was no work for her, no room for her and no money to pay her," Mrs. Stone reported. (William Milton later assured Mrs. Henley she was still on the payroll, but the upset woman packed up and left town rather than endure more verbal abuse from Daughtry.)[3]

A newspaper reporter witnessed Daughtry's breakdown at City Hospital the morning after the fire. The commandant arrived mid-morning, looking as if he had slept in his clothes. Seeing the inmates safe in hospital beds and knowing how close they had all come to perishing in the conflagration, Daughtry collapsed in deep, heaving sobs. Several of the decrepit old veterans left their beds to comfort the distraught commandant. It was understandable, perhaps, that an exhausted seventy-four-year-old man might become overly emotional in the aftermath of a near-disaster, but the public nature of his breakdown caused some to question his fitness for the job.[4]

The trustees were aware of Daughtry's increasingly mercurial behavior, but they chose to ignore it until rumors reached John Leathers about Daughtry and Imogene Nall, his twenty-one-year-old bookkeeper. In the wake of the fire, Daughtry had taken rooms for the two of them at a guesthouse. Pewee Valley neighbors, having seen the couple together, were saying that the relationship involved more than the business of the Home.

Milton and Leathers wasted no time convening a private hearing of the executive committee on April 9, 1920.

"Various rumors have been afloat, in many cases amounting to scandal, which involves the fair name and reputation of the Confederate Home," Leathers announced. He had asked several interested parties to make themselves available for testimony; they were waiting outside the boardroom.

"I have no personal knowledge whatever of any of these matters," Leathers continued. "I cannot conceive anyone . . . could start charges of this sort through any malicious intent or idle gossip. They must be actuated by good motives."

Six witnesses were called before the committee. Most of them described a spiteful commandant out of control, a pattern of petty persecutions and arbitrary withholding of meals and medicines. With their testimony completed, Leathers spoke again.

"We have not touched on the most important matter we came here to investigate," he said: "[accusations against] Daughtry of living a double life here at the institution. This is the vital question at issue."

None of the witnesses, however, could provide absolute, ironclad, firsthand evidence of impropriety between Daughtry and Nall.

"I think there are many other reasons why the man is not fitted to be Commandant of the institution, beside the charge that he is guilty of immoral conduct," one witness said.

Leathers didn't see it that way; his focus was on Daughtry and Nall, and it was frustrating that no one had a speck of hard evidence.

"If anyone has a charge to make, now is the time to speak and come up to tell us what you know," Leathers practically begged the group. "I want to get at the bottom of this."

After a grueling afternoon of testimony and discussion, no one could bring honorable evidence, and Leathers was forced to close the hearing, leaving himself and the others in an awkward position. Because there was no direct evidence supporting rumors of Daughtry's impropriety with the young woman who worked for him, the committee would be forced to defend Daughtry against his accusers.[5]

It was a position that would become increasingly uncomfortable.

Too many people were hearing too many stories about Daughtry's behavior toward inmates and employees for the matter to simply disappear.

During her visits to the Home, Charlotte Woodbury asked inmates about mistreatment. No one would say anything. Finally, an inmate she spent much time with in Pewee Valley called at the Woodbury residence. He spent the afternoon describing Daughtry's tyrannical actions.

"Why did you never tell me?" Woodbury asked the man. At that, Woodbury said, "He turned away and shook his head and his eyes filled with tears and said, 'I was afraid I'd lose my Home.'"

"I will see that this thing is sifted to the bottom," she promised.

Mrs. H. J. Stone was president of the reactivated Confederate Home chapter of the United Daughters of the Confederacy, and she visited the Home daily. She reported that the men "were afraid to make complaints, as those few who did were thrown out." Also, she said, "employees were turned out if they made complaint."

Mrs. Stone and her chapter members wrote the state UDC organization, telling women across the state "we are convinced that the present Commandant is unfit for the place." (Five months after Mrs. Stone's letter was circulated by the UDC, Daughtry prohibited inmates of the Home from attending her chapter's annual memorial service at Pewee Valley's Confederate Cemetery.)[6]

Oldham County attorney Judge R. T. Crowe was no fan of Daughtry's, either. Crowe had successfully defended the Reverend Alexander N. White against one of the commandant's vendettas and had made a point of getting to know White's fellow inmates and Home employees. He was blunt in his opinion to John Leathers: "I do believe that Colonel Daughtry is not temperamentally suited to be Commandant of the Home."

Florence Barlow, the Home bookkeeper who had worked with Henry George and was turned out of the Home following Bennett Young's death, kept up a steady correspondence with inmates, veterans across the state, and Pewee Valley residents. She painted Daughtry as a despot and a bully, and she wasn't shy about accusing the commandant of impropriety with his young employee.[7]

Daughtry was aware of the discontent swirling about him. He blamed a small group of disloyal employees and disgruntled inmates for spreading grievances. The ringleader, he believed, was wheelchair-bound Dr. Alexander N. White.

Alexander N. White had come to the Kentucky Confederate Home in 1903 after a ministerial career that, as he described it, "has not been an especially conspicuous one, yet it has not been an obscure one."

Born in Mississippi in 1844, White left his family farm in 1861, enlisting in the Forty-second Mississippi Infantry. After the war, he attended seminary, married, and moved to Kentucky in 1875 as minister of a small Baptist church in Paris. Within a year his wife, Jennie, had left him and returned to Mississippi.

Heaviness in the heart of man maketh it stoop, but a good word maketh it glad. White threw himself into reading, more Bible study, and preaching. Called to the Baptist church of Carlisle, he was an

enthusiastic minister who could parse a single Pauline sentence for
hours from the pulpit. Thin and loose-limbed, his blue eyes blazing
with the Holy Spirit, White had a clear sense of Christian right and
wrong, and was never too reserved to rejoice with the saints and cry
with the sinners.

He was a joiner, a tireless handshaker always on the lookout for
another soul to bring to Jesus. He was a member of the local Commercial Club and the county United Confederate Veterans camp.
(He avoided the secret societies, however, believing them to be clan-
destine organizations with un-Christian loyalties.)

The Reverend Dr. A. N. White was an exceptionally smart man;
too smart, perhaps, for small-town Baptists who wanted their Gospel
dispensed in easy-to-understand doses. Though inadvertent, White's
scholarly condescension and evangelical pushiness could become irritating to plainer people.

He spent the last two decades of the nineteenth century preaching at and organizing a series of increasingly smaller Baptist churches in central Kentucky, a career not especially conspicuous, but not
entirely obscure.

In 1896 a fall exacerbated an old war wound, and his left hip
crumbled like chalk.

"When misfortune overtook me and I became physically incapacitated for earning the means of support," he wrote, "I was compelled to ask for the protection and benefits of this Home."

Bespectacled Salem Ford welcomed him to the Home on January 12, 1903, ten weeks after it opened. Ford arranged for the crippled preacher to receive a new wood-and-wicker rolling chair, and
White—never one to be lost in the bitter smoke of regret—
embarked on the next stage of his ministerial career.

By 1920 A. N. White had lived in the Kentucky Confederate
Home for seventeen years, longer than any other inmate. White
wrote the petition to retain Salem Ford, the Home's first superintendent, but Commandant Coleman considered the old preacher
obstructive and impertinent (and one Home matron termed him "a
meddler, a sneak and a hypocrite"). Commandant Henry George,
however, enjoyed talking the Bible with White, and used him to

organize religious activities in the new Duke Hall, with White scheduling visiting ministers, selecting hymnals, and inviting evangelists. (White desperately wanted to be named chaplain of the Home, but Bennett Young resisted the idea.)[8]

Chaplain or not, White was doing the Lord's work among the old veterans of the Kentucky Confederate Home.

W. T. Calmes was a retired bachelor schoolteacher diagnosed with cancer shortly after arriving in the Home. He asked White to accompany him on trips to Louisville for treatment. Calmes had no close family, and White visited his sickroom daily, telling the invalid stories and helping Calmes with his final correspondence. At the end, Calmes greeted death holding White's hand and comforted by an assurance of everlasting life. The funeral of W. T. Calmes was one of dozens White preached in Duke Hall at the request of dying inmates.

White also wrote obituaries for his fellow inmates, providing dying men of little accomplishment the opportunity to look at their lives and organize their thoughts about what it all meant. In the obituaries he wrote, White would recount a veteran's war record on behalf of the Lost Cause, but it pleased him most to add that the subject "was no less loyal to his convictions as a soldier of Jesus Christ."[9]

Having outlasted three commandants and outlived three hundred inmates, White could be excused some officiousness. He could be high-handed with Home employees, and he had little patience for official ignorance or sloth. When caught in a transgression, he could affect the air of an injured innocent, a simple minister trying to do God's will.

Commandant Daughtry was certain that the sanctimonious preacher in the wheelchair was feeding tales of impropriety and mismanagement to Charlotte Woodbury, Mrs. Stone, Judge Crowe, and Florence Barlow. Shortly before the fire, he caught White helping inmate Pearce B. Bohannon draft an affidavit alleging mismanagement and brought charges, but White's attorney and a court order thwarted the expulsion.[10]

For more than a decade White had scheduled local ministers to preach weekly in the Home. Without giving notice to White, however, Daughtry started bringing in his own ministers to preach in the same place at the same time.

"On one occasion the Commandant brought in a preacher from Louisville after the services had begun," White later testified. Daughtry "interrupted the preacher present and the Louisville man preached."

The preacher who was interrupted that day—the man who witnessed Daughtry's petty action and White's humiliation—was the Reverend Father George W. Dow, new rector of St. James's Episcopal Church.[11]

Father Dow was new to the friendly little church across the road from the Home, new to Pewee Valley, and new to Kentucky. Father McAllister had retired from the ministry shortly after the Home fire, and George W. Dow took the pulpit in April 1921. Pewee Valley vestrymen had called Dow from a diocese in New York, where he had been an activist clergyman with a working-class parish.

Dow grew up in Lowell, Massachusetts, but he was hardly the cold codfish-and-molasses Yankee many expected him to be. Instead, he was a round, balding, jolly man who never rationed his smiles. Growing up, Dow had heard war stories from the many GAR members in Lowell, and he was intrigued to be living near 150 old Confederate veterans.

Shortly after Dow's arrival, White wheeled himself across the road from the Home to welcome the new pastor and his wife, and the fifty-three-year-old Episcopalian was charmed by the seventy-six-year-old wheelchair-bound Baptist minister from Mississippi. Both men were well read, and White especially appreciated the company of another educated theologian. Dow loved White's stories of Kentucky's different religious sects, particularly the energetic Primitive Baptists. (Episcopalians, Dow joked, were known as God's Frozen People.) The two men shared a special appreciation for the Book of Proverbs and would recite alternating verses until Dow's wife made them stop. ("A virtuous woman is a crown to her husband," White reminded Dow.)

In short order, the reverend and the rector became fast friends.

Dow soon began hearing disturbing stories from White, other inmates, and his parishioners about poor conditions and mistreatment in the Home. In his own visits to the Home, Dow observed inmates wearing ragged uniforms for want of a seamstress, sour milk served at mealtime, dirty bedpans left next to food trays on infirmary tables, and sick men left to moan in pain all night because there was no night nurse.

And he witnessed White's humiliation at the hands of the small-minded commandant.

Dow had seen his share of oppressive bosses and petty tyrants in the factories of his old parish, and he was rarely shocked by bad intentions. He quietly convened a meeting of others troubled by conditions at the Kentucky Confederate Home. For the first time, Daughtry's accusers gathered to build a dossier documenting the commandant's mismanagement, misdeeds, and neglect.

Aware that John Leathers's earlier hearing had exonerated Daughtry due to lack of direct evidence, the group chose to compile a document consisting only of sworn eyewitness testimony. Mrs. Stone, president of the Confederate Home UDC chapter, alleged that substandard food was served to inmates and only one meal a day was available on Sunday. Florence Barlow wrote of seeing Daughtry and his young bookkeeper together in compromising situations. Former Home physician Dr. Rowan B. Pryor documented cases of prescriptions ignored and special food orders disregarded. Matron Lela Henley described Daughtry's erratic behavior and her unwarranted discharge. Ten inmates, including White, prepared sworn affidavits with details of mistreatment and neglect. The dossier also cited several cases of inmates discharged from the Home without justification or due process.

Reminding himself that by truth and mercy is inequity purged, Father Dow wrote a covering letter and attached it to the dossier. "Local feeling toward the management is ready to break in a storm of scandal," he warned in his letter.[12]

The storm of scandal broke in May 1921 when Dow's cover letter and the dossier landed on Governor Edwin P. Morrow's desk and the front pages of Kentucky's newspapers.

Governor Morrow was a Coolidge Republican who owed nothing to the old ex-Confederate Democratic constituency, but he had run on a platform of amputating corruption and patronage from Kentucky's charitable and penal institutions. Statewide headlines triggered by the dossier—and perhaps a desire to demonstrate his commitment to nonpolitical boards of control—spurred Morrow to launch an investigation of the charges against Daughtry and the Kentucky Confederate Home. On June 7 he directed State Inspector and Examiner Henry E. James to delve into the allegations.[13]

For weeks, as Inspector James conducted his public investigation, newspaper columns were awash with charges, countercharges, claims, and lurid speculation. Florence Barlow, Mrs. Stone, and Father Dow repeated their charges to reporters; Dr. Pryor, Lela Henley, and other former employees were hounded for details of Daughtry's relationship with "a defenseless orphan girl" (as newspapers described the twenty-two-year-old Imogene Nall).[14] John Leathers mounted a public and resolute defense of the Home's board of trustees—never mentioning Daughtry by name.

Back in Frankfort, Inspector James was proving to be a ham-fisted investigator with the instincts of a street cop. He compiled a list of more than 119 names of everyone mentioned in either news accounts or the dossier (including seventy of the old inmates) and swore out subpoenas for each. Using sheriff's deputies from Jefferson and Oldham counties, he surprised his witnesses with visits at their residences and requests for immediate depositions. At the Home, James brought the old inmates one by one into a room and questioned them in front of a state attorney and Commandant Daughtry. Most of the witnesses were rattled and unprepared; the frightened inmates were suddenly deaf and blind to anything that may or may not have occurred around them.[15]

James's final report, forwarded to Governor Morrow in midsummer, did more to excoriate the accusers than answer the charges.

"It is a regrettable fact," James reported to the governor, "that a rebellion has sprung up among some eight or ten inmates of the

Home led by the Rev. A. N. White, an inmate, and a dozen or more discharged employees." He wrote off Dow and other Pewee Valley residents as "a half-dozen good and well-meaning, but deceived and misled people."

In the details of his report, however, James validated many of the claims of the original dossier.

The inspector admitted that, while the inmates received only one meal a day on Sunday and that he had earlier recommended otherwise, the inmates themselves were accepting of the situation and "they always took something to their rooms from the table at noon."

Yes, James wrote, there were some problems with the freshness of the food on the days he inspected the Home. "Relative to the milk, it is proper to say that the ice supply was so reduced for a few days that the milk could not at all times be kept sweet."

As for the charge that inmates had been discharged from the Home without notice or trial, Inspector James wrote, "The minutes of the Board of Trustees show, and the Board admits, that in some cases this charge is true."

James acknowledged that, at seventy-four years old, Daughtry naturally made errors and failed to use perfect tact or diplomacy, but "there is not sufficient proof to justify the charge that he is unkind, crabbed, partial or temperamentally unfit to manage an institution of this kind."

Only Imogene Nall remained white as a church lily. For all his subpoenas, depositions, and interrogations, Inspector James—like John Leathers before him—found no absolute, ironclad, firsthand evidence of a dalliance between Daughtry and Nall. ("Your good name remains untarnished and clean," Leathers wrote her after the report was released.)

Newspaper headline writers, apparently, never got beyond the report's one-page summary when they wrote: "Report Approves of Conduct of Home" and "Col. Daughtry Is Exonerated."

The matter should have ended there, but Father George W. Dow would not allow the reputation of his Confederate friend to be smeared.[16] "I cannot allow this published report to go unchallenged," he wrote in August to newspaper editors in Louisville, Frankfort, and Lexington.

Dow's righteous defense of "such a sweet-natured Christian gentleman as the Reverend Dr. A. N. White" was everything a friend could desire. The rector defended White's motives while questioning those of Inspector James. He described unsanitary conditions that still existed at the Home and faulted James for his intimidating interrogations of inmates at the Home. "There are many ways to make helpless men uncomfortable when they are not in the good graces of those in authority," he wrote.

The inspector's response to Dow's "vicious attack" appeared in newspapers three days later. "I am thoroughly convinced of his insincerity in his latest attack," James snarled. "Mr. Dow is either ignorant of the facts or seeks to purposely mislead or deceive the public."[17]

This sulfurous personal attack provoked still others to write in defense of Father Dow.

In the end, all the charges and countercharges, claims and counterclaims, finally faded away to nothing, as Kentuckians eventually grew sick of the story and the press wandered off in search of fresher meat.

Kentucky's memories of the candlelit days of sixty years before were fading like old photographs, and—except when drawn by stories of disaster or scandal—the public was becoming indifferent to the veterans of the Kentucky Confederate Home. It was the 1920s, and the state was hurtling into a frenetic decade of new roads, rural electrification, installment buying, general prosperity, and rampant optimism. In this modern age the bewhiskered old relics of America's Civil War were little but museum curios.

On May 30, 1923, twenty-four veterans from the Kentucky Confederate Home, accompanied by Commandant Daughtry, left Pewee Valley on the electric car to participate in Louisville's first Memorial Day observance for veterans of all American wars. Blue sky and sunshine promised a perfect day for the massive parade that was planned, down Broadway to ceremonies at the National Military Cemetery.[18]

Dress uniforms clean and creased, the ex-Confederates, having arrived at the rail station, formed in two lines for a short walk to the Armory, where they would join in the parade with Spanish War veterans, American Legionnaires, GAR members, Kentucky National Guardsmen, and other men who had borne arms in defense of their nation.

The Confederate veterans unfurled their colors—Stars and Stripes in the place of honor at the head of the right-hand column, Stars and Bars on the left—for the march up Fourth Street to the parade assembly point. Pedestrians on their way to the parade stopped to gawk at the old fellows and, recognizing who they were by their uniforms and banner, broke into applause and delighted cheers. Men removed straw boaters and waved them in the air. Office workers, drawn to open windows by the noise on the street, looked down and shouted encouragement. Children danced along behind the shuffling veterans as if following a circus parade, and the old men's steps grew crisp when Daughtry began calling cadence. Brass uniform buttons, polished with care the night before, gleamed in the sunlight as the proud old men marched several blocks up Fourth Street behind their side-by-side flags.[19]

John W. Hammond, chairman of the parade arrangements committee, intercepted Daughtry at the assembly area before the Confederate veterans could join the parade. Hammond told the ex-Confederates that the group would not be allowed to march in the main parade with the Confederate Stars and Bars.

"One God, one country, one flag," Hammond told them.

The inmates took a hurried vote; the result was unanimous. The Confederate veterans folded both flags and walked back to the station for an early return to Pewee Valley.

That short march along Fourth Street on Memorial Day 1923 was the last time veterans of the Kentucky Confederate Home would march in public under the folds of their old banner.

The allegations by Father George Dow, the Reverend Alexander White, and others sparked the meanest, most personal dispute in the history of the Kentucky Confederate Home, and the consequences touched almost everyone involved.

A few concerned citizens, including Florence Barlow and Father Dow, convinced state representative Mary Flannery to introduce legislation disbanding the Home's board of trustees. Fifty-three Pewee Valley residents, many of them Father Dow's parishioners, successfully petitioned other legislators to kill the bill.[20]

John H. Leathers was too smart to consider the rancor of recent years a verdict on the four decades—half his life—spent tending to the welfare of Confederate comrades, but the controversy and public bitterness must have sucked away the old banker's remaining energy. A lingering summer cold turned into pneumonia and took his life on June 29, 1923.[21]

Charles L. Daughtry, too, was hurt and weakened by three years of allegations and acrimony. He died on July 31, 1923, after a short illness. Confederate veterans escorted Daughtry's body to Bowling Green and his wife, who had never relocated to Pewee Valley with her husband. Imogene Nall did not attend the funeral service.[22]

Meeting after Daughtry's death, the board of trustees could find no Confederate veteran of sufficient stamina or health to manage the Home. On August 3, 1923, they turned to the Home's longtime engineer, fifty-five-year-old Alexander S. McFarlan, giving command of the Home for the first time to someone who had not been a Confederate veteran.[23]

McFarlan's appointment received scant notice outside Pewee Valley and the community of ex-Confederates, but the application for admission by a black man from Bourbon County threatened to put the Kentucky Confederate Home back on the front pages.

The issue of black Confederate veterans was an awkward one for ex-Confederates at the beginning of the twentieth century (and remains a contentious one even now).

While it is certain that some black men marched with, bivouacked with, and even fought with Confederate troops, those black men were—virtually without exception—doing so at the direction of the white men who enslaved them, a fact conveniently overlooked by most Southerners in the years after the war. Ignoring the issue of slavery, Lost Cause adherents painted the Civil War as a sectional conflict where strong-willed Southerners, wishing to retain their agrarian independence, vainly defended their homeland against Northern aggressors. The Lost Cause was a common cause for *all* Southerners, they said, and as proof they publicly (but only figuratively) embraced men of color who marched with the Southern Confederacy.

"Uncle Josh" was the property of the Robinson family of Warren County in 1862. He was returning from the mill with a sack of meal when a Confederate cavalry troop stopped to ask the black man if he wanted to go with them. "I threw the sack of meal over the fence and left," Josh told a reporter more than fifty years later. He joined the cavalrymen on the spot, he said, and spent the rest of the war caring for their horses.[24]

Early in the twentieth century, black men with stories similar to Josh Robinson's—former slaves who had dodged Federal lead on the battlefront—began showing up at reunions of Confederate veterans. (The Morganfield UCV camp paid Robinson's expenses to attend national reunions.) These black Confederates never appeared on UCV membership rolls and certainly didn't attend the (all-white) veterans' banquets or smokers, but some were issued uniforms and marched in reunion parades with their white "comrades." White Southerners often passed the hat at these events, collecting a tidy sum to send home with the black Confederates.

"Ten-Cent Bill" Yopp was one of the better known of the black Confederates. He was born a slave on the Yopp plantation in Laurens County, Georgia. At age seven he was given to the son of the family, who later became Captain Thomas M. Yopp of the Fourteenth Georgia Regiment. Bill accompanied his master into combat as a manservant, nursing the captain back to health after he was wounded at the Battle of Seven Pines. A tenant farmer after the war, Bill brought fresh fruits and vegetables to his old master, who had gone to live in Georgia's Confederate soldiers' home. "Ten-Cent Bill" earned his nickname at the home by running errands for the inmates, charging them at the flat rate of a dime apiece. When his master died in 1920, the Georgia trustees allowed Bill Yopp to stay on at the home as an employee.[25]

In August 1924 Commandant McFarlan received a letter asking for application forms for "William Pete, a colored Confederate soldier." Lot D. Young, respected veteran, author, and Bourbon County politico, was sponsoring Pete's application for admission to the Kentucky Confederate Home.[26]

Willie Pete had been an itinerant handyman around Bourbon County for longer than most people remembered. He claimed to have been a personal servant of General Joseph Wheeler, acting as Wheeler's stableboy and groom throughout the Civil War. The old black man attended reunions of the Morgan's Men Association, where he was accepted as "Wheeler's aged hostler."[27]

Lot D. Young, who occasionally employed Pete for odd jobs, helped the illiterate black man complete his admission application. "I am fully sensible of the effects of my recommendation to the Board in setting this precedent," Young wrote. "But I felt that Pete's history and his loyalty, with his good behavior, quitted him to this recognition."[28]

Allowing a black man to march with white men in a parade was one thing, but to allow a black man—Confederate veteran or not—to live in the Home and take his meals alongside white men was simply unacceptable in 1924 Kentucky. Yet turning away a needy ex-Confederate—even if he was a black man—might spark another round of bad publicity for the Home.

The board of trustees thus faced a dilemma at their September 3 meeting, but the pragmatic new commandant proposed an acceptable solution. In effect, Willie Pete would become an employee of the Home, sleeping and eating with the black employees.[29]

"This old darky could not be regularly admitted as our ex-Confederate soldiers," McFarlan explained to Young. "However, he can come to the Home and be accorded the comforts and benefits thereof. I will be able to give him odd jobs, feeling sure that he can do many little things about the Home."[30]

Young was pleased with McFarlan's plan and the progressivism it demonstrated. "You will find Pete an old-time obedient nigger, proud of his record as a Confederate and fond of the associations of these, his soldier friends," replied Young. "It is a fine tribute the

Board pays him, and the sentiment it implies is a refutation of insinuations sometimes indulged by prejudiced people."[31]

Willie Pete, the black Confederate, lived and worked at the Kentucky Confederate Home off and on for the next decade.

George W. Dow, rector of St. James Episcopal Church, may have had a different impression of progressivism in Pewee Valley. Father Dow had expected to serve the Pewee Valley parish for the rest of his career, but the vestry concluded that his activist style was perhaps not suited to that small community.

The rector and the Reverend Dr. White may have shared a few Proverbs ("They would have none of my counsel; they despised all my reproof") before Dow and his wife departed for a new parish in Maryland in 1924.[32]

Chapter 15

The Engineer and the Little Girl

For children growing up in Pewee Valley in the mid-1920s, the Kentucky Confederate Home grounds was a huge neighborhood playground: eight acres in the center of the village, sloping lawns crisscrossed with broad walkways, neat landscaping, tall trees, and well-tended buildings. During the warming days of spring, the grounds made a fine place for boys and girls to ride a bicycle, fly a kite, or just run for the sheer joy of running. On summer evenings, especially, there were always other children ready to put together a quick game of Red Rover or Swing the Statue before mothers began calling their families indoors for supper.

The old men didn't mind; they seemed to enjoy being outdoors, too. Some would stroll the grounds or walk to the depot on sunny days; others sat on metal chairs enjoying the warmth. Except for the occasional crazy one, the old men were always proper, seldom yelling at the children or telling them to be quiet.

Like benign gray ghosts, the veterans of the Kentucky Confederate Home floated around the children's world—always present but scarcely visible.

The children barely noticed that there were fewer and fewer of them as each year passed.[1]

Miss Evie Temple, secretary of the Kate M. Breckenridge Chapter, United Daughters of the Confederacy, wrote Commandant McFarlan on April 12, 1924, asking for a report on conditions at the Kentucky Confederate Home.

244

"At present there are seventy-eight veterans in the Home," Mc-
Farlan replied. "There are twenty-four men in the infirmary: none
are critically ill, a great many, however, are very feeble."[2]

The new commandant went on to tell Miss Temple of his efforts
to provide a respectable place for the inmates living there: "We strive
to make this a real home; their every reasonable want is provided for,
such as a variety of good wholesome food, good medical attention and
kind nursing. A Christian influence is always present. Religious services are held every Sunday afternoon, the pastors of different local
churches conducting the services.

"As a means of contributing to the happiness of the veterans," he
added, "we would suggest that you write each one a bright, cheerful
letter or card, as all of them enjoy getting mail."

McFarlan was furnishing decent care for the old veterans in his
charge, and cheery mail might provide some pleasant moments for
the aging inmates. But the Kentucky Confederate Home was becoming increasingly isolated from the world outside Pewee Valley.

By the mid-1920s the foundations that had supported the Kentucky
Confederate Home for more than two decades—energetic Confederate veterans' groups, a generous state government, and a sympathetic public—were beginning to crumble.

"The world gets more lonesome every year," Thomas Osborne
told the 1924 annual meeting of the Kentucky Division, United
Confederate Veterans. "Our great camp at Louisville once enrolled
over four hundred [members]." Osborne was one of only four remaining charter members of that camp.[3] Of 3,000 active Kentucky
UCV members in 1900, less than a tenth remained active in 1925.

State government continued to support the Kentucky Confederate Home with its regular appropriation, but without the same
enthusiasm as when thousands of ex-Confederates and their family
members could swing the outcome of a statewide election. Kentucky had introduced a modest pension program for its Confederate veterans and widows in 1912, and politicians in Frankfort
increasingly questioned why the state should continue to fund the
Pewee Valley Home instead of just pensioning the old men off with

a monthly check for $12. (Lawmakers increased the pension to $20 in 1928.)

By 1925 nine out of ten Kentuckians had been born after Lee's surrender. Cultural memory of the war remained strong in Kentucky, but the old men of the Civil War generation seemed impossibly distant to a generation growing up on radio, airmail, bobbed hair, and jazz. The newspaper-reading public might enjoy an occasional sentimental feature story about one of the Home's aging veterans, but there was little about the Home to sustain wide public interest.

Kentucky's UDC membership was flourishing, however, and Charlotte Woodbury still made her weekly visits to Pewee Valley on behalf of the Women's Advisory Committee. Despite their involvement in so many other state and national projects—completing the Jefferson Davis Monument in Hopkinsville; supporting needy Confederate widows; reviewing school curriculums; promoting books by Southern writers; compiling records of Great War veterans; lobbying for the Jefferson Davis Highway—the Daughters maintained their steadfast support of the living relics at the Home.

Residents of Pewee Valley could hardly ignore the institution in their midst. The Home's economic impact on the village had decreased as the inmate population declined, but the facility and the old inmates were a visible presence every day. They were "just part of our neighborhood," according to one resident.

Chief Engineer A. S. McFarlan had worked at the Home for fifteen years repairing boilers, patching leaky pipes, and maintaining the old structure using every tool in his kit. As commandant of the Kentucky Confederate Home during its final years, McFarlan would make good use of the Daughters and his Pewee Valley neighbors to help maintain an aging—and dwindling—population of old men.

On Commandant Daughtry's death, Alexander S. McFarlan was the default choice to assume charge of the Home. McFarlan was not a Confederate veteran and had no management experience to speak of, but he was in many ways the ideal man to manage the Home during its final years.

Born in Missouri three years after the end of the Civil War, Mc-Farlan came to Louisville in his twenties to play baseball for the Kentucky Colonels, an early National League team. The young baseballer found himself in an industrial city in the midst of a mechanical revolution, a time when men were learning to use electricity and petroleum products to drive machines more efficiently. McFarlan had little formal training, only general apprenticeships here and there, but he had a knack for getting disparate parts of a complicated system to work together. He acquired a series of increasingly higher-paying jobs as a mechanical engineer when the Home's board of trustees hired him in 1908 to maintain the expanding facility in Pewee Valley.

Some men may awake to the sound of birdsong and the smell of bacon frying in a skillet; Alexander S. McFarlan awoke with his ears attuned to the sound of a failing motor bearing and his nose sniffing for overheated lubricating oil. He was on call twenty-four hours a day, working indoors or out to coax hot water through a faulty heater or patch a hole in the roof of the old resort hotel. More than a handyman, the engineer devised systems for water, heat, electricity, and sewage, then installed the necessary equipment from blueprints he drew himself.

Busy as McFarlan was, he was an attentive family man. He and his wife raised their children in a rented home in nearby Crestwood, and despite his odd hours at work, he found time to play baseball with his two youngest sons. McFarlan was a hardy man, not particularly tall, but well muscled from working with sledges and pipe wrenches. He had a square, open face marked by a neat mustache, and his hair was plentiful, remaining dark even into his sixties. Children, particularly, remembered McFarlan's hands: huge mitts with scarred knuckles as big as walnuts. He was an easygoing man with the power to crush a brass doorknob in a single hand.

McFarlan knew every foot of pipe and every inch of wiring in the Home's buildings, but during his years as engineer he came to know more than the mechanical systems. Without involving himself in workplace politics and drama, he gauged the human forces at work in the Home and learned to read the management traits, good and bad, of the men he worked for. W. O. Coleman had been flummoxed by the paperwork necessary to do the job; he lost the confidence of the board of trustees because he couldn't organize his desk. Henry George managed a happy Home with regular entertainments and events, but George had never really been engaged in the daily operations of the institution. Charles L. Daughtry's egotism squandered the support of the Daughters and the Home's Pewee Valley neighbors.

When Commandant McFarlan moved his family to Pewee Valley, he had already created a mental blueprint for the respectable place he intended to provide the remaining inmates of the Kentucky Confederate Home.

"A. S. McFarlan and his wife," wrote inmate George W. Noble, "are as kind and as good to all the inmates as if they were their own children. We have a fine farm, laundry, bathing tubs and each man can wash and dress once a week. We have nothing to do but eat and sleep. If we are not able to wash ourselves, they furnish a man to wash us; and if we are unable to feed ourselves, they furnish a man to feed us."[4]

Though McFarlan was a generation younger than his charges, he set out like a dutiful father to provide a safe, comfortable, and entertaining domicile for the Home's inmates. Doing much of the work himself, he removed the trees ruined by fire and planted new ones, staked out flowerbeds, resurfaced walkways, and strung outdoor lights. He posted a night watchman, hired night nurses, and made sure a physician was never more than thirty minutes away.

Having observed his share of lazy and inattentive employees over the years, he sacked most of the stewards, laundresses, and helpers, replacing them with Pewee Valley residents he knew to be energetic and diligent. "Every employee is and must be kind and forbearing toward the inmates," he insisted. "Cheerful and courteous treatment is rigidly observed by the employees." To be certain his standards were met, he hired his wife as chief stewardess.[5]

Like Henry George, Commandant McFarlan recognized the importance of entertainments to the happiness of the old men in his care. "For amusements, motion picture shows are given twice a week; radio every day and night." He organized field trips for the veterans, often taking groups to "inspect" the operation of a Home vendor.

During one of those inspection tours, fifteen Home veterans visited Louisville Provision Company. The inmates—all but one in his eighties—shuffled through big refrigerated rooms watching workers assemble crates of bacon, butter, lard, and eggs for delivery. The old men graciously pronounced the operation "fit" before receiving a meal in the company lunchroom and returning on an early train to Pewee Valley.[6]

At the time of the trip—April 1925—eighty-five veterans remained in the Home.

Christmas Day 1925 had been spare of much celebration at the Home. Commandant McFarlan and his wife made sure there was a decorated tree in the vestibule, but few of the inmates had relatives to remember them with calls, cards, or gifts.

Charlotte Woodbury and seven other women of the Louisville UDC chapter arrived at the Home while the men were at lunch. Out of sight of the inmates, the women tied little gifts to the Christmas tree and placed wrapped packages under it.

A visitor described what happened when the men emerged from the mess hall: "Merriment, even hilarity, echoed through the halls of the old Home and in the hospital lobby, where the happy old men gathered around the large Christmas tree."

At ninety-four, H. R. Crabtree was the oldest inmate in the Home, and he left his room in the infirmary to join the celebration. George Tandy, who had turned eighty-six the day before, had to be convinced the event wasn't his birthday party. Eighty-one-year-old George Booze, a new arrival from Corbin, boasted that he was "the only man on the place who could dance the waltz and the schottische," then proceeded to demonstrate. Soon dozens of men were on their feet, each "trying to out-Charleston one another."

The UDC women handed out gifts of tobacco, socks, handkerchiefs, candy, and fruit while a photographer flashed pictures of the old men. The men shared tales of earlier Christmases, "while here and there a tear was brushed away with an impatient gesture as the name of a comrade, no longer among those present, was mentioned."[7]

Charlotte Woodbury and the other Daughters departed just before sunset, leaving behind the seventy-two remaining inmates of the Kentucky Confederate Home.

William and Ada Herdt's youngest daughter, Virginia, was born in 1921, and the little girl grew up surrounded by the old men in their gray uniforms. The Herdts operated Herdt Motor Company, building wagons and repairing engines, and Home inmates regularly stopped by the shop for an idle visit or to pick up a part for the commandant.

The little girl and her family saw inmates on the streets of Pewee Valley, too. Some of the old men carried jugs to an old spring wellhead, bottling the warm sulfurous water they believed might ease their aches; others hung around the depot, greeting arrivals and keeping up on the latest news. Occasionally a veteran came to the door of the Herdt's Tulip Avenue home, selling handmade brooms or craft items.

"The old veterans are very nice," George W. Noble said about his fellow inmates. "They have reared daughters and have great respect for the female. Some of the inmates here have been wealthy men and have loving wives, myself is one of them who once owned a nice home and a nice wife who was the mother of thirteen children. I owned a fine farm and raised them all, educated them to read and write."[8]

Seven-year-old Gin Herdt—no one called her "Virginia" except schoolteachers and preachers—didn't know or particularly care about the personal histories of the men of the Kentucky Confederate Home. The inmates were immaterial to the world inhabited by small-town children. However, like most of the others growing up in Pewee Valley, Gin knew most of the old veterans by sight, if not by name: Mr. Kern was short and barrel-chested; he sometimes delivered the mail around Pewee Valley. Mr. Shearin was tall and skinny with thick round spectacles that made him look like an owl. Mr. White rolled along the walkways in his wheelchair, but he was going blind and mostly stayed on the porch unless he had someone to push him. Mr. Herring had snow-white hair and a bowlegged walk; Mr. Metcalfe's mouth was caved in from lack of teeth. Mr. Kemper always had money, and he sometimes gave nickels to children who ran errands for him.

Every house in Pewee Valley, it seemed, had its favorite veteran, an inmate who might show up to do a little gardening or a few odd jobs for tobacco money. The Herdts had John Thomas Laws of Louisville, a ninety-year-old former sergeant of the Second Kentucky Infantry, Company K.

"'Uncle Tom,' we all called him," Gin recalled. "He was like a member of the family."

Tall, gentle Uncle Tom Laws spent time in the Herdt home doing errands and, now and then, babysitting Gin and the other Herdt children while their parents took some time away. Tom also helped at the wagon shop, occasionally driving into Louisville with William to deliver a job or pick up a part.

The Herdts visited Tom at the Home, too. "Momma would bake him a cake on his birthday, and we'd take it over to him," Gin said.

Gin remembered the last time that she and her family walked from their house to the Kentucky Confederate Home to see Uncle Tom. She sat with her father, sister, and brother on folding chairs in Duke Hall while her mother played piano for the funeral service of Confederate Sergeant John Thomas Laws, who fought at Fort Donelson, Stones River, Jackson, Chickamauga, Mission Ridge, Resaca, Dallas, Peachtree Creek, and Jonesboro.

The little girl grew up in a neighborhood surrounded by old men who, sixty years before, had left their homes and families to fight for a cause that was lost before the first battle was joined. By August 31, 1928, forty-six of them remained in the Home.[9]

The winter of 1928–1929 was a hard one for the inmates of the Kentucky Confederate Home; a particularly virulent strain of flu took the lives of nineteen veterans in twenty-two days.[10]

In the midst of the epidemic, State Inspector John N. Ashcraft arrived in Pewee Valley to audit the institution. Ashcraft made no recommendations in his report, but stated as fact what everyone knew: "So long as the Home is maintained in these large quarters with a capacity for around 250 persons, the overhead expense and per capita cost of taking care of these veterans is bound to be large."

On February 11, 1929, the day Ashcraft forwarded his report to the governor, thirty-five veterans remained in the Home.[11]

"When a man dies he is dressed in a nice Confederate soldier's uniform, put in a nice coffin and his funeral preached; buried in the Confederate Soldier's Cemetery one mile from the Home and tombstones put at the head of his grave," inmate George W. Noble wrote in 1928.[12]

Commandant McFarlan was conscientious about his paperwork, and the imminent death of an inmate triggered a process unique to the Home. First, McFarlan would consult his death book, a ledger entitled "Information about Inmates Requests and Kinfolks." In it, an inmate might list his next of kin, contact information, burial instructions, or special requests. Veteran D. B. Bennett wanted his body returned to Dawson Springs for burial, and he entered the name of a funeral director there. Lavan M. Shearin asked that someone telephone his daughter in Indianapolis in the event of his death, but if "at night, send telegram." Ninety-two-year-old widower M. N. Webster wanted "no kind of dope administered when sick." George Booze had built up an account in Pewee Valley State Bank sufficient to ship his body back to Corbin for burial, and he left a note in the death book authorizing McFarlan to withdraw the money for that purpose.[13]

"The doctor has reported to us that Mr. George C. Wells is failing very fast and in all probability will not last long," McFarlan wrote to the veteran's daughter in August 1925, following Wells's request in the death book. "At his age, you understand a change may come for the worse at any time."[14]

When an inmate passed away and the family was notified, Mc-

Farlan called undertaker Milton Stoess in Crestwood. McFarlan had negotiated a package price for veterans who were to be buried in the Confederate Cemetery. For $14, the funeral director would retrieve the body, wash it, dress it in a fresh uniform supplied by the Home, place it in a wood coffin for the funeral service in Duke Hall, then transport it to the cemetery and inter it there.[15]

By the 1920s Stoess was using an automotive hearse to carry coffins from the Home to the cemetery. A few inmate mourners might ride in the funeral car, but most, wearing dress uniforms, would march in silence, bareheaded under the old banners, north on Maple Avenue.

Little Gin Herdt and other Pewee Valley residents would watch the solemn procession to the cemetery, then later see a handful of old men walk back down Maple to the Home, yipping and yawping like schoolboys, full of the giddy and guilty exhilaration of having outlived another comrade.

With the funeral of George L. Tandy on May 23, 1929, twenty-nine veterans remained in the Home.[16]

Political vultures were circling Pewee Valley, but the women of Kentucky's UDC chapters were not about to see their hallowed Home carried away.

At its state convention in October 1929, the UDC voted to press for legislation converting the Kentucky Confederate Home into an institution for the care of Kentucky veterans of the Spanish-American War and the recent World War. Such action, they pointed out, would avert sending the remaining Confederate veterans to poorhouses and at the same time would inaugurate a service for needy veterans of other wars. The women had helped pay for the Home, they supported it with their hearts and purses, and they were determined to keep it open as a Lost Cause memorial. The state UDC president pledged to field a full-time delegation of Daughters at the next legislative session.[17]

Politicos cast covetous eyes on the plum Pewee Valley property—forty-two prime acres of land, including a working farm and like-new institutional buildings—even as the remaining veterans passed away. The state examiner noted, "The grounds and buildings now used for the Home could be used to relieve the congested condition at some other institution."[18]

Directors of the state's eleemosynary facilities began lining up support with the governor's office and favored legislators, hoping to inherit the buildings and grounds. Kentucky's major newspapers, which had once consistently editorialized on behalf of the veterans, now ran columns speculating on who should inherit the property and what should become of the ex-Confederates remaining there.[19]

Governor Flem D. Sampson had little interest in the Kentucky Confederate Home. At the beginning of the 1930 legislative session, he appointed two dead men to the board of trustees, a mistake discovered only after the dead men were confirmed as trustees and telegrams sent to inform them of their appointment.[20]

There were few remaining veterans able to serve on the board of trustees, so by 1930 the board was made up of an equal number of veterans and sons of veterans. Governor Sampson appointed Charles F. Leathers, son of late Louisville banker John H. Leathers, to the board in 1930. Veterans who founded and operated the Kentucky Confederate Home in its early years—the original trustees—managed a home for the benefit of former comrades, often men whom they had commanded in combat, many of whom they had known personally for decades. The new generation of trustees—the sons of veterans—sought merely the orderly disposition of affairs, respectful guardianship of old men who were more like distant uncles than comrades.

Commandant McFarlan's competence earned him free rein from the passive board. Remaining ex-Confederates, the Daughters, and inmates lauded his operation of the Home; best of all, he ended each year with a slight budget surplus. Over the years the board raised McFarlan's salary to $200 a month, and his wife earned an additional $60 for her duties as matron. In addition, McFarlan's oldest son was on the payroll at $120 a month as engineer, providing the commandant's household a comfortable $4,560 annual income.[21]

The Daughters failed in their attempt to expand the role of the Kentucky Confederate Home during the 1930 legislative session, but their furious lobbying managed to defeat several bills that would have abolished the Home.[22]

By October 1931, as the Daughters debated their strategy for another legislative session and the effects of the Great Depression deepened in Kentucky, twelve veterans remained in the Home.[23]

The United States experienced financial panics in 1873, 1893, and 1907, but never had all areas of the country and all classes of people been affected as deeply and as personally as during the Great Depression of the 1930s.

Kentucky tax revenues were shrinking as farm prices bottomed out and mines shut down. Factories slowed their output; fewer boats visited Kentucky river ports. By 1933 one fourth of Kentucky's banks had failed. (George Booze lost most of the money he had banked for his burial.)

The Home's trustees reacted to worsening economic news by reducing the number of employees and cutting the salaries of the remaining employees by 10 percent, but expenses could be curtailed only so much.[24] Sentiment in Frankfort seemed to be in favor of closing the Home, especially when the state examiner reported it was costing more than $1,000 a year per resident to house and feed the ex-Confederates in Pewee Valley (this at a time when many Kentucky families were struggling by on a third of that amount).[25]

"As a taxpayer, may I suggest that there seems to be a glaring waste of state funds" on the Home in Pewee Valley, one reader wrote to the editor of the *Louisville Courier-Journal*. The writer's father was a Confederate veteran, and he fully appreciated the tender feelings the Home carried with it, but the fact that it required twelve employees to care for eleven inmates "in itself seems to be a strong impetus toward closing this institution."[26]

Charlotte Woodbury and the women of the UDC flooded legislative offices with letters of their own. While they acknowledged the high cost of caring for the inmates, they again proposed that other dependents of the state be placed there with the veterans. ("It has been suggested that the crippled children be moved to this beautiful country place," Woodbury wrote.)[27] The Daughters were still a political force to be reckoned with, and they enlisted members of the Daughters of the American Republic and the Kentucky Federation of Women's Clubs to join their lobbying effort. Camping out in Senate offices, women described the hardships to be visited on the old veterans if they were to be moved "to new, unfamiliar and lonely surroundings."

Incredibly, the UDC prevailed. Though the State Budget Commission supported closing the Home and moving the veterans elsewhere, and a state assemblyman proposed legislation to that effect, the measure failed. When the legislature passed several temporary funding bills to sustain the Home through 1934, the national UDC organization lauded Kentucky's Daughters for having "saved the Confederate Home," noting that lawmakers "yielded to patriotic and sentimental pleas not to evict the aged men."[28]

On July 6, 1932, when the state examiner urged new Governor Ruby Laffoon to take executive action to close it, nine veterans remained in the Home.[29]

"The Home as an institution may now be likened with those it fosters," Commandant McFarlan acknowledged in September 1933. "It is nearing the end of its existence and there is no doubt of the next General Assembly making some provision regarding the Home and the future care of the few inmates now in it."[30]

Economic conditions in the state continued to worsen, and it was glaringly apparent to everyone that the life of the Home was coming to a close.

Lawmakers and newspaper editors heard daily from Kentuckians who viewed the Home as an unnecessary waste. "The enormity of over-expenditure of taxpayer funds in this institution grows more apparent and more appalling," wrote one disgruntled Oldham County resident. The commandant took his share of criticism, too: "The material assets of the various members of the family who operates the Home have risen to a most comforting point."[31]

Everyone had to get along on less, and the McFarlan family was no exception. McFarlan had taken further pay cuts, and by 1933 was making just $125 a month. His wife had been cut from the payroll (though she still worked at the Home), and his oldest son had left Pewee Valley to look for another job.[32] Gin Herdt's father had converted his motor business to a Ford motorcar dealership in 1925, but by 1933, with no one buying new cars, William Herdt and his sixteen-year-old son struggled to make a living repairing trucks and automobiles for those who could afford to operate them.

If times were hard, the children of Pewee Valley barely noticed. The Kentucky Confederate Home grounds was still a fine neighborhood playground. The children trooped to Duke Hall for graduation ceremonies, piano recitals, and, once, even a Charleston contest. The benign gray ghosts in their Home uniforms still floated around the children's world, but so few remained they were hardly a presence.

Gin Herdt was twelve years old in 1933, her scabby-knee-and-bare-feet years about to end. One of the veterans—eighty-six-year-old Tennessee-born Charles Morris, perhaps, who served in the Twelfth Kentucky Cavalry seventy years before—gave the little girl a quarter for singing a favorite song. She ran to the drugstore, using the coin to buy her first lipstick.

The children wouldn't have noticed on December 26, 1933, when State Examiner Nat B. Sewell, in the strongest official language yet, urged that the Kentucky Confederate Home be closed and the property be sold or leased to raise revenues for the state.[33]

Six Kentucky Confederate veterans remained in the Home.

In March 1934 a state representative introduced a bill calling for the abolishment of the Kentucky Confederate Home. According to the bill, inmates remaining in the Home on July 1, 1934, would be transferred to the care of the Pewee Valley Sanitarium and Hospital, which would receive $2.00 a day per inmate for their care. The grounds and buildings would be turned over to the state's Department of Public Property for final disposal.[34]

The Daughters made a halfhearted effort to block the legislation, but even the most devoted among them realized that the handwriting was on the wall. As the board of trustees instructed McFarlan to begin closing out the books and inventorying items, Pewee Valley residents began to daydream about what might become of the grounds on which the elegant Villa Ridge Inn once stood.

Recalling Charlotte Woodbury's earlier suggestion, many in the village favored a proposal that the Home be converted "into an orthopedic hospital for the care and treatment of crippled children." Ebullient new president Franklin D. Roosevelt, crippled by polio, encouraged the hope that children disabled by disease or defect might be made to walk again, and neighbors of the Home noted that "the spacious grounds would provide plenty of outdoor recreation for the juvenile patients."[35]

Others suggested that Pewee Valley secure Federal Public Works Administration monies and dedicate the land as a state park. Still others desired that the property become a permanent Confederate memorial park.[36]

Those pastoral dreams crashed into bureaucratic reality on April 16, 1934, when a delegation arrived in town to evaluate the property's fitness as an overflow facility for the Lakeland Asylum. Pewee Valley residents' vision of brave little children frolicking over the grounds was replaced overnight by the prospect of having hundreds of violent, drooling lunatics housed in their midst. Frank E. Gatchel, chairman of the Pewee Valley town board, called for mass meetings, and howls of protest could be heard as far as Frankfort.[37]

Rather disingenuously, Governor Laffoon pronounced that he "hoped to dispose of the property as advantageously as possible to the state, without doing any injustice to the community of Pewee Valley." First, however, the ex-Confederates must be moved.[38]

With the death of ninety-one-year-old Ike Humphrey, five Kentucky Confederate veterans remained in the Home.

Members of the board of trustees conferred by phone with Kentucky attorney general Bailey Wooton on matters related to the July 1 closure.

Men and women from all over the state were showing up at the Home's door asking for the return of items they had donated over the years. Confederate-era flags, firearms, and furniture—some quite valuable—decorated the public rooms of the Home, and the board had no reliable record of the original donor. Retain the items for disposition by the Kentucky Department of Public Property, Wooton instructed. Birdie Parr Marshall and her attorney arrived in Pewee Valley with a court order demanding the portrait of Captain Daniel G. Parr commissioned by the Parr family thirty years before. The portrait was hanging in Duke Hall, and the boat captain's daughter wanted it back. Give it to her, the attorney general said.[39]

The board also dealt with the matter of the donation jar, a sum of $131 in cash that had accumulated over the years from small gifts given by visitors. Wooton told the board that they were free to hand the money over to Charlotte Woodbury and the Confederate Home chapter of the UDC for improvements to the Confederate Cemetery at Pewee Valley.[40]

As July 1 approached, Commandant McFarlan completed his inventory of every book, every painting, every piece of furniture, every appliance, every frying pan—everything in the Kentucky Confederate Home. Facing unemployment himself, McFarlan did his best to buoy the spirits of the five remaining inmates; he made final arrangements to release the employees and move the old men on Friday, June 29.

A week before the move, Attorney General Wooton phoned Charles F. Leathers, and Leathers phoned McFarlan at the Home. There had been a hitch. The law abolishing the Home had never been published and was therefore not yet legally in force. Hold everything.

For three weeks Commandant McFarlan, his wife, and the five remaining inmates rattled around the empty rooms, among the crates and draped furniture of the Kentucky Confederate Home, entertaining one another with stories they had shared a hundred times.

McFarlan received the final word on July 18.

The next morning Mrs. McFarlan cooked breakfast for her husband and the ex-Confederates. After breakfast, Commandant McFarlan answered the knock at the door; two attendants dressed in white entered the foyer.

Two ambulances were parked in the driveway. The attendants escorted five old men—two on cots, one in a rolling chair, and all five dressed in fresh gray uniforms—out the door of the Kentucky Confederate Home and into the big cars that would take them to their new quarters.

After the ambulances had driven away, the engineer went back inside to make a final memo entry in his logbook: "Commandant A. S. McFarlan continued to operate the Home until after breakfast on Thursday, July 19, 1934, when the veterans, Geo. Crystal, W. R. Hardin, Chas. K. Morris, Wm. Southerland and A. N. White were removed to the Pewee Valley Sanitarium, and the building then became vacant."[41]

During its thirty-two years of operation the Kentucky Confederate Home served as a respectable dwelling place for almost a thousand veterans of America's Civil War. Now it was time for the Home to enter its own respectable place in Kentucky history.

Epilogue

Three of the five ex-Confederates who moved to the Pewee Valley Sanitarium in July 1934 passed away before the end of the year: Charles K. Morris, George Crystal, and William Sutherland died of causes not unusual for men of their advanced age. Though bedridden, William R. Hardin thrived for another two years until an April morning in 1936 when the nurse was unable to waken him.[1] The Reverend Dr. Alexander. N. White, still wheelchair bound and losing his sight, was occasionally reprimanded by the management of the sanitarium for the enthusiasm with which he shared the Gospel message with other patients.

Shortly after the last inmates vacated the Home, the Kentucky Board of Public Property authorized letting bids for the property and buildings, but no agency expressed sufficient interest and the buildings remained vacant. Former commandant Alexander McFarlan was hired to maintain the property, and in 1937 the buildings temporarily housed hundreds of families left homeless by Ohio River flooding. McFarlan eventually left Pewee Valley to join his children in Lexington, and the buildings quickly fell into disrepair. Hoboes found residence there; scavengers removed carpets and lumber.[2]

With the inmates gone and the property out of their control, there was no further need for the Home's trustees. Governor A. B. "Happy" Chandler called a special legislative session to streamline state government, and the Reorganization Act of 1936 abolished the Kentucky Confederate Home board of trustees along with two dozen other state boards and commissions.[3]

A newspaper reporter, researching a Sunday supplement travel piece on the community, visited Pewee Valley in 1936 and met the two men he called "The Last Confederates."

The Reverend Dr. White, ninety-two years old and totally blind, was still rolling around Pewee Valley, still with a full head of white hair, full mustache, and narrow goatee, and the reporter was taken with the old man's quiet dignity and faith. "A man of education, calmly poised, he awaits philosophically and with patience the last 'Taps'—and with inspired confidence the last reveille."

George Booze was back in Pewee Valley, too, having lost his burial money in the bank failures. Booze had left the Home before it closed to live with his son in Corbin; now he was living at the sanitarium with White. "Life is not over yet for George A. Booze," the reporter wrote of the ninety-one-year-old Confederate veteran. "He tells his stories with crackling humor—and there's always someone to listen to them."[4]

White lived another two years before succumbing to heart disease. He was the last Confederate veteran, and the last resident of the Kentucky Confederate Home, to be buried in the Confederate Cemetery at Pewee Valley. George Booze died in 1939; his body was shipped back to Corbin. He was likely the last ex-Confederate to have lived in the Home.

In 1937 Pewee Valley residents again held mass protest meetings when the state announced plans to house a hundred women convicts on the grounds of the former Kentucky Confederate Home. Their protests managed to derail the plan, and the Home buildings continued to disintegrate.[5]

The Rural Education Association, the same organization that owned and operated the Pewee Valley Sanitarium and Hospital, struck a deal to buy the Home property for $8,750 in 1938. The association planned a community for underprivileged youth, including schoolrooms, a dormitory, and a working farm. They razed the ramshackle buildings, but plans failed to materialize, and the property was eventually resold for residential development.[6]

When a Louisville dentist and his wife acquired nineteen acres of the property in the late 1940s, they built an estate incorporating parts of the foundation and walls of the Home's old laundry building. The couple named their estate Confederate Hill.[7]

The same financial and chronological imperatives that ended the active life of the Kentucky Confederate Home were affecting the other Confederate soldiers' homes.

The Maryland, Tennessee, Alabama, North Carolina, and Florida homes all closed in the 1930s with the death of the their last inmates or with the final handful of ex-Confederates packed off to another institution. Virginia's home closed in 1941 when its last veteran passed away; the Louisiana home closed shortly after.

South Carolina opened its home to widows and daughters of Confederate veterans and the home operated until 1957, four years short of the centennial of America's Civil War.

Beauvoir, in Biloxi, Mississippi, ended its life as a veteran's home in 1947, but remains open today for tours after reconstruction in the wake of Hurricane Katrina. Following the death of its final remaining Confederate widow, the Oklahoma Confederate Home building in Ardmore was turned over to the U.S. Veterans Administration, and veterans of other wars now walk the hallways there.[8]

With the Kentucky veterans long gone, their Pewee Valley cemetery became overgrown. The work of clearing brush, pulling stumps, leveling sunken graves, and resetting headstones was too much for the dozen clubwomen of the Confederate Home Chapter (renamed the Pewee Valley Chapter) of the UDC. Oldham County sheriff Buford Renaker—the grandson of a Confederate veteran—pitched in, often detailing county prisoners to work on the property.

True Daughter Charlotte Woodbury still had some political clout in Frankfort, and in 1957 she prevailed on Governor Chandler to direct state monies toward restoring the cemetery. A coordinated effort between the state, the Kentucky Division of the United Daughters of the Confederacy, the Kentucky Sons of Confederate Veterans, and the Morgan's Men heritage association resulted in a rededication of the Confederate Cemetery at Pewee Valley on Confederate Memorial Day, June 3, 1957.[9]

A thousand Kentuckians attended the ceremony, and Governor Chandler gave a dedicatory address honoring the men and women of the Confederate generation. But the event was a minor echo of the day in 1902 when Bennett Young turned over the keys of the Kentucky Confederate Home to Governor J. W. C. Beckham and the Commonwealth of Kentucky.

Visit Pewee Valley today and it's easy to imagine how it must have appeared a century ago. I drove there on one of those perfect pre-Derby spring afternoons that Kentucky is famous for, where the sky is the bright blue of wildflowers and fat marshmallow clouds clump and bump their way along overhead.

Sixteen miles east of Louisville (and about that far south of the Ohio River), Pewee Valley hasn't yet been overrun by the residential and commercial development inching its way eastward from the larger city. Pewee Valley is much as it was at the beginning of the twentieth century: a quiet village of well-bred estate homes in the Queen Anne and Colonial Revival styles, unpretentious stone church buildings, and polite residential lanes more suited for strolling than driving. It's a not-quite-country, not-quite-city type of place where a favorite great-aunt might have lived, the kindly old maiden aunt you always wanted to spend more time with.

I was visiting the Confederate veteran burial section of the Pewee Valley Cemetery—310 identical gray-white stones in perfect rank—when I met Susan, the great-granddaughter of John T. Jones, Company C, First Battalion, Kentucky Mounted Rifles. Susan was from Arkansas, traveling through Kentucky on business, and she had taken the afternoon off to find out more about her long-dead Confederate ancestor. We introduced ourselves, and she did what a lot of family historians do: pull out a couple of three-ring binders crammed with documents, letters, photocopies, and notes about hundreds of people who were long dead by the time she was born.

She had inherited a stack of papers from a distant cousin, papers that described John T. Jones's admission to and life in the Kentucky Confederate Home, and she showed them to me. I recognized on the documents the signatures and names of people who, in prior

months, had become familiar to me: Henry George. Florence Barlow. Milton Sea. Bennett Young.

After the Civil War, Susan's great-grandfather had married, raised
a family, and spent the last years of the nineteenth century as an
itinerant horse trainer in Texas. In 1914, at age seventy-six, with his
children gone and his wife dead, John T. Jones entered the Kentucky Confederate Home. Apart from a short furlough or two, he
lived in the Home until his death there in 1922. There were few
family memories of Jones's final years, and Susan had come to Pewee Valley to learn more about the Kentucky Confederate Home.

"Is the Home still here?" she asked as we stood next to the veteran's grave marker.

No, I told her. Much of it burned to the ground in 1920, but it
continued to operate until 1934. The property was sold off a few
years later. I asked if she wanted to see where it stood, and she followed me in her car back to the highway.

We left the cemetery and drove a mile north on Maple Avenue,
a tree-shaded residential lane spotted here and there with just-
budding dogwood, rosebud, and crimson rambler. I drove slowly up
the street, knowing (although Susan didn't) that this was the road
down which a dozen uniformed Confederate veterans marched
when they accompanied the casket of her great-grandfather to a final salute and a last rest in the Pewee Valley cemetery.

Susan and I looped into a gravel drive that winds up a short slope
to St. James Episcopal Church. We got out of our cars, and I directed her to the historical marker standing at the corner of Maple
Avenue and State Highway 42 near the center of Pewee Valley.[10]

CSA Cemetery
In burying ground 1 mile south, marked by granite obelisk, lie
remains of 313 soldiers who died while residents of the Kentucky Confederate Home. The Home was located on high
ground just northwest of here. It was used for CSA veterans,
1902 to 1934.

Susan stared for a while at the little hill across the highway as I told

265

her what the Home looked like when her great-grandfather lived there: the elegant four-story main building that had once been a fashionable resort hotel; the wide carriageway that wound up to the front of the main building; an assembly hall hung with portraits of Robert E. Lee and his generals; a gleaming white infirmary building; an electric commuter rail line that ran back into Louisville; comfortable chairs on the wide porches; and the twelve-foot-long guidon, a gift from Virginia Parr Sale, that flew from a flagpole at the very top of the cupola roof.

I described to her a cloudless October morning in 1902: ten thousand men and women from all sections of Kentucky crowding the hill across from us for the dedication of the Kentucky Confederate Home. Starting just after dawn, they arrived by train, trolley, carriage, cart, and wagon to open the Home with bands, buntings, celebration, and oration. It was the largest gathering of Kentucky Confederates since Lee surrendered at Appomattox thirty-seven years before.

Among the orators that day was W. T. Ellis, former Confederate cavalryman and popular U.S. congressman from Owensboro. The crowd interrupted Ellis time after time with thunderous applause during his hour-long Lost Cause oration, but he earned the greatest roars of approval when he spoke of the debt his audience owed men of the Confederate generation. "The young men Kentucky gave to the Confederate army," he said, "rendered their state some service and are . . . entitled to a respectable place in its history."

After a while, Susan turned and began asking the same questions I'd asked when I saw the historical marker for the first time: Who built the Home? Was it a poorhouse? Were the people who lived here forced to come here? What was it like to live there? Were they all disabled? Crippled? Homeless? How did they spend their days? Were they taken care of? What happened to the last remaining residents?

Finally, Susan—a woman who had traveled a thousand miles to Pewee Valley, Kentucky, to find out more about a long-dead great-grandfather—asked the question she wanted to ask all along:

"Was he happy here?"

I didn't know.

But I could tell her I was sure that by the end of his life John T. Jones—and all the others who lived at the Kentucky Confederate Home—had found a respectable place.

Notes

Abbreviations

C-J	*Louisville Courier-Journal*
ConVet	*Confederate Veteran*
Filson	Filson Historical Society, Louisville, Kentucky
KDLA	Kentucky Department for Libraries and Archives, Frankfort
KyHS	Special Collections, Kentucky History Center, Kentucky Historical Society, Frankfort
Messenger	*Confederate Home Messenger*

Introduction

1. *Going Back to Civilian Life*, iv.
2. Lincoln quote from "VA History in Brief," 5.
3. Klotter, *A Concise History of Kentucky*.

1. The Cripple and the Banker

1. The description of Beasley's funeral service and interment that begins and ends this chapter comes from the *Louisville Courier-Journal* (hereafter *C-J*), March 6–7, 1898, and the *Louisville Times*, March 6, 1898.

2. Confederate casualty figures are problematic. The "one in five" and "a quarter-million" figures are "commonly cited by historians today," according to Faust, *This Republic of Suffering*. The "20 percent" is from Rosenburg, *Living Monuments*, citing an extrapolation in Livermore, *Numbers and Losses in the Civil War in America, 1861–65*. The "tens of thousands" comes from an estimate in Dean, *Shook over Hell*.

3. Beasley's enlistment and service record and unit history comes from the Alabama Department of Archives and History, www.archives.alabama.gov/civilwar/soldier.cfm.

4. Trammell, "Battles Leave an Army of Disabled," *Washington Times*, June 21, 2003.

5. "VA History in Brief"; Blanck and Millender, "Before Civil Rights."

6. Wines, "Paupers in Almshouses," in *Report on Crime, Pauperism and Benevolence in the United States at the Eleventh Census: 1890* (Part 1, Analysis), 303.

7. "VA History in Brief," 5–6.

8. Even as Louisville's Confederate veterans gathered to organize their own relief organization, a letter to the editor of the *Courier-Journal* lamented the closing of the Sadd Mission, a relief organization founded by J. M. Sadd and funded by public contributions. The Sadd Mission had provided meals, vocational training, and religious instruction to hundreds of Louisville's homeless and destitute each year. *C-J*, April 3, 1888.

9. *C-J*, April 1, 1888.

10. Horan, *Confederate Agent*, 137–140; H. Levin, *Lawyers and Lawmakers of Kentucky*, 94.

11. *C-J* and *Louisville Evening Post*, April 3, 1888; Johnston, *Memorial History of Louisville*, vol. 1, 215–219.

12. *Biographical Encyclopedia of Kentucky of the Dead and Living Men of the Nineteenth Century;* "Louisville of To-Day."

13. For more on John Leathers, see Johnson, *History of Kentucky;* Evans, *Confederate Military History;* and *City of Louisville and a Glimpse of Kentucky.*

14. For a more complete listing of these earlier groups, see W. W. White, *The Confederate Veteran.*

15. A copy of the dinner program for the AAT reunion dinner is in the United Confederate Veterans Association Records, Louisiana and Lower Mississippi Valley Collections, LSU Libraries, Baton Rouge, Louisiana.

16. The names of the association's charter members appeared in *C-J* and the *Louisville Evening Post*, April 3, 1888; their occupations can be found in contemporary city directories and biographical compilations. They were, almost without exception, professional men, Louisville's business, political, educational, religious, and social leaders. For a financial accounting of the organization's first nine years, see *C-J*, April 14, 1897, and "Confederates in Kentucky," *Confederate Veteran* (hereafter *ConVet*) 5, no. 5 (May 1897): 209.

17. Allen, *The Big Change*, discusses the stigma charity carried with it at the time. For a more thorough discussion of how men like Leathers determined the worthiness of Confederate veterans like Beasley, see Rosenburg, *Living Monuments.*

18. Mrs. Williams wrote about her visit to Beasley's newsstand in "One of the Real Heroes," *ConVet* 5, no. 4 (April 1897): 167.

19. The generosity exhibited by Louisville's ex-Confederates toward Billy Beasley did not end with his death. His widow, daughter, and step-daughter received regular assistance from the Confederate Association of Kentucky for the next fifteen months. Mrs. Beasley was hospitalized with typhoid fever in June 1899 and died on July 9. The ex-Confederates paid her medical expense and arranged for her burial and for a marker next to her husband in Cave Hill Cemetery. *C-J*, July 10, 1899.

2. The Private and the Clubwoman

1. For a detailed description of the memorial and dedication service (including speeches), see *Kentucky Leader*, June 11, 1893; and "Unveiling a Monument at Lexington, Ky.," *ConVet* 1, no. 7 (July 1893): 196. For preparations, see the *Lexington Press*, May 28–30, 1893.

2. Quoted in Halberstam, *Coldest Winter*, 645.

3. "Reunion at Augusta," *ConVet* 1, no. 11 (November 1893): 323; and untitled article in *ConVet* 2, no. 10 (October 1894): 290. See also W. W. White, *The Confederate Veteran*.

4. *C-J*, September 21, 1889.

5. Biographical information on Boyd comes from Peter, *History of Fayette County, Kentucky*, 528; and "John Boyd, Maj. Gen. U.C.V.," *ConVet* 2, no. 4 (April 1894): 121. He was also profiled in the *Dallas News*, May 22, 1895, as part of its Houston reunion coverage.

6. "John Boyd, Maj. Gen. U.C.V.," 121.

7. *Lexington Herald*, April 15, 1918.

8. Confederate Veteran Association of Kentucky, "Constitution," Special Collections, Kentucky History Center, Kentucky Historical Society, Frankfort (hereafter KyHS).

9. *Lexington Leader*, March 20, 1892.

10. For brief histories of the founding of the United Confederate Veterans and its grassroots origins, see Foster, *Ghosts of the Confederacy*, and W. W. White, *The Confederate Veteran*.

11. "United Confederate Veteran Camps," *ConVet* 1, no. 3 (March 1893): 85; and "U.C.V. Camps," *ConVet* 2, no. 3 (March 1894): 94.

12. For an early history of the Kentucky UCV, see "History of U.C.V. of Kentucky," *ConVet* 1, no. 11 (November 1893): 340.

13. *Lexington Leader*, March 20, 1892.

14. *Lexington Leader*, June 1, 1893.

15. *C-J*, September 20, 1889.

16. Kinkead, *A History of Kentucky;* Deiss, "Thirteen Stars—Thirteen States," 7.

17. Thirty years later Mrs. John B. Castleman still seethed as she recalled her treatment during wartime at a Federal checkpoint. Mrs. Castleman and her sister, both girls barely into their teens, were stopped while trying to return to their home on the outskirts of Louisville. The Union officer in charge of the checkpoint refused them passage and took the children into custody, where they were interrogated as possible spies. Only the intervention of a family friend prevented the frightened girls from being jailed and held for charges when they refused to take a Union loyalty oath. *C-J*, September 9, 1895.

18. From a speech by Louisville mayor Charles D. Jacob at an Orphan Brigade reunion, *C-J*, September 20, 1889.

19. "Our Dead at Lexington, Kentucky," *ConVet* 4, no. 3 (March 1896): 89.

20. Ironically, a year later the Women's Auxiliary to the Confederate Veterans Association would threaten to boycott Confederate Decoration Day if Breckinridge were allowed to attend. The "silver-tongued orator" had been caught in a messy affair with a woman young enough to be his granddaughter. In the twelve months following his speech at the dedication, Breckinridge would lose a $15,000 breach-of-promise lawsuit, reelection to the House, and most of his reputation. *Lexington Leader,* May 23, 1894.

21. The memorial ritual remained the same, year after year. See *Lexington Press,* May 27, 1894, and *Sunday Leader,* June 6, 1897.

22. This treatment of battlefield dead was not unusual. See Faust, *This Republic of Suffering.*

23. Bennett Young tells the Dorothea Burton story in "Dedication of Zollicoffer Monument," *ConVet* 18, no. 12 (December 1910).

24. Blair, *Cities of the Dead,* sees memorialization as an act of resistance against a Federal occupation. For a description of Decoration Day in Louisville, see "The Lesson of Decoration Day," *Southern Bivouac* 1, no. 9–10 (May–June 1883): 390.

25. *Cynthiana Democrat,* May 28, 1929.

26. Peter, *History of Fayette County, Kentucky,* 616. Also, social club news and announcements in Lexington newspapers, 1885 to 1905, demonstrate the breadth of Adeline Graves's club activities.

27. "One Hundred Years Old," *ConVet* 5, no. 6 (June 1897): 254–255.

28. "History of U.C.V. of Kentucky," *ConVet* 1, no. 3 (November 1893): 340.

29. *C-J*, September 19, 1889.

30. On the organization of the UDC, see Poppenheim, *History of the United Daughters of the Confederacy*. The quotations are from ibid., 4, 7.

31. *Lexington Leader*, March 23, 1896. Also "United Confederate Daughters," *ConVet* 4, no. 1 (January 1896): 22; and *Lexington Herald*, April 15, 1918.

32. "Kentucky," *ConVet* 4, no. 12 (December 1896): 408.

3. The Boat Captain and the Bank Robber

1. The account of the meeting between Daniel Parr and Bennett Young that opens and closes this chapter comes from *C-J*, April 19, 1901; "Home for Disabled Confederates," *The Lost Cause* 4, no. 9 (April 1901): 131; and *Mt. Sterling (Ky.) Advocate*, April 30, 1901. Bennett Young is quoted extensively in the *C-J* account.

2. Duke, *History of Morgan's Cavalry*, and Young, *Reminiscences of a Soldier of the Orphan Brigade*.

3. *Georgetown (Ky.) Weekly Times*, July 13, 1881.

4. *Georgetown (Ky.) Weekly Times*, November 30, 1881.

5. "Taps," *Bivouac* 1, no. 1 (September 1882): 36; and untitled article in *Southern Historical Society Papers* 11, no. 8–9 (August–September 1883): 432.

6. A Boyd County newspaper editor grumbled about the state's refusal to provide financial support: "The sum required would not affect the taxpayers . . . any more than the weight of a feather would check the speed of a horse," he wrote. *Catlettsburg (Ky.) Democrat*, quoted in *Georgetown (Ky.) Weekly Times*, November 30, 1881.

7. *Georgetown (Ky.) Weekly Times*, November 14, 1883.

8. The best study of the Confederate soldiers' homes in the states of the Southern Confederacy (and the schemes that financed them) is Rosenburg, *Living Monuments*.

9. "The Blue and the Gray," *Southern Bivouac* 2, no. 9 (May 1884): 431.

10. *ConVet* 6, no. 3 (March 1898): 156–157.

11. *ConVet* 30, no. 1 (January 1923): 48.

12. Plante, "National Home for Disabled Volunteer Soldiers," 57–59.

13. "Confederates in Kentucky," *ConVet* 5, no. 5 (May 1897): 209.

14. During an oration entitled "Reconciliation," Bennett Young would hold up to the crowd a bullet-ridden old gray jacket, which he would then slowly and reverently fold and put away as he recited a familiar Confederate poem: "Fold it up carefully, / Lay it aside; / Tenderly touch it, / Look

on it with pride." "Confederate Memorial, Columbus, O.," *ConVet* 3, no. 9 (September 1897): 455–456.

15. *C-J*, January 12, 1898.

16. Bennett H. Young was an extraordinary part of Kentucky politics, commerce, jurisprudence, and popular culture during the twenty years either side of 1900, and it's surprising that he is largely forgotten today. The information here was drawn mainly from Kinchen, *General Bennett H. Young*, a hagiographic, but the only existing, book-length biography. He is, however, listed in many biographical compilations, and I have consulted Johnson, *History of Kentucky*; Johnston, *Memorial History of Louisville*; LaBree, *Notable Men of Kentucky* and *Press Reference Book*; H. Levin, *Lawyers and Lawmakers*; and Seekamp and Burlingame, *Who's Who in Louisville*. See also McAfee, *Kentucky Politicians*; and *City of Louisville and a Glimpse of Kentucky*. Young was a fascinating figure, and he deserves a full-length, critical biography.

17. Edward G. Longacre, "Terror Strikes the Northern Heartland," *Civil War Times* 42, no. 3 (August 2003): 36.

18. My account of the St. Albans raid comes primarily from Wilson, "The Hit-and-Run Raid." (Unfortunately, Wilson changes Young's middle name to "Hiram.") For contrasts, see Harris, *Assassination of Lincoln*, which seethes with Union rage over the Vermont raid, and Headley, *Confederate Operations in Canada and New York*, which tries to justify it militarily. Kinchen's *Daredevils of the Confederate Army* is good for contemporary readers who wish to know more about the strategic and political contexts of the raid.

19. J. L. Driscol, "Capture of St. Albans, Vt.," *ConVet* 5, no. 2 (February 1897): 74–75.

20. Kinchen, *General Bennett H. Young*, 79–80.

21. For more on Young, see Evans, *Confederate Military History*.

22. Untitled article, *ConVet* 2, no. 8 (August 1894): 251.

23. "The Sun Shines Bright," *ConVet* 4, no. 10 (October 1896): 325–330; and "Delightful Reunion at Nashville," *ConVet* 4, no. 11 (November 1896): 261–265.

24. For a description of Missouri's scheme, see "History of the Missouri Confederate Home," *ConVet* 1, no. 5 (November 1893): 147; for Kentucky's emulation of the scheme, see *Lexington Leader*, October 17, 1901.

25. *C-J*, January 18, 1898, and "Confederate Home Wanted in Kentucky," *ConVet* 6, no. 2 (February 1898): 38.

26. *C-J*, November 19, 1898; and "Daughters of the Confederacy in Kentucky," *ConVet* 6, no. 12 (December 1898): 553.

27. "Louisville Wants Reunion Next Year," *ConVet* 6, no. 4 (April 1898): 158.

28. The text of the speech is printed in "Reunion News," *ConVet* 7, no. 6 (June 1899): 251. See also *C-J*, July 12, 1899.

29. "Reunion," *ConVet* 18, no. 6 (June 1910): 259–261.

30. W. W. White, *The Confederate Veteran*, 64; and *Bourbon News*, February 9, 1900.

31. "The Louisville Reunion: Address by Col. B. H. Young, Chairman," *ConVet* 8, no. 6 (June 1900): 244–247.

32. Kirwan, *Johnny Green*, 206–207.

33. This biographical information comes from Parr's expansive obituary in *C-J*, January 20, 1904. During the bitter probate litigation that followed his death, however, it was revealed that Parr was probably from an Italian-American family named "Parero." He got his start as a riverbank barkeep and huckster before entering the shipping business. See *Kentucky Irish American*, April 9, 1904.

34. *C-J*, October 23, 1902.

35. Donation of the bells to Walnut Street Baptist Church: *C-J*, October 5, 1902. Endowment of Parr's Rest: *Louisville Times*, December 5, 1914.

36. For more about Virginia Marmaduke Parr Sale, see Seekamp and Burlingame, *Who's Who in Louisville*.

37. Indenture accompanying the deed transferring ownership of Parr's Chestnut property to the ex-Confederates. *C-J*, April 19, 1901.

4. The Auditor and the Stockman

1. Evans, *Confederate Military History*, 389–390.

2. For biographical information about Hewitt, see Kentucky Auditor of Public Accounts History, www.auditor.ky.gov/Public/About_Us/APA_History.asp; and "Gen. Fayette Hewitt," *ConVet* 17, no. 4 (April 1909): 177. The stories of the embezzlement and Hewitt's resignation are told in *Dallas (Tex.) News*, March 23, 1888, and November 21, 1889.

3. *Lexington Leader*, February 5, 1896, and *Lexington Herald*, February 7, 1896.

4. *Lexington Leader*, May 23, 1901.

5. "Maj. Gen. J. M. Poyntz, Richmond, Ky.," *ConVet* 7, no. 11 (November 1899): 493.

6. Crichton, *America 1900*, 53–57. For a wry take on Goebel, the assassination, and the aftermath by a reporter who covered the events, see Cobb, *Exit Laughing*, 242–261.

7. Kleber, *Kentucky Encyclopedia.*

8. *C-J*, October 22, 1901.

9. For a description of the meeting, including all the speeches quoted here (unless otherwise noted), see *C-J*, October 23, 1901.

10. Judge R. H. Cunningham's entire speech is reprinted in *ConVet* 8, no. 1 (January 1902).

11. *Owingsville (Ky.) Outlook*, March 19, 1903, and October 10, 1908; *Lexington Leader*, February 24, 1912.

12. *Mt. Sterling (Ky.) Advocate*, November 19, 1901.

13. For verbal pledges and optimistic estimates of financial support, see *Lexington Leader*, October 17, 1901, *C-J*, October 23, 1901, and *Bourbon (Ky.) News*, January 17, 1902.

14. *Bourbon (Ky.) News*, November 15, 1901.

15. "A Home in Kentucky," *Lost Cause* 5, no. 5 (December 1901); and Minutes of the Sixth Annual Convention, Kentucky UDC, Winter 1902, KyHS.

16. There is little evidence that Union veterans provided large amounts of money, but Kentucky's ex-Confederate fundraisers delighted in showcasing contributions from their former foes as a way of emphasizing the nonpartisan nature of their effort. A dubious claim that the first subscription came from a Union veteran who lost his arm in battle against Kentuckians at Franklin, Tennessee, was dutifully reported in newspapers across the state. *Bourbon (Ky.) News*, December 6, 1901.

17. See *Journals* of the Kentucky House and Senate, 1902.

18. *Hickman (Ky.) Courier*, February 14, 1902.

19. *Lexington Leader*, January 19, 1902, and *Richmond (Ky.) Climax*, January 15, 1902.

20. The nay vote was cast by Republican Robert G. Hanna of Lewis County. Fleming's quote is from *Lancaster (Ky.) Central Record*, February 27, 1902.

21. Board of Trustees, Minutes, May 6, 1902, KyHS (hereafter, Minutes).

22. From an undated typewritten sheet, "Statement of Resources in Sight for Confederate Home," KyHS. See also "Confederate Home in Kentucky," *Lost Cause* 7, no. 2 (September 1902): 23.

23. *Lexington Leader*, February 26, 1902.

24. Minutes, July 2, 1902.

25. *Lexington Leader*, February 26, 1902.

26. *C-J*, May 19, 1902.

27. Subscription Ledger, May 31, 1902, KyHS.

28. Minutes, July 2, 1902.

29. Minutes, July 30, 1902.

30. Minutes, September 4, 1902.

31. *C-J* and *Lexington Leader*, September 5, 1902.

32. News of the protests, including all quotes by Pewee Valley residents, is in *C-J*, September 6, 1902.

33. *Hickman (Ky.) Courier*, September 12, 1902.

34. Letter from J. E. Vincent to Fayette Hewitt, September 13, 1902, KyHS.

35. *Bourbon (Ky.) News*, October 3, 1902.

36. *Richmond (Ky.) Climax*, September 25, 1902.

37. For more on the Dukes, see *C-J*, October 21, 1906; and L. McF. Blakemore, "Mrs. Basil W. Duke," *ConVet* 17, no. 12 (December 1909): 610. See also Matthews, *Basil Wilson Duke*, and Duke, *Reminiscences*.

38. The minutes of the board from October 2 show that the trustees accepted and deposited the chapter's $1,000 (and even discussed scheduling the chapter's reception), but the minutes are equally clear that the money was returned. (See Minutes, October 2 and 24, 1902.) For the next twenty years, however, the Albert Sidney Johnston Chapter would contend that their last-minute donation of $1,000 "made the Confederate Home possible." See *C-J*, March 30, 1919, and Charlotte Woodbury's letter to the editor, *C-J*, February 15, 1932.

39. Letter from A. W. Bascom to Fayette Hewitt, September 22, 1902, KyHS.

5. The Governor and the Prisoner

1. The description of the opening of the Kentucky Confederate Home, including all speeches and quotations (except where noted) are from *C-J*, October 23–26, 1902; *Louisville Commercial*, October 24, 1902; "The Sun Shines Bright on the Old Kentucky Home," *Lost Cause* 7, no. 3 (October 1902): 43–45; and "The Kentucky Confederate Home," *ConVet* 8, no. 12 (December 1902): 558–560; and 9, no. 1 (January 1903): 15–16.

2. Other Confederate veterans' homes weren't as ecumenical. The Louisiana soldier's home, known as Camp Nicholls, didn't allow a U.S. flag to fly overhead from the time the home opened in 1884 until 1912. See *New York Times*, July 6, 1912.

3. This and later quotations from Holloway in prison are from Ainsworth and Kirkley, *The War of the Rebellion*, 421.

4. For conditions at Fort Delaware, see Sturgis, *Prisoners of War, 1861–65*, 275–276.

5. The *New York Times*, November 2, 1902, was skeptical about Beckham's chances for reelection; and the *Lexington Leader*, April 9, 1902, speculated that Young would run against Beckham in the primary.

6. The *New York Times*, September 14, 1903, notes that Beckham's reelection might be decided by the ex-Confederate vote.

7. Though the newspaper reporter says the veterans marched "under the Stars and Bars," they more likely carried a version of the Confederate Battle Flag, the red flag with a diagonal cross of blue bars and white stars on the blue. The battle flag was adopted as a copyrighted emblem of the United Confederate Veterans. For clear illustrations of the different Confederate flags and their history, see Cannon, *Flags of the Confederacy*. For more about how the veterans viewed their flags, see *Historical Sketch Explanatory of Memorial or Certificate of Membership in U.C.V's*.

8. Letter from Mary Bascom to "Cousin Anna," October 27, 1902, Filson.

9. H. Levin, *Lawyers and Lawmakers of Kentucky*, 54.

10. For information on Ellis, see Evans, *Confederate Military History*, and online at the Biographical Directory of the United States Congress (http://bioguide.congress.gov).

11. *New York Times*, June 12, 1902.

12. During the previous presidential campaign, candidate William Jennings Bryan made seventeen hour-long speeches in one day while traveling from Indianapolis to Louisville, addressing more than 100,000 people. See *Bourbon (Ky.) News*, October 10, 1900.

13. Clift, *Governors of Kentucky*.

6. The Druggist and the Sheriff

1. Handwritten petition to Capt. S. H. Ford, February 4, 1903, Filson.

2. Hay and Appleton, *Roadside History*, 126, 223, 75.

3. Vertical files at the KyHS Library include an unidentified, undated clipping of a bylined article by Louisville civic leader and columnist Adele Brandeis describing her family's summer vacation at Villa Ridge Inn.

4. Interestingly, Bennett H. Young knew something about operating a resort hotel. He and Walter N. Haldeman were active investors in the Crab Orchard Springs Resort in Lincoln County in the 1880s. See *City of Louisville and a Glimpse of Kentucky*, 146.

5. *C-J*, October 16, 1895.

6. *C-J*, September 6, 1902.

7. Biographical information on Salem H. Ford from "Maj. S. H. Ford, Maj. Gen. Pontz's Staff, Kentucky Division, M.C.V," *Lost Cause* 4, no. 4 (November 1900): 21; *History of Daviess County*, 225, 364, 393, 403–405; Edwards, *Shelby and His Men*, 149–150; and Ford, "Reminiscences," typewritten manuscript, Filson.

8. Ford's descriptions of the preparatory work are in *C-J*, September 11, 1902, and October 23, 1902.

9. An untitled ledger book in KyHS includes a list of gifts given to the Home during its first year of operation. On the hogshead of tobacco, see *Bourbon (Ky.) News*, January 9, 1903.

10. For the fern, see letter from Mary Bascom to "Cousin Anna," October 27, 1902, Filson; the other gifts are described in *C-J*, October 23 and 24, 1902.

11. Letter from Commandant Coleman to the Tom Barrett Chapter, UDC, Ghent, August 18, 1903, Filson.

12. *C-J*, January 27, 1903.

13. Though the application form changed slightly over the years, the required information described in the text that follows remained consistent.

14. Quotations here and following are from the Home's application form, many of which are on file at KDLA.

15. Minutes, October 24, 1902. The quotation is from the standard form acceptance letter; thanks to Susan Reedy for showing me a copy of the acceptance letter received by her great-grandfather, John T. Jones.

16. Register of Inmates Received, KyHS.

17. *The Gray Book*, 32–33.

18. *C-J*, November 23, 1901, and "Kentucky Confederate Home," *Lost Cause* 6, no. 4 (May 1902).

19. Both quotes come from newspaper coverage of the Kentucky Division UCV reunion, *C-J*, October 23, 1901.

20. Young's comment comes from his report to the Board of Trustees, Minutes, May 6, 1903. Some of the inmates come to the Home from county poorhouses, he observed, and are "in many instances grotesquely clad."

21. Compare rules discussed in Minutes, September 4, 1902, and December 1, 1902, with text of "Rules and Regulations of Residents and Employees at Fitch's Home for Soldiers" and "Rules and Regulations for Inmates of Kentucky Confederate Home," both KyHS.

22. Home management continually warned camps about recommending inebriates for admission. See *Messenger* 1, no. 2 (November 1907).

23. Register of Inmates Received, KyHS.

24. *C-J*, December 1, 1902; "ample justice" quote from *Bourbon (Ky.) News*, December 2, 1902.

25. Board members authorized the purchase of uniforms on January 7, 1903, according to the minutes of that meeting. Levy Bros. of Louisville would supply uniforms to inmates of the Home for more than thirty years.

26. Milliken's report is attached to Minutes, January 27, 1903.

27. Minutes, February 10, 1903. The *Paducah Sun* reported on February 4, 1903, that Ford left the job "because the duties are too hard for him."

28. *C-J*, February 8, 1928; and George D. Ewing, "William Oscar Coleman," *ConVet* 36, no. 3 (March 1928): 107. See also Mosgrove, *Kentucky Cavaliers*, 66, 232; and Willis, *Kentucky Democracy*, 456–457.

7. The General's Sister and the Stockman's Wife

1. Cox's *Dixie's Daughters* describes a UDC more elite, perhaps, than that found in Kentucky. True, members were more likely to be town women than farm women, but leadership of Kentucky's statewide organization was shared by big-city women and the (presumably) more middle-class small-town women during the years the Home was in operation.

2. Board minutes state clearly that Ford was hired as "Superintendent" and Coleman was hired as "Commandant." Nevertheless, board members, UCV officers, and newswriters referred to Salem Ford by both titles. In later years, Coleman would describe himself as "the first Commandant of the Confederate Home." Salem Ford's legitimate claim to being the first manager of the Home would be largely overlooked. See *C-J*, February 8, 1928.

3. Letter from Bennett H. Young to Board of Trustees, attached to Minutes, May 6, 1903.

4. The offenses and punishments described in this chapter (except where noted) are from the Home's Discipline Reports, Kentucky Department for Libraries and Archives, Frankfort (hereafter KDLA).

5. Minutes, May 6, 1903.

6. For Paducah and Lexington pledges, see *Bourbon (Ky.) News*, January 30, 1903, and *Lexington Leader*, October 4, 1903. W. J. Stone's letter to Fayette Hewitt, October 25, 1902, KyHS.

7. The commission agreements are among the Home's miscellaneous correspondence at KyHS. See *New York Times*, April 23, 1903, for notice of Cantrell's fundraising visit to that city.

8. Minutes, May 6, 1903.

9. From a speech by Judge R. H. Cunningham to the first statewide meeting of the Kentucky Division, UCV, October 22, 1901. The entire speech is in *C-J*, October 23, 1901.

10. The most complete listing of named rooms and the donors who named and decorated them is found in *Messenger* 1, no. 2 (November 1907).

11. *C-J*, January 23, 1903.

12. Gen. Joseph H. Lewis, *C-J*, October 24, 1902.

13. *C-J*, October 24, 1902.

14. For some reports of poorhouse horrors, see *Adair County News*, July 22, 1903; *Owingsville (Ky.) Outlook*, October 1, 1903; *Breathitt County News*, March 25, 1904; and *Springfield (Ky.) Sun*, August 8, 1905.

15. Florence Barlow's quote is from "Kentucky Confederate Home," *Lost Cause* 10, no. 9 (April 1904); Bennett Young's is from Minutes, May 6, 1903.

16. Quote from the Report to the President, Seventh Annual Convention, Kentucky UDC, Winter 1903, KyHS.

17. Circular Letter to Kentucky United Daughters of the Confederacy Chapter, October 19, 1902, KyHS.

18. Letter from Mary Bascom to "Cousin Anna," October 27, 1902, Filson.

19. Letter from Bennett H. Young to Board of Trustees, attached to Minutes, September 2, 1903.

20. Mrs. J. M. Arnold to Executive Committee, Confederate Home Board, January 14, 1904, KyHS.

21. Minutes of the Seventh Annual Convention, Kentucky UDC, Winter 1903, KyHS.

8. The Knight and the Icemaker

1. The *Courier-Journal*'s Sunday rotogravure section for October 26, 1902, included a spread of photos of the Home's guest rooms and common areas.

2. The room numbering system changed from time to time as the Home was remodeled and rebuilt. Based on the Home's "Report of Occupation and Use of Rooms in Home" and its "Report of Inmates in the Home" (both KyHS) for the applicable periods, I believe these men were in Room 52.

3. Minutes, September 3, 1903.

4. "Reunion of Kentucky Division, U.C.V.," *ConVet* 12, no. 1 (January 1904): 9–10.

5. *Richmond Climax*, January 27, 1904, and *Bourbon (Ky.) News*, January 29, 1904.

6. Mrs. J. M. Arnold to Executive Committee, Confederate Home Board, January 14, 1904, KyHS.

7. *Bourbon (Ky.) News*, November 21, 1902.

8. *Bourbon (Ky.) News*, October 3, 1905.

9. *Bourbon (Ky.) News*, June 29, 1909.

10. An engineering school chum wrote of how he and Norvell enlisted together in "From Baltimore to First Bull Run," *ConVet* 7, no. 2 (February 1899): 62–63. Norvell wrote about his experiences in Camp Douglas in "Organized Prisoners in Camp Douglas," *ConVet* 11, no. 4 (April 1903): 168–170.

11. Richardson, *Field of Disease*, 477. The description of Norvell is from the editor's introduction to O. B. Norvell, "Organized Prisoners in Camp Douglas," *ConVet* 11, no. 4 (April 1903): 168.

12. Norvell's application for admission to the Virginia home (and correspondence about his illness with Basil Duke) are available at Library of Virginia, Richmond.

13. J. R. Deering, "Lieut. O. B. Norvell," *ConVet* 8, no. 9 (September 1905): 425–426.

14. Report of Inmates in Home, December 1902 (for Norvell) and January 1903 (for Lovely).

15. "Kentucky's Munificence to the Confederate Home," *Lost Cause* 10, no. 7 (February 1904): 51.

16. The confusion at this time over whether women would be accommodated at the Home seems purposeful. They certainly could not be housed in the dormitory-style main building. See "Kentucky's Munificence to the Confederate Home" and "Kentucky Confederate Home," *Lost Cause* 10, no. 9 (April 1904); also *Bourbon (Ky.) News*, January 29, 1904, and February 26, 1904; and *Richmond (Ky.) Climax*, January 27, 1904.

17. Minutes, May 4, 1904.

18. *Adair County News*, February 15, 1905.

19. Rosenburg, *Living Monuments*, attributes the high mortality rates in Confederate Homes to the high percentage of "war-wounded" housed there (as many as a third of the veterans at some homes). He also points to a lifetime of poverty and stress-related disabilities as factors in the mortality rates. Most studies citing higher-than-average mortality rates among Civil War veterans (notably the Silver, Pizarro, and Strauss study reported by Aaron Levin in his article in *Psychiatric News*, April 21, 2006) have focused on Union veterans, due to better postwar medical record-keeping.

Their conclusions, however, would doubtless apply to Confederate veterans as well.

20. Minutes, January 7, 1903.

21. Bowles's letter is dated January 7, 1903, and included in Minutes, January 7, 1903.

22. Minutes, January 7, 1903.

23. *Bourbon (Ky.) News*, June 30, 1903.

24. "Kentucky Confederate Home."

25. Minutes, May 4, 1904.

26. Letter from Andrew M. Sea to Confederate Home Board of Trustees, January 6, 1903, KyHS.

27. "Kentucky Confederate Home." Though their minutes indicate no discussion of the matter, the board was probably aware of the cost inefficiencies inherent in cottage-style housing. Trustees of the Confederate Soldiers' Home of Georgia estimated that fifteen family cottages would cost about $1,000 each, while the same $15,000 would pay for a single large building that could house up to a hundred inmates. See Rosenburg, *Living Monuments*, 53.

28. For a description of the cemetery, monument, and dedication ceremony, see Emerson, *Historic Southern Monuments*, 146–150, and "Monument to Kentucky Confederates," *ConVet* 12, no. 8 (August 1904): 383. For more about Hindman's gift, see *Semi-Weekly Interior Journal*, September 1, 1903, and Minutes, September 2, 1903.

29. As long as he lived, L. D. Holloway carried the flag at the head of every funeral procession. See *Messenger* 1, no. 6 (March 1908).

30. The fire equipment is described in Minutes, May 4, 1904.

31. Description of the dedication of the infirmary, including Thorne's behavior, is from *C-J* and *Lexington Leader*, November 12, 1904. Bennett Young later issued a statement denying there was anything untoward about Thorne's appearance. See *Earlington (Ky.) Bee*, November 17, 1904.

32. Annual Report of the Kentucky Confederate Home, for year ending December 21, 1905, KDLA. Infirmary crowding is described in *Messenger* 1, no. 2 (November 1907).

33. *Bourbon (Ky.) News*, June 29, 1909.

9. The Railroad Man and the Barber

1. Unless otherwise noted, all reports of inmate misbehavior, charges preferred, and punishment handed out are from Discipline Reports, KDLA.

2. *Laurel (Ky.) Mountain Echo*, June 2, 1904.

3. Letter from Fayette Hewitt to Bennett Young, March 9, 1903, KyHS.

4. Minutes, January 4, 1905.

5. Mrs. Leer describes her visit to the Home in "A Visit to the Confederate Home at Pewee Valley, Ky.," *Lost Cause* 10, no. 8 (March 1904).

6. The history, explanation, symptoms, and treatment of war-related stress disorders come from Slone and Friedman, *After the War Zone*, and Rosen, *Understanding Post-Traumatic Stress Disorder*. Written for the families of troops returning from deployment for America's Global War on Terror, *After the War Zone* is informative, sympathetic, practical, and highly recommended. Dean, *Shook over Hell*, presents some quantifiable data showing that the incidence of post-traumatic stress disorder was greater among Civil War veterans than veterans of any other American war since.

7. The "mistaken kindness" quote is from Annual Report of the Kentucky Confederate Home for year ending December 21, 1905. The Discipline Reports enumerate more categories of inebriation than most professionals would ever encounter. Both, KDLA.

8. Minutes, July 1, 1904.

9. *Messenger* 1, no. 10 (July 1908). O'Brien recovered from his injuries and lived in the Home until he died in 1922. He is buried in the Confederate Cemetery at Pewee Valley.

10. Thompson, *History of the Orphan Brigade*, 236–238.

11. Young's description of the disciplinary process comes from Annual Report of the Kentucky Confederate Home for year ending December 21, 1905.

12. Minutes, August 9, 1904.

13. *Messenger* 2, no. 8 (June 1909). He returned to the Home just before his death and is buried in the Confederate Cemetery.

14. See the information on H. C. Melbourne in Minutes, July 1, 1904.

15. Annual Report of the Kentucky Confederate Home for year ending December 21, 1905.

16. Minutes, August 9, 1904.

17. Minutes, July 9, 1904.

18. Minutes, August 9, 1904.

19. Letter from John H. Leathers to Andrew M. Sea, October 27, 1904, KyHS.

20. Undated clipping included in Minutes, January 4, 1905.

21. The inspection committee, chaired by Charles L. Daughtry, pre-

sented its initial report at the board meeting of January 4, 1905. The Oldham County complaint is in *Springfield (Ky.) Sun*, March 22, 1905.

22. *Hartford (Ky.) Republican* and *Stanford (Ky.) Interior Journal*, July 21, 1905.

23. Undated clippings attached to Minutes, January 3, 1906.

24. See Minutes, January 3, 1906, and *Bourbon (Ky.) News*, February 2, 1906.

25. George wrote his note on a copy of a Senate appropriations bill for the Home that apparently was never brought to a vote. "I am certain that this bill will not be funded," George wrote, before adding the good news about the inspection report. The handwritten note, signed by George, follows Minutes, January 6, 1906.

26. Annual Report of the Kentucky Confederate Home for year ending December 21, 1905.

10. The Socialite and the Editor

1. *Messenger* 1, no. 1 (October 1907).

2. The inmates consumed up to five gallons of fruit jam at a meal. *Messenger* 1, no. 2 (November 1907).

3. *C-J*, November 12, 1904, and *Messenger* 3, no. 3 (January 1910).

4. *C-J*, November 12, 1904.

5. *Messenger* 1, no. 12 (September 1908); 2, no. 1 (October 1908); and 2, no. 6 (April 1909).

6. *Messenger* 1, no. 1 (October 1907).

7. Minutes, June 3, 1904.

8. Minutes, March 2, 1906.

9. *Mount Vernon (Ky.) Signal*, October 13, 1905.

10. *C-J*, March 3, 1906.

11. Minutes, March 14, 1906.

12. This endorsement of Henry George is from *Hopkinsville Kentuckian*, March 31, 1906.

13. The Florence Barlow biographical information and quotes that follow, unless otherwise noted, are from Eagle, *Congress of Women*, 797–803; *Lexington City Directory*; and Seekamp and Burlingame, *Who's Who in Louisville*. The stories of Barlow's father and grandfather come from Perrin, Battle, and Kniffin, *Kentucky*; and Sofia Fox Sea, "Capt. Milton Balow," *Lost Cause* 4, no. 10 (May 1901): 71.

14. Letter from Florence Barlow to Henry L. Martin, May 8, 1917, KyHS.

15. Ibid.

16. Lizzie Duke's biography is recounted in *Messenger* 1, no. 1 (October 1907).

17. Minutes, September 5, 1906.

18. Writer Jim Wheat of Dallas, Texas, first wrote of the Lizzie Howe–Handley–Duke connection on the Dallas County history Web site (http://freepages.history.rootsweb.ancestry.com/~jwheat/). This article, one of several on well-known Dallas madams, is carefully documented. I have checked Wheat's sources, and found some records of my own, confirming that Lizzie Howe left Kentucky and earned her fortune in Dallas as Lizzie Handley, then returned to the Bluegrass (via New York) as wealthy bene-factress Mrs. L. Z. Duke.

19. *New York Times*, June 16, 1903; April 28, 1905; and February 10, 1910.

20. Whatever her origins, Mrs. L. Z. Duke gave liberally to ex-Confederates and Confederate causes. She was one of three major donors for the monument to General Felix K. Zollicoffer in Pulaski County ("Dedication of Zollicoffer Monument," *ConVet* 18, no. 12 [December 1910]: 567–571) and contributed $3,000 toward an addition to the Oklahoma Confederate veterans' home (*Messenger* 4, no. 2, December 1910).

21. Description of the opening of Duke Hall (including quotes) comes from "Kentucky's Confederate Soldiers' Home," *ConVet* 16, no. 9 (September 1908): 466–467; and *Messenger* 1, no. 2 (November 1907).

22. Young himself was in similar hot water twenty years before, when his Louisville Southern Railroad was alleged to have given gifts of stock to the Louisville mayor and city council members. See *New York Times*, October 14, 1885.

23. Lizzie Duke's past remained shrouded in Kentucky, even after her death on April 9, 1912. Her remains were shipped to Louisville for burial in the Confederate Section at Cave Hill Cemetery by an honor guard of ex-Confederates. Florence Barlow spoke on behalf of the Confederate Home chapter, but no other Daughters of the Confederacy participated in the funeral service. See *C-J*, April 10–12, 1912.

11. The Fiddlers and the Indian Agent

1. *Messenger* 4, no. 5 (March 1911). The Old Soldier Fiddlers was a popular act nationwide. Six months before they appeared in Pewee Valley, they were booked for a week at the Orpheum Theater in San Francisco on a bill headlined by Lionel Barrymore. At the end of the week the Fiddlers

were held over by audience demand; Barrymore wasn't. *San Francisco Call*, October 30, 1910. The description of their act comes from several sources, notably the review of their Orpheum performance, *San Francisco Call*, October 31, 1910.

2. *Hazel Green (Ky.) Herald*, April 30, 1908.

3. For biographical information on George, see *Memorial Record of Western Kentucky*, 117–118; and "Col. Henry George," *ConVet* 27, no. 9 (September 1919): 346. For more about his military service, read George, *History of the 3d, 7th, 8th, and 12th Kentucky C.S.A.*, written while he was commandant at the Home.

4. *New York Times*, May 4, 1888, and *Messenger* 1, no. 8 (June 1908).

5. Evans, *Confederate Military History*, 360–361.

6. The best comparative history of Confederate homes is Rosenburg, *Living Monuments*, the source of most information in this section.

7. For Oklahoma, see "From Annual Report of the Trustees of the Oklahoma Soldiers' Home," *ConVet* 21, no. 6 (June 1913): 310–312; for Texas, *Dallas News*, January 15, 1899.

8. Only the Mississippi veterans' home came close to the comfortable elegance and setting of the Kentucky Home. Varina Davis, former First Lady of the Confederacy, turned over the family home, Beauvoir, for use as a soldiers' home. Facing the Gulf shore in the little resort town of Biloxi, Beauvoir was not nearly as spacious as Kentucky's old Villa Ridge Inn.

9. Tennessee visitor: Mrs. T. H. Baker, "The Confederate Home of Kentucky," *ConVet* 23, no. 11 (October 1915): 462–463; Florida visitor, *Pensacola Journal*, June 20, 1905.

10. *Messenger* 1, no. 8 (June 1908).

11. All reported in the "Religion" column of the *Confederate Home Messenger* from 1907 through 1911.

12. *Messenger* 2, no. 2 (December 1908).

13. *Messenger* 1, no. 2 (November 1907), and 1, no. 4 (January 1908).

14. *Messenger* 2, no. 7 (May 1909).

15. *Messenger* 1, no. 4 (January 1908).

16. *Messenger* 4, no. 2 (December 1910).

17. *Messenger* 4, no. 3 (January 1911).

18. *Messenger* 4, no. 5 (March 1911).

19. From untitled ledger of bills paid, 1911 and 1912, KyHS.

20. Issues of the *Confederate Home Messenger* from 1907 through 1911 include announcements and reports of dozens of Pewee Valley community events held at L. Z. Duke Hall.

21. Interview by author with Virginia Herdt Chaudoin, July 11, 2007.

22. *Messenger* 1, no. 1 (October 1907).

23. *Messenger* 3, no. 10 (August 1910).

24. *Messenger* 4, no. 7 (May 1911).

25. *Messenger* 1, no. 8 (June 1908).

26. Letter from T. W. Duncan, used with permission of Rebecca C. Myers.

27. *Messenger* 4, no. 7 (May 1911), and 4, no. 8 (June 1911).

28. *Messenger* 2, no. 11 (September 1909).

29. *Messenger* 2, no. 1 (October 1908), and 3, no. 6 (April 1910).

30. *Hazel Green Herald*, April 4, 1908.

31. Interview with Virginia Herdt Chaudoin.

32. *Messenger* 3, no. 2 (December 1909).

33. Biographical information on the Tree Man from, and letters used with permission of, Rebecca C. Myers.

12. The Farmer and the Daughter

1. Minutes of the Twenty-third Annual Convention, Kentucky UDC, Winter 1919, KyHS.

2. Minutes, December 27, 1918, record approval of a "Women's Advisory Committee." Minutes, February 19, 1919, incorrectly refers to the "Ladies Advisory Committee," and the mistake occurs occasionally thereafter.

3. Report by Henry George to Board of Trustees, December 31, 1914, KyHS.

4. For a while, George enlisted able-bodied inmates to reroof and repaint the main building; but when inmate Elisha L. Herndon fell off a ladder and broke both legs, the commandant decided it wasn't such a good idea to send seventy-year-old men scuttling over the roof and scaffolding. *Messenger* 1, no. 8 (May 1908).

5. Minutes, January 5, 1916.

6. Minutes of the Twentieth Annual Convention, Kentucky UDC, Winter 1916, KyHS.

7. Poppenheim, *History of the United Daughters of the Confederacy*, 202–213.

8. Minutes of the Twenty-first Annual Convention, Kentucky UDC, Winter 1917, KyHS. The national organization was urging chapters to turn their hands to war work. See *Dallas News*, January 27, 1918, and *C-J*, April 23, 1918.

9. Minutes of the Twenty-first Annual Convention, Kentucky UDC, Winter 1917, KyHS.

10. Minutes of the Twenty-second Annual Convention, Kentucky UDC, Winter 1918, KyHS.

11. *C-J*, September 26, 1917.

12. Minutes, August 29, 1917.

13. *Louisville Herald*, September 24, 1917.

14. Ibid.

15. Ibid.

16. Ibid.

17. For Young's statement, complete with item-by-item price comparisons, see *C-J*, September 26, 1917.

18. The *Herald* was the first to pick up the two-meals-a-day story, and the paper rode it hard, staying ahead of the other Louisville papers. However, when Young gave his statement (and full access to the Home) exclusively to the *Courier-Journal*, the *Herald* found itself frozen out of its own story. Aside from a few brief follow-ups, the story died away. See also *C-J*, October 6–7, 1917, and November 8, 1917.

19. The book was *History of the 3d, 7th, 8th and 12th Kentucky C.S.A.*, published by the Dearing Printing Co. in 1911. "The matter was prepared while the author was busy discharging the intricate duties as Commandant of the Kentucky Confederate Home," George says in the preface.

20. Letter from Florent D. Jaudon to Mrs. George L. Danforth, September 26, 1916, Filson.

21. Ibid.

22. Minutes, December 4, 1917.

23. *C-J*, July 31 and August 1, 1923; and "Col. C. L. Daughtry," *ConVet* 31, no. 9 (September 1923): 348. For some of Daughtry's war stories, see C. L. Daughtry, "Stealing a Yankee Captain," *ConVet* 10, no. 7 (July 1902): 308; and Daughtry, "Three Comrades of the Sixties," *ConVet* 21, no. 1 (January 1913): 18–19.

24. *Lancaster (Ky.) Central Record*, July 10, 1903.

25. Minutes, January 5, 1918.

26. *C-J*, April 27, 1918.

27. Minutes, March 5, 1918.

28. Rosenburg, in *Living Monuments*, writes about the changing role of women at other Confederate homes; see especially 139–141.

29. Minutes, December 27, 1918.

30. *C-J*, May 23, 1922, and Johnson, *History of Kentucky*, 1016.

31. Billy Beasley and his family lived rent-free for a time in an apartment owned by Thomas D. Osborne. See chapter 1.

32. Seekamp and Burlingame, *Who's Who in Louisville*, 247; and *Louisville Times*, June 13, 1919.

33. Southard, *Who's Who in Kentucky*, 443.

34. *Louisville Times*, June 13, 1919.

35. *Messenger* 2, no. 2 (November 1908).

36. He was invited in 1909 to return to St. Albans, Vermont, scene of his wartime raid and bank robbery, as principal orator for a regional historical celebration. A group of diehard Union veterans spun up an angry protest, and Young graciously withdrew his acceptance. *Bourbon (Ky.) News*, May 7, 1909, and *Messenger* 2, no. 6 (April 1909).

37. "The Passing of the Gray," *ConVet* 27, no. 3 (March 1919): 76.

38. Young's cross-country race with death is described in *C-J*, February 23–24, 1919.

39. Lengthy coverage of Young's life may be found in *C-J*, February 24, 1919, and "The Passing of the Gray."

40. Minutes, May 7, 1919.

41. Minutes, January 2, 1920.

42. Letter from Commandant C. L. Daughtry to Executive Committee, Board of Trustees, March 31, 1919.

43. Daughtry's letters and reports to trustees are increasingly peppered with stories of "friction among the employees," "bickering and recriminations," and "tracing the blame" during 1919 and early 1920. See letters dated March 31, 1919; September 5, 1919; and circa Summer 1919.

44. Letter from Commandant C. L. Daughtry to Board of Trustees, undated (ca. Summer 1919).

13. The Trainer and the Undertaker

1. The chronology, description, and details of the fire on March 25, 1920, unless otherwise noted, are constructed from contemporary newspaper accounts and reports of those who were present. I particularly relied on coverage in the *Courier-Journal* and the *Louisville Herald*, March 26–28, 1920. Charlotte Woodbury's report of the fire, much of which quotes Commandant Daughtry, appears in Mrs. John L. Woodbury, "The Confederate Home of Kentucky," *ConVet* 28, no. 5 (May 1920): 196. Inmates gave reporters different versions of George Wells's shouted warning; I've assembled a version that makes sense (and inserted "goddam" where the papers' editors left only dashes).

2. Minutes, May 7, 1919.

3. For a more detailed description of the 1908 fire (including extant

equipment and procedures), see *Messenger* 2, no. 1 (October 1908). See also *Stanford (Ky.) Interior Journal*, October 13, 1908, and *Hartford (Ky.) Herald*, October 14, 1908.

4. Minutes, August 29, 1917.

5. San Francisco: *New York Times*, September 5, 1915. Chicago: *New York Times*, December 28, 1923. Quebec: *New York Times*, October 27, 1916.

6. Ripley, *Unthinkable*, helped me make sense of the confusing (and dangerous) behavior of people in the Home that evening.

7. Interview by author with Bill Herdt Jr., July 11, 2006.

8. The story of Ida Ochsner is from *Hartford (Ky.) Herald*, July 10, 1912.

9. Biographical information on Jones is from Susan Reedy and Jones's application to the Home, KDLA.

10. Coincidentally, the *Courier-Journal* Sunday rotogravure section had already gone to press with a lengthy article about the history of the Louisville Fire Department, accompanied by a great photo of the department's massive new American LaFrance motor-driven, motor-pumping fire engine. See it at *C-J*, March 28, 1920.

11. Some Pewee Valley locals say that the American LaFrance pumper was mounted on a railcar for the trip to Pewee Valley. I find no evidence of that being the case. Instead, it's more likely that the disabled behemoth was *returned* to Louisville on a flatbed railcar for repairs.

12. *C-J*, March 27, 1920.

13. *C-J*, March 28, 1920.

14. *Louisville Herald*, March 29, 1920.

15. *C-J*, March 27, 1920.

16. *C-J*, April 8, 1920, and Minutes, April 9, 1920.

17. Letter from Commandant Daughtry to Executive Committee, Board of Trustees, July 31, 1920.

18. Plans described in *C-J*, June 22, 1920. See also Minutes, April 9, 1920, and Minutes of the Twenty-fourth Annual Convention, Kentucky UDC, Winter 1920, KyHS.

14. The Reverend and the Rector

1. Minutes, May 7, 1919.

2. The nurse story is in the letter from Commandant C. L. Daughtry to Board of Trustees, September 5, 1920. In the same letter he writes that inmates are conspiring with employees to disregard his orders. His letter

to Board of Trustees, July 31, 1920, expresses annoyance at Woodbury's oversight. The letters are appended to Minutes.

3. Minutes, April 9, 1920.

4. *C-J*, March 28, 1920.

5. A direct transcript of Leathers's hearing is in Minutes, April 9, 1920.

6. Minutes of the Twenty-fourth Annual Convention, Kentucky UDC, Winter 1920, KyHS.

7. The Woodbury, Stone, and Crowe information (including direct quotes) are recorded in Minutes, April 9, 1920.

8. White had a habit of writing lengthy "apologies" when charged with some infraction at the Home. (Most other inmates offered a verbal apology to the commandant or board.) One of White's apologies is a ten-page justification, including a detailed autobiography, from which the quotes in this section are taken. The apology is undated, but it appears White had been charged with having spoken in a cross manner to a matron. Only on the final page does he apologize for having "had the temerity to ask a very simple question." KyHS.

9. A. N. White, obituary for H. H. Hockersmith, *ConVet* 20, no. 7 (July 1912): 334.

10. Minutes, May 7, 1919.

11. *Louisville Times*, August 5, 1921.

12. Contents of the dossier are described in an article in the *Louisville Herald*, June 7, 1921.

13. *Louisville Times*, June 7, 1921.

14. *Louisville Times*, August 10, 1921. According to Federal Census records, Imogene Nall was born to William E. and Emma Nall of Meade County in 1898. She was still living with both parents in 1910. In 1920 her mother was unemployed and living as a boarder in a house off Frankfort Avenue in Louisville.

15. The inspector's means of gathering evidence, along with the text of the report, is described in *Louisville Times*, July 22, 1921.

16. Dow's response is printed as a letter to the editor in *Louisville Times*, August 5, 1921.

17. *Louisville Times*, August 10, 1921.

18. The story of this Memorial Day observance earned headlines across the country. I used accounts in *C-J*, the *New York Times*, and the *Dallas News*, all appearing on May 31, 1923.

19. Though the Louisville newspaper reporter says the veterans were carrying the "Stars and Bars," a photo of their furled flag taken that day

shows what very well could be the Confederate Battle Flag. I defer, however, to the reporter's description.

20. *Louisville Times*, February 13, 1922.

21. *C-J*, June 29, 1923.

22. *Louisville Herald*, July 31, 1923. After Daughtry died, Florence Barlow, who remained embittered by her treatment, and that of Home veterans, lived on in a rented carriage house in Pewee Valley, churning out letters to veterans and legislators. She died, alone, in 1925.

23. *C-J*, August 4, 1923.

24. *C-J*, March 18, 1917.

25. *New York Times*, January 25, 1920, and *Atlanta Daily World* (reprinting a story published by the Confederate Soldier's Home of Georgia), June 6, 1936.

26. Letter from Inez Caudel, Bourbon County Chapter, American Red Cross, to A. S. McFarlan, August 18, 1924.

27. William Pete (sometimes spelled "Peet" or "Peat") didn't leave many paper footprints, and it's hard to determine the veracity of his claim. The Morgan's Men Association often listed his attendance at its reunions; see, for example, *C-J*, October 15, 1929.

28. Letter from L. D. Young to Commandant McFarlan, September 17, 1924.

29. Minutes, September 3, 1924.

30. Letter from Commandant McFarlan to L. D. Young, September 4, 1924.

31. Letter from L. D. Young to Commandant McFarlan, November 21, 1924.

32. Dow resettled in Maryland, where he continued to speak up for the underdog. In 1928 he called on President Calvin Coolidge to plead for clemency for a teenager involved in the murder of a D.C. policeman. See *Washington Post*, June 10, 1928.

15. The Engineer and the Little Girl

1. On July 11, 2007, I met siblings Virginia Herdt Chaudoin, Louise Herdt Marker, and Bill A. Herdt Jr. in Pewee Valley to discuss—and record—their memories of the Kentucky Confederate Home. We met at the Herdts' place of business, an auto parts store located a few hundred yards from where the Home once stood. (Their father and grandfather operated wagon repair and blacksmithing businesses from the same location for most of a century, and I had noted the Herdt business name on the Home's

chart of accounts payable.) During the four hours I spent there, a dozen of the Herdts' friends and contemporaries dropped in to add their recollections of Pewee Valley and the Home. At different times, with different words, they described the inmates as ghostlike, evanescent, walking wisps of memory from a past time and a distant place. These childhood impressions come from the last generation to have walked the paths of the Home and met the men who lived there, and their memories inform this chapter.

2. Letter from Commandant McFarlan to Evie Temple, April 14, 1924, KyHS.

3. *C-J*, October 18, 1924.

4. Noble, *New Age*, 18. Jerri Conrad, a descendant of George Noble, shared a copy of his self-published book with me. During Noble's three years and eight months in the Home, he developed and put to paper a complicated theosophy. He asked for an honorable discharge from the Home in 1926, paid to have his *New Age* printed, then lived the rest of his life as an itinerant on the proceeds of his book sales.

5. Letter from Commandant McFarlan to Evie Temple, April 14, 1924, KyHS.

6. *Louisville Post*, June 20, 1925.

7. This Christmas celebration, including photographs of veterans admiring the tree, comes from the *Louisville Times*, December 31, 1925.

8. Noble, *New Age*, 18.

9. Letter from Commandant McFarlan to Board of Trustees, August 31, 1928, KyHS.

10. *Louisville Herald-Post*, December 1, 1929.

11. *Louisville Herald-Post*, February 11, 1929.

12. Noble, *New Age*, 18.

13. Information about Inmates Requests and Kinfolks, KyHS.

14. Letter from Commandant McFarlan to Alice Hall, August 18, 1925, KyHS.

15. From a loose typewritten sheet in the death book, lists of "What Home furnishes in case an inmate desires to be buried in the Home cemetery" and "What friends or relatives must furnish if they desire body to be buried away from Home." The page includes itemized prices for each. KyHS.

16. "U.D.C. Notes," *ConVet* 37, no. 7 (July 1929): 271.

17. *Louisville Times*, October 14, 1929, and *Louisville Herald-Post*, December 1, 1929.

18. *Louisville Herald-Post*, February 11, 1929.

19. See, for example, *C-J*, March 3, 1929, and May 18, 1930.

20. *Lexington Leader*, March 21, 1930.

21. Monthly Payroll of Officers and Employees, April 30, 1930, KyHS.

22. *C-J*, February 15, 1932.

23. *Lexington Herald*, October 21, 1931.

24. Letter from Board of Trustees to Commandant McFarlan, marked as received February 1, 1932, KyHS.

25. *Louisville Times*, October 21, 1931.

26. *C-J*, February 12, 1932.

27. *C-J*, February 15, 1932, and *Louisville Times*, November 17, 1933.

28. "Chapter Reports," *ConVet* 40, no. 5 (May 1932): 192.

29. *Louisville Herald-Post* and *Louisville Times*, July 6, 1932.

30. Letter from Commandant McFarlan to Board of Trustees, September 6, 1933, KyHS.

31. *C-J*, July 17, 1932.

32. Monthly Payroll of Officers and Employees, April 30, 1933, KyHS.

33. *C-J*, December 27, 1933.

34. Minutes, April 4, 1934.

35. Pewee Valley's reaction to the possibility that the grounds might be used for juvenile orthopedic patients is described in *C-J*, February 18, 1934.

36. *C-J*, April 18, 1934.

37. *C-J*, April 17–18, 1934.

38. *C-J*, April 18, 1934.

39. Minutes, May 2, 1934.

40. Letter from Attorney General Wooton to Board of Trustees, May 24, 1934, KyHS.

41. Final entry in payroll ledger book, signed by Commandant McFarlan.

Epilogue

1. Kentucky birth, marriage, and death records.

2. For letting bids, see *C-J*, August 21 and November 15, 1934. For disrepair, see *Louisville Times*, April 29, 1937.

3. Legislative Research Commission, "The Executive Branch of Kentucky State Government," www.e-archives.ky.gov.

4. *Louisville Herald-Post*, August 29, 1936.

5. *Louisville Times*, April 28, 1937.

6. *Oldham (County, Ky.) Era*, October 7, 1938.

7. *C-J*, June 2, 1957.

8. Rosenburg, *Living Monuments*, and author's visits.

9. Dedication of Confederate Cemetery at Pewee Valley, June 3, 1957, KyHS.

10. Hay and Appleton, *Roadside History*, 14–15.

Bibliography

Manuscripts

Official Home Records

When the Kentucky Confederate Home closed in July 1934, Commandant Alexander McFarlan shipped more than fifty crates of library books, paintings, lithographs, flags, firearms, and furniture to the Kentucky Historical Society in Frankfort. Many of the items remain there today (including Florence Barlow's framed military button collection). Browse through the open stacks of the Schmidt Research Library of the Kentucky Historical Society and you're likely to find a book with an inscription or stamp indicating that it came from the Home.

McFarlan and the board of trustees turned over most of the Home's operational documents to the Department of Public Property, but most made their way to the Kentucky Historical Society as well. Many of the operational documents—those not destroyed by the 1920 fire—were microfilmed in 1950, then destroyed. Various canceled checks, bills, and inventories were destroyed without microfilming. Several boxes of original materials have been cataloged (2007M07) and are available for study in Special Collections, Kentucky History Center, Kentucky Historical Society.

The Kentucky Department for Libraries and Archives in Frankfort maintains some original and microform materials relating to the Home.

The brief biographies of inmates included in this book are most often derived from information included on their applications for admission, their Kentucky death certificates, and the Federal census rolls. Where I have supplemented this basic information with other Home records, newspaper accounts, family correspondence, or other miscellaneous records, I've cited those sources in the notes.

Listed below are the Home documents I made greatest use of when researching this book and the institutions in which they can be found.

Kentucky Department for Libraries and Archives, Frankfort

Annual Report of the Kentucky Confederate Home
Applications for admission
Discipline reports

Kentucky Historical Society, Frankfort

Board of Trustees, Minutes
Miscellaneous correspondence
Register of Inmates Received
Report of Inmates in the Home
Report of Occupation and Use of Rooms in Home
Statement of Resources in Sight for Confederate Home
Subscription Ledger

Other Manuscript Sources

Kentucky Historical Society, Frankfort

Confederate Veteran Association of Kentucky. *Constitution, By-Laws and Membership*. [Lexington, Ky.:] Transylvania Printing Co., 1890.
Kentucky United Daughters of the Confederacy. Annual Meeting Minutes.
United Daughters of the Confederacy Records, 1855–1999.

Filson Historical Society, Louisville, Kentucky

Charter, Confederate Home Chapter, United Daughters of the Confederacy, May 7, 1904.
Ford, Emmett B. "Reminiscences of S. H. Ford, Captain of Company 'F,' 2nd Reg.—General Jos. O. Shelby's Brigade of Missouri Confederate Cavalry—1861–1865." Typewritten manuscript dated April 2, 1956, from handwritten original dated March 8, 1909.
Letter from Florence Barlow to Henry L. Martin, May 8, 1917.
Letter from Mrs. A. W. (Mary) Bascom to "Cousin Anna," October 27, 1902.
Letter from Commandant Coleman to the Tom Barrett Chapter, UDC, Ghent, August 18, 1903.
Letter from Florent D. Jaudon to Mrs. George L. Danforth, September 26, 1916.
Petition to Capt. S. H. Ford, signed by inmates and employees, February 4, 1903.
St. James Episcopal Church, Rev. E. C. McAllister's Journal, 1911–1929.

State Records

Alabama Department of Archives and History, Montgomery. Civil War
  Service Database.
Kentucky Auditor of Public Accounts History, Frankfort.
Kentucky birth, marriage, and death records.
Kentucky *Journal of the Regular Session of the House of Representatives.*
Kentucky *Journal of the Regular Session of the Senate.*
Kentucky Vital Statistics. Original death certificates.

Published Works

Two books are especially useful on the days of the Lost Cause and the
Confederate soldiers' home movement. R. B. Rosenburg's *Living Monuments: Confederate Soldiers' Homes in the New South* (Chapel Hill: University
of North Carolina Press, 1993) is the definitive study of Confederate veterans' homes: why they were created, who built them, who lived there, and
how they were operated. Rosenburg laments that "the Confederate soldiers' home movement, which began in the 1880s, has received scant attention" (5). He provides a partial remedy, offering concise institutional
histories of the homes and statistical analyses of inmates, but from the
states of the original Confederacy only. The challenges of Kentucky, a
state that was never officially part of the Confederacy, in establishing, financing, and operating a Confederate veterans' home earn just a few para-
graphs in Rosenburg's volume.

  Gaines M. Foster's *Ghosts of the Confederacy: Defeat, the Lost Cause, and
the Emergence of the New South* (New York: Oxford University Press,
1988) describes the attraction of the Confederate celebration during the
half-century following Gettysburg. The work is scholarly, the writing
sprightly.

Abel, E. Lawrence. *Singing the New Nation: How Music Shaped the Confed-
  eracy, 1861–1865.* Mechanicsburg, Pa.: Stackpole Books, 1999.
Ainsworth, Fred C., and Joseph W. Kirkley, eds. *The War of the Rebellion: A
  Compilation of the Official Records of the Union and Confederate Armies.*
  Series 2, Vol. 6. Washington, D.C.: Government Printing Office, 1899.
Allen, Frederick Lewis. *The Big Change: America Transforms Itself, 1900–
  1950.* New Brunswick, N.J.: Transaction Publishers, 1993.
Barry, John M. *The Great Influenza: The Epic Story of the Deadliest Plague in
  History.* New York: Viking, 2004.
Biographical Directory of the United States Congress, 1774–2005. Washington,

D.C.: U.S. Government Printing Office, 2005. (Online at http://bioguide .congress.gov/biosearch/biosearch.asp.)

Biographical Encyclopedia of Kentucky of the Dead and Living Men of the Nineteenth Century. Cincinnati: J. M. Armstrong & Co., 1878.

Blair, William A. *Cities of the Dead: Contesting the Memory of the Civil War in the South, 1865–1914.* Chapel Hill: University of North Carolina Press, 2004.

Blanck, Peter David, and Michael Millender. "Before Civil Rights: Civil War Pensions and the Politics of Disability in America." *Alabama Law Review* 52, no. 1 (Fall 2000): 1–50.

Boswell, Harry James. *Representative Kentuckians: City Builders.* Louisville, Ky: [self-published,] 1913.

Brady, William. *Personal Health: A Doctor Book for Discriminating People.* Philadelphia: W. B. Saunders Co., 1916.

Cannon, Devereaux D., Jr. *The Flags of the Confederacy: An Illustrated History.* Gretna, La.: Pelican Publishing Co., 1994.

Caron's Louisville Directory. Vol. 32. N.p., 1902.

City of Louisville and a Glimpse of Kentucky. Louisville: Committee on Industrial and Commercial Improvement of the Louisville Board of Trade, 1887.

Clift, G. Glenn. *Governors of Kentucky, 1792–1942.* Cynthiana, Ky.: The Hobson Press, 1943.

Cobb, Irwin S. *Exit Laughing.* Indianapolis: The Bobbs-Merrill Co., 1941.

Cox, Karen. *Dixie's Daughters: The United Daughters of the Confederacy and the Preservation of Confederate Culture.* Gainesville: University Press of Florida, 2003.

Crichton, Judy. *America 1900: The Turning Point.* New York: Henry Holt and Co., 1998.

Davis, William C. *The Orphan Brigade: The Kentucky Confederates Who Couldn't Go Home.* Baton Rouge: Louisiana State University Press, 1983.

Dean, Eric T. *Shook over Hell: Post-Traumatic Stress, Vietnam, and the Civil War.* Cambridge, Mass.: Harvard University Press, 1997.

Deiss, Ruth. "Thirteen Stars—Thirteen States." *United Daughters of the Confederacy Magazine* 15, no. 1 (January 1952): 7.

Dennett, John Richard. *The South as It Is: 1865–1866.* New York: Viking Press, 1965.

Duke, Basil W. *History of Morgan's Cavalry.* Cincinnati: Miami Printing & Pub. Co., 1867.

————. *Reminiscences of General Basil W. Duke.* Garden City, N.Y: Doubleday, Page & Co., 1911.

Eagle, Mary Kavanaugh Oldham, ed. *The Congress of Women: Held in the Woman's Building, World's Columbian Exposition, Chicago, U.S.A., 1893.* Chicago: Monarch Book Co., 1894.

Edwards, John N. *Shelby and His Men; or, The War in the West.* Kansas City, Mo.: Hudson-Kimberly Publishing Co., 1897.

Emerson, Mrs. B. A. C., ed. *Historic Southern Monuments.* New York: The Neale Publishing Co., 1911.

Evans, Clement A., ed. *Confederate Military History: A Library of Confederate States History.* Extended ed. Atlanta, Ga.: Confederate Publishing Company, 1899 (reprinted, Wilmington, N.C.: Broadfoot Publishing Company, 1988).

The Executive Branch of Kentucky State Government. Informational Bulletin no. 171. Frankfort: Legislative Research Commission, 2002.

Faust, Drew Gilpin. *This Republic of Suffering: Death and the American Civil War.* New York: Vintage Books, 2008.

Foster, Gaines M. *Ghosts of the Confederacy: Defeat, the Lost Cause, and the Emergence of the New South, 1865–1913.* New York: Oxford University Press, 1988.

George, Henry. *History of the 3d, 7th, 8th and 12th Kentucky C.S.A.* Louisville, Ky.: C. T. Dearing Printing Co., 1911.

Going Back to Civilian Life. War Department Pamphlet no. 21–4. [Washington, D.C.:] War and Navy Departments, 1945.

The Gray Book. N.p.: Gray Book Committee, Sons of Confederate Veterans, 1920.

Halberstam, David. *The Coldest Winter: America and the Korean War.* New York: Hyperion, 2007.

Harris, T. M. *Assassination of Lincoln: A History of the Great Conspiracy.* Boston: American Citizen Co., 1892.

Hay, Melba Porter, and Thomas H. Appleton Jr., eds. *Roadside History: A Guide to Kentucky Highway Markers.* Frankfort: Kentucky Historical Society, 2002.

Headley, John W. *Confederate Operations in Canada and New York.* New York: Neale Publishing Co., 1906.

Historical Sketch Explanatory of Memorial or Certificate of Membership in the U.C.V.'s. New Orleans: Hopkins' Printing Office, 1897.

History of Daviess County, Kentucky. Chicago: Inter-State Publishing Co., 1883.

Horan, James D. *Confederate Agent, a Discovery in History.* New York: Crown Publishers, 1954.

Johnson, E. Polk. *A History of Kentucky and Kentuckians.* Chicago: Lewis Publishing Co., 1912.

Johnston, J. Stoddard. *Memorial History of Louisville.* Vol. 1. Chicago: American Biographical Publishing Co., 1896.

Kentucky: A Guide to the Bluegrass State. American Guide Series. New York: Harcourt, Brace & Co., 1939.

Kerr, Charles, ed. *History of Kentucky.* 5 vols. Chicago: American Historical Society, 1922.

Kinchen, Oscar A. *Daredevils of the Confederate Army: The Story of the St. Albans Raiders.* Boston: Christopher Publishing House, 1959.

———. *General Bennett H. Young, Confederate Raider and a Man of Many Adventures.* Boston: Christopher Publishing House, 1981.

Kinkead, Elizabeth Shelby. *A History of Kentucky.* Boston: American Book Co., 1924.

Kirwan, A. D., ed. *Johnny Green of the Orphan Brigade: The Journal of a Confederate Soldier.* [Lexington:] University of Kentucky Press, 1956.

Kleber, John E., ed. *The Encyclopedia of Louisville.* Lexington: University Press of Kentucky, 2001.

Kleber, John E., ed. *The Kentucky Encyclopedia.* Lexington: University Press of Kentucky, 1992.

Klotter, Freda C. *A Concise History of Kentucky.* Lexington: University Press of Kentucky, 2008.

Kolb, Richard K. "Thin Gray Line: Confederate Veterans in the New South." *VFW Magazine* 46, no. 6 (June 1997).

Krock, Arthur. *Myself When Young: Growing Up in the 1890s.* Boston: Little, Brown, 1973.

La Bree, Ben, ed. *Camp Fires of the Confederacy.* Louisville, Ky.: Courier-Journal Job Printing Co., 1898.

———, ed. *The Confederate Soldier in the Civil War, 1861–1865.* Louisville, Ky.: Courier-Journal Job Printing Co., 1895.

———, ed. *Notable Men of Kentucky at the Beginning of the 20th Century.* Louisville, Ky.: Geo. G. Fetter Printing Co., 1902.

———, ed. *Press Reference Book of Prominent Kentuckians.* Louisville, Ky.: Standard Printing Co., 1916.

Levin, Aaron. "Civil War Trauma Led to Combination of Nervous and Physical Disease." *Psychiatric News* 41, no. 8 (April 21, 2006): 2.

Levin, H., ed. *The Lawyers and Lawmakers of Kentucky.* Chicago: Lewis Publishing Co., 1897.

Lewis, Samuel E. *The Treatment of Prisoners-of-War, 1861–1865.* Richmond, Va.: W. E. Jones, Printer, 1910.

Lexington Cemetery, Meeting of the Lot Owners Held March 11th, 1895. Lexington, Ky.: Transylvania Printing Co., 1895.

Lexington City Directory. Lexington, Ky.: R. L. Polk & Co., 1909.

Livermore, Thomas L. *Numbers and Losses in the Civil War in America, 1861–65.* Boston: Houghton, Mifflin and Co., 1900.

Longacre, Edward G. "July 2–26, 1863: John Hunt Morgan's Ohio Raid." *Civil War Times* 42, no. 3 (August 2003).

"Louisville of To-Day: A Souvenir of the City for Distribution during the G.A.R. Encampment." Louisville, Ky.: Consolidated Illustrating Co., 1895.

Matthews, Gary Robert. *Basil Wilson Duke, CSA: The Right Man in the Right Place.* Lexington: University Press of Kentucky, 2005.

McAfee, John J. *Kentucky Politicians—Sketches of Representative Corn-Crackers and Other Miscellany.* Louisville, Ky.: Press of the Courier-Journal Job Printing Co., 1886.

McDowell, Robert E. *City of Conflict: Louisville in the Civil War, 1861–1865.* Louisville, Ky.: Louisville Civil War Roundtable, 1962.

McMeekin, Isabella McLennan. *Louisville, the Gateway City.* A Cities of America Biography. New York: J. Messner, 1946.

Memorial Record of Western Kentucky. 2 vols. Chicago: Lewis Publishing Co., 1904.

Morgan, Mrs. Irby. *How It Was: Four Years among the Rebels.* Nashville, Tenn.: Publishing House, Methodist Episcopal Church, South, 1892.

Mosgrove, George Dallas. *Kentucky Cavaliers in Dixie; or, The Reminiscences of a Confederate Cavalryman.* Louisville, Ky.: Courier Journal Job Printing Co., 1895.

Nicosia, Gerald. *Home to War: A History of the Vietnam Veterans' Movement.* New York: Crown, 2001.

Noble, G. W. *New Age.* Jackson, Ky.: Jackson Times Printing Co., 1928.

Perrin, W. H., J. H. Battle, and G. C. Kniffin. *Kentucky: A History of the State.* 6th ed. Louisville, Ky.: F. A. Battey and Co., 1887.

Peter, Robert. *History of Fayette County, Kentucky.* Chicago: O. L. Baskin & Co., 1882.

Plante, Trevor K. "The National Home for Disabled Volunteer Soldiers." Prologue. *U.S. National Archives and Records Administration* 36, no. 1 (Summer 2004): 57–59.

Poems and Songs of the Civil War. New York: Barnes & Noble, 1996.

Poppenheim, Mary Barnett. *The History of the United Daughters of the Confederacy.* Vol. 1. N.p.: Richmond, Garrett and Massie, 1938.

Prince, Cathryn J. *Burn the Town and Sack the Banks! Confederates Attack Vermont!* New York: Carroll & Graf, 2006.

Richardson, Benjamin Ward. *The Field of Disease: A Book of Preventive Medicine*. Philadelphia: Henry C. Lea's Son & Co., 1884.

Ripley, Amanda. *The Unthinkable: Who Survives When Disaster Strikes—and Why*. New York: Random House, 2008.

Rosen, Marvin. *Understanding Post-Traumatic Stress Disorder*. New York: Chelsea House, 2003.

Rosenburg, R. B. *Living Monuments: Confederate Soldiers' Homes in the New South*. Chapel Hill: University of North Carolina Press, 1993.

Scott, Anne Firor. *The Southern Lady: From Pedestal to Politics, 1830–1930*. Chicago: University of Chicago Press, 1970.

Seekamp, Alwin, and Roger Burlingame, eds. *Who's Who in Louisville*. Louisville, Ky.: Louisville Press Club, 1912.

Short, Joanna. "Confederate Veterans Pensions, Occupation, and Men's Retirement in the New South." *Social Science History* 30, no. 1 (2006): 75–101.

Simpson, Alicia, ed. *Kentucky Confederate Veteran and Widows Pension Index*. Hartford, Ky.: Cook & McDowell, 1979.

Slone, Laurie B., and Matthew J. Friedman. *After the War Zone: A Practical Guide for Returning Troops and Their Families*. Cambrdige, Mass.: Da Capo Press, 2008.

Smith, Suzanne Wooley. "The Tennessee Monument to the Women of the Confederacy: A Study in Conflicting Ideas of Public Commemoration and Collective Memory, 1895–1926." *Border States: Journal of the Kentucky-Tennessee American Studies Association*, no. 11 (1997): 1–7.

Southard, Mary Young, ed. *Who's Who in Kentucky: A Biographical Assembly of Notable Kentuckians*. Louisville, Ky.: Standard Printing Co., 1936.

Sturgis, Thomas. *Prisoners of War, 1861–65: A Record of Personal Experiences, and a Study of the Condition and Treatment of Prisoners on Both Sides during the War of the Rebellion*. New York: G. P. Putnam's Sons, 1912.

Thompson, Edwin Porter. *History of the Orphan Brigade*. Louisville, Ky.: Lewis N. Thompson, 1898.

Townsend, John Wilson. *Kentucky in American Letters, 1784–1912*. Vol. 1. Cedar Rapids, Ia.: Torch Press, 1913.

Trammell, Jack. "Battles Leave an Army of Disabled." *Washington Times*, June 21, 2003.

United States Sanitary Commission. *Narrative of Privations and Sufferings of United States Officers and Soldiers while Prisoners of War in the Hands of the Rebel Authorities*. Boston: Littell's Living Age, 1864.

"VA History in Brief." Washington, D.C.: Department of Veterans Affairs. Online at http://www1.va.gov/opa/publications/archives/docs/history_in_brief.pdf.

Vogel, Jeffrey E. "Redefining Reconciliation: Confederate Veterans and the Southern Responses to Federal Civil War Pensions." *Civil War History* 51, no. 1 (2005): 67–93.

Waller, Willard Walter. *The Veteran Comes Back.* New York: Dryden Press, 1944.

Wetherington, Mark V. "Kentucky Joins the Confederacy." *Kentucky Humanities*, April 1999.

White, A. N. *Cleon Keyes: An Appreciation.* Louisville, Ky.: Published under the Auspices of Kentucky Baptist Historical Society, [1912?].

White, William W. *The Confederate Veteran.* Tuscaloosa, Ala.: Confederate Publishing Co., 1962.

Willis, George Lee. *Kentucky Democracy: A History of the Party and Its Representative Members—Past and Present.* Louisville, Ky.: Democratic Historical Society, 1935.

Wilson, Charles Morrow. "The Hit-and-Run Raid." *American Heritage* 12, issue 5 (August 1961): 28–32.

Wilson, Charles Reagan. *Baptized in Blood: The Religion of the Lost Cause, 1865–1920.* Athens: University of Georgia Press, 1982.

Wines, Frederick H. *Report on Crime, Pauperism and Benevolence in the United States at the Eleventh Census: 1890 (Part 1, Analysis).* Washington, D.C.: Government Printing Office, 1896.

Wols, H. D., and J. E. Baker. "Dental Health of Elderly Confederate Veterans: Evidence from the Texas State Cemetery." *American Journal of Physical Anthropology* 124, no. 1 (May 2004): 59–72.

Young, Bennett H. *Confederate Wizards of the Saddle.* Boston: Chapple Publishing Co., 1914.

Young, Lot D. *Reminiscences of a Soldier of the Orphan Brigade.* Louisville, Ky.: Courier-Journal Job Printing Co, 1918.

Index

Index

Index